Analysis of 18th- and 19th-Century Musical Works in the Classical Tradition

Analysis of 18th- and 19th-Century Musical Works in the Classical Tradition

David Beach
University of Toronto

Ryan McClelland
University of Toronto

 Routledge
Taylor & Francis Group

NEW YORK AND LONDON

First published 2012
by Routledge
711 Third Avenue, New York, NY 10017

Simultaneously published in the UK
by Routledge
2 Park Square, Milton Park, Abingdon, Oxon OX14 4RN

Routledge is an imprint of the Taylor & Francis Group, an informa business

Library of Congress Cataloging in Publication Data
Beach, David, 1938– author.
  Analysis of 18th- and 19th-century musical works in the classical tradition/
  David Beach, Ryan McClelland.
    p. cm.
  Includes bibliographical references and index.
  1. Musical analysis—Textbooks. 2. Harmony—Textbooks. 3. Musical form—
  Textbooks. I. McClelland, Ryan C., author. II. Title.
  MT6.B294 2012
  780.9′033—dc23   2011042055

ISBN: 978-0-415-80665-7 (hbk)
ISBN: 978-0-415-80666-4 (pbk)
ISBN: 978-0-203-12183-2 (ebk)

Typeset in Bembo
by Florence Production Ltd, Stoodleigh, Devon

Contents

Preface

This is a book about analyzing music. What does this mean? Analysis is a process of discovering how a piece of music "works." A fuller answer to this question depends both on the methodological choices of the analyst and the type of music under consideration. This text focuses on instrumental music composed in the eighteenth and nineteenth centuries by Bach, Haydn, Mozart, Beethoven, Schubert, Schumann, Chopin, and Brahms. All of these composers created music within a relatively consistent set of organizational principles referred to as the *common-practice tonal system*. Central to this system is the domain of *harmony*— of chords and their progressions. Of particular importance is the way successive harmonies relate to one another, as these harmonic progressions define key areas and also create the sense of a musical journey, with its rising and falling tension, across a composition. Like much poetry, musical works of common-practice tonality generally fall into a specific type of *form*, in other words a conventional layout of melodic themes and key relationships. Analysis recognizes formal types and then identifies how individual works satisfy or challenge formal expectations throughout their musical journeys. Recurring principles of musical form operate on all levels of musical structure from that of an entire piece (e.g., a sonata form or a rondo form) down to the individual phrase. Closely allied with form is the temporal dimension of music, broadly referred to as *rhythm*. In the music we are studying, the relative lengths of formal units, especially at the level of the musical phrase, shape musical experience in significant ways. Thus, our approach to this repertoire emphasizes elements of harmony, form, and rhythm.

This text is directed at upper-level undergraduate and graduate students from all musical disciplines who are required or elect to take a course in music analysis. Although we assume that musicians in such courses will have completed several courses in music theory earlier in their studies, we do provide a review of foundational principles in Part I.[1] Even those who are secure in their understanding of tonal harmony should spend some time with these introductory chapters to acquaint themselves with our approach to this material. Chapter 1 reviews chord construction and labeling and then discusses harmonic progression within a single key (diatonic harmony). Chapters 2 and 4 consider change of key (modulation) and chords created through accidental alterations (chromatic harmony). Our approach to harmony emphasizes that in music, just as with words in language, not all harmonies are equally significant. Recognizing the multi-leveled, or hierarchical, nature of tonal harmony is essential to understanding the larger arcs of directed motion that animate tonal music. Satisfying performances of the repertoire we are studying invariably balance local detail with long, sweeping gesture; a hierarchical approach to harmonic analysis nurtures sensitivity to the latter. In addition, we probe how melodic lines similarly embed multiple levels of structure, revealing correlations between simpler underlying melodic frameworks and the harmonic pillars supporting them. Chapter 3 discusses the basic element of musical form, the phrase, and we explain some concepts that might not be as frequently included in introductory theory courses as are harmonic topics. In particular, we devote considerable attention to techniques that expand phrases beyond their expected lengths and also to the notion that, like beats within a measure, not all musical measures are equally strong. This latter phenomenon, now known as *hypermeter*, was recognized by eighteenth-century writers as the alternation of "strong" and "weak" measures, and hypermetric analysis again develops awareness of longer musical motions. Our hierarchical approach to tonal and rhythmic structures is influenced by, and fully consistent with, the theories of Heinrich Schenker, but this book is not a text in Schenkerian analysis. That is, many of Schenker's ideas are present without attempting to convey all that is required to construct graphic analyses that are consistent with his concept of multi-leveled musical organization.

Part II is primarily devoted to detailed analyses of twelve compositions. These chapters are organized by formal types, proceeding from binary and rounded binary forms (Chapter 5) to sonata forms (Chapters 6 and 7), ternary form (Chapter 8), and finally rondo form (Chapter 9). For each of the twelve pieces that we discuss thoroughly, we provide a complete score along with some annotations. These annotations identify formal sections, offer an interpretation of hypermeter, and label harmonic progressions. It is strongly recommended that the student listen to each piece, preferably more than once, before reading the analytic discussion. Listening to each piece while following the annotated score will greatly facilitate reading the analytic discussion. Due to their greater length, the pieces in Chapters 6–9 are also accompanied by outlines of formal-tonal organization, and these figures should be scanned before reading our analytic commentary. Typically, our discussion begins with a survey of the formal organization, usually with some mention of the piece's main key areas. Then we enter the composition more deeply, focusing principally on the hierarchical nature of tonal and rhythmic structures and the manipulation of pitch motives. Often we visually depict our analytic understanding through voice-leading simplifications or representations, as explained in the Appendix. For instructors who find there are too many pieces included in Part II or that our discussions are too challenging, two suggested remedies would be to skip Chapter 7 or to omit the last piece analyzed in each of Chapters 7–9.

In choosing the twelve pieces for detailed analysis, we have been guided by two primary considerations. First, we have selected substantial works that are studied by university-level students in their applied lessons and chamber music coachings and that in the broader musical community are frequently performed and recorded. As a result, we cannot pursue every phrase of these pieces in as much detail as we might like, but we fervently believe that analysis courses should tackle pieces that are as long and as intricate as the ones students are preparing for juries or recitals. Second, we have included pieces for varying instrumentation, including two duos (one for clarinet and piano, the other for violin and piano), a piano trio, and an orchestral movement, to the extent possible given the limitations of space. The suggested assignments at the end of each chapter similarly involve a significant number of chamber works.

Due to the detailed nature of analysis and our choice to include complete scores, we have had to restrict ourselves to a particular subset of the musical works composed in the eighteenth and nineteenth centuries. Although Bach's music appears quite often in Chapters 1, 2, and 4 as we review tonal harmony, we do not examine any of his works in detail in Part II. Such a study would require explication of types of pieces that were not much pursued by composers of the late eighteenth and nineteenth centuries. Put differently, the formal conventions applicable to Baroque music differ quite markedly from those applicable to Classical and Romantic music. At the later end of our chronological spectrum, we have focused on those composers most directly within the Classical tradition of Haydn, Mozart, and Beethoven; composers such as Berlioz, Liszt, Wagner, Tchaikovsky, and Strauss are not studied. These and other composers of the later nineteenth century began to extend both formal and tonal conventions in fundamentally new directions, and any serious engagement with their music would stretch our book to an impractical length. We have opted to provide numerous illustrations of analysis within a repertoire that is relatively uniform in organizing principles rather than deliver a more diffuse sampling of analyses of widely differing compositions. Even within our core group of composers, we decided eventually not to include a detailed study of any of their vocal music. This decision was a practical one of space, but also it has been our experience that students who can find their way through a ternary-form piano piece by Schubert or Brahms, for example, can easily navigate one of their songs; the reverse is less often the case. In part, this results from the generally shorter lengths of vocal works, but the presence of a text also makes the identification of phrases and sections more straightforward and the text's meaning provides an accessible avenue to beginning analysis of a vocal work.[2]

We have also had to restrict the topics we address in our analytic commentary due to our principal emphases on tonal, formal, rhythmic, and motivic organization. Although we are aware of performance implications of our analytic observations, we only address them occasionally. This is due, in part, to practical limitations of space, but it is also due to the magical way that differing performance interpretations can realize a particular analytic observation. We believe that in-class demonstrations by instructors or student performers as well as comparative assessment of recordings will generate sounds and class discussions that are much more evocative than words we might commit to paper. Closely related to performance concerns is musical expressivity. Throughout the analyses, we suggest how particular musical features have expressive effects, but we do not do so consistently, and we leave the happy task of exploring this topic further to instructors and students. And it is important to bear in mind that ours is a text on music analysis, not music history. While we give a general sense of how tonal harmony and musical forms evolved during the nineteenth century, we do not do so in any comprehensive way. And we certainly make no attempt to address how familiarity with composers' biographies, their social milieus, and the intended functions of their musical works enrich understanding. The ability to analyze music is among the tools musicians need, and it is an important one. It is the topic of the present text, but it is by no means the only intellectual enterprise that can enhance the lifelong development of the musically sensitive mind.

We want to thank Constance Ditzel, Senior Editor (Music), and Denny Tek, Senior Editorial Assistant (Music), for their enthusiastic support of this book from its initial stages through its publication. We also acknowledge Mhairi Bennett, production manager, for her expert transformation of our manuscript into its present form.

PART I

Principles of Harmony and Phrase Design

1 A Review of Diatonic Harmony

Designation of Pitch and Chords

A preliminary step in our review of diatonic harmony must be to establish how we will designate pitches and chords throughout this text. When we want to specify a particular pitch in a specific octave, we will follow the system adopted by the Acoustical Society of America, where middle C is C4, as indicated in Example 1.1.

EXAMPLE 1.1 Pitch Designation

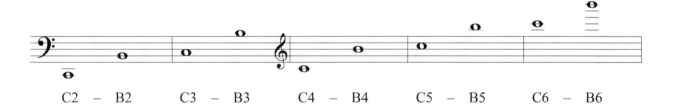

C2 – B2   C3 – B3   C4 – B4   C5 – B5   C6 – B6

Triads are designated by Roman numerals specifying the degree of the scale on which they are built, and in this text we will designate the quality of each triad by upper- and lower-case numerals, upper-case for major and lower-case for minor. Diminished triads are indicated by a lower-case numeral followed by a superscript zero, e.g., vii°. Inversions of triads are indicated by the addition of figured-bass symbols (Arabic numbers and/or accidentals) to the right of the Roman numeral, 6 for first inversion and $\frac{6}{4}$ for second inversion.[1] Accidentals are needed where the interval above the bass is altered in relation to the key signature. An accidental alone indicates that the third above the bass is altered; otherwise, the accidental precedes the Arabic numeral, indicating the interval above the bass that is affected, e.g., ♯6.

Example 1.2 shows the triads and their inversions in both the major and minor modes. Note, however, that we have listed only those $\frac{6}{4}$ chords representing I, IV and V, since these are the only ones commonly employed.[2] In the minor mode we have included the major triad built on the natural seventh degree of the scale as well as the diminished triad on the leading tone. Recall that in the minor mode the leading tone requires an accidental (♮ or ♯).

EXAMPLE 1.2 Triads and Inversions in Major and in Minor

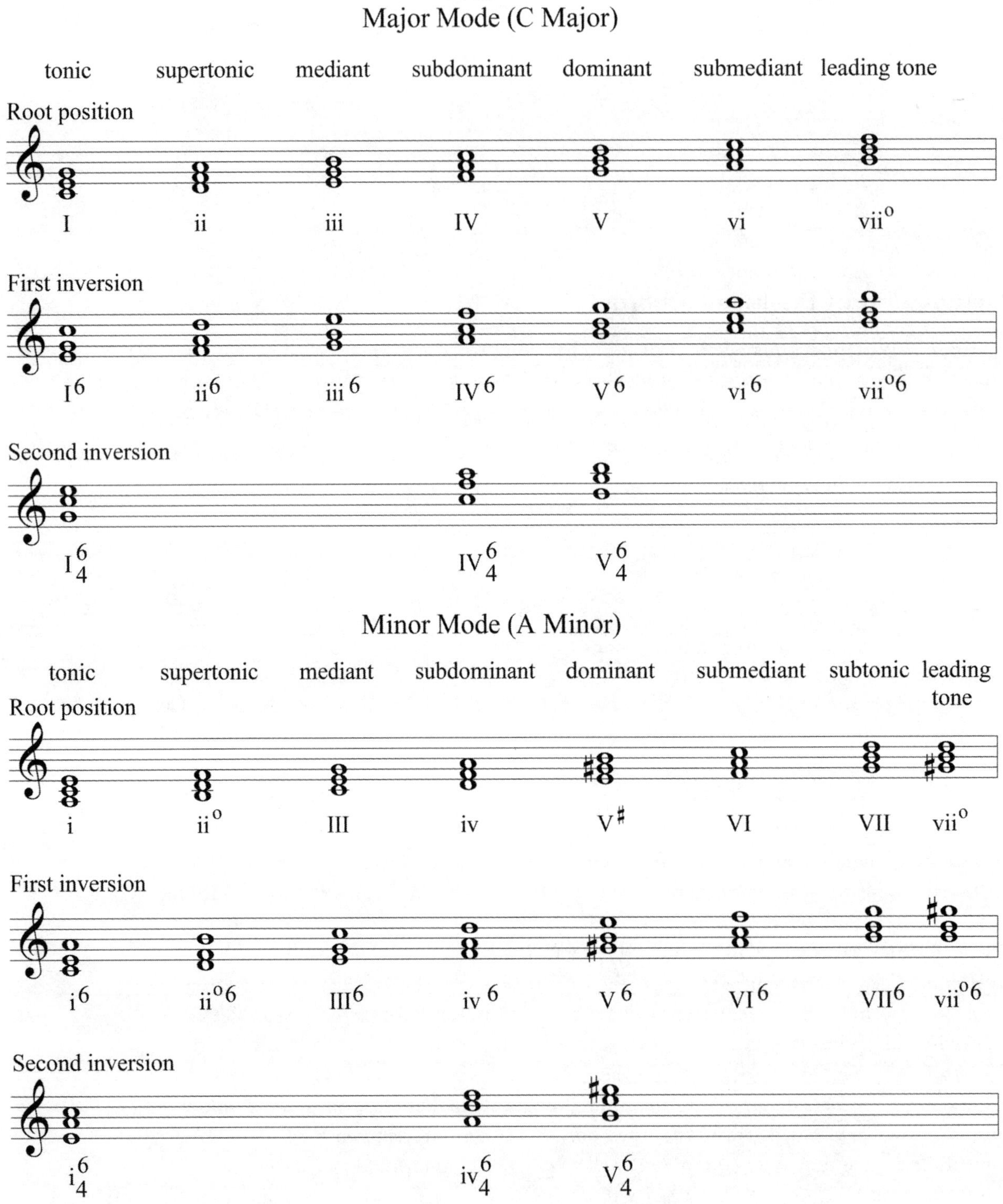

Major Mode (C Major)

tonic	supertonic	mediant	subdominant	dominant	submediant	leading tone

Root position

I   ii   iii   IV   V   vi   vii°

First inversion

I⁶   ii⁶   iii⁶   IV⁶   V⁶   vi⁶   vii°⁶

Second inversion

I⁶₄   IV⁶₄   V⁶₄

Minor Mode (A Minor)

tonic	supertonic	mediant	subdominant	dominant	submediant	subtonic	leading tone

Root position

i   ii°   III   iv   V♯   VI   VII   vii°

First inversion

i⁶   ii°⁶   III⁶   iv⁶   V⁶   VI⁶   VII⁶   vii°⁶

Second inversion

i⁶₄   iv⁶₄   V⁶₄

Triads within a key are commonly referred to by the following names beginning with I/i and ascending to vii°: tonic, supertonic, mediant, subdominant, dominant, submediant, and leading-tone triad. These names are easy to remember once you realize the origin of the terminology, which implies a symmetry around the tonic. The dominant is the fifth above the tonic, and the subdominant is a fifth below. The mediant is midway between tonic and dominant, and the submediant is midway between tonic and subdominant. This leaves the supertonic, meaning the triad above the tonic (*super* is the Latin word for "above").[3]

During the eighteenth century, the gradual acceptance of the passing seventh (8–7) as a legitimate chord tone gave rise to seventh chords built on each degree of the scale. In the major mode, there are four different types of seventh chord: 1) the major triad with major seventh on scale degrees 1 and 4; 2) the major triad with minor seventh on scale degree 5; 3) the minor triad with minor seventh on scale degrees 2, 3, and 6; and 4) the diminished triad with minor seventh (known as the half-diminished seventh chord) built on the leading tone. In the minor mode, the major triad with major seventh occurs on scale degrees 3 and 6; the major triad with minor seventh on scale degree 5 (with the raised leading tone), but also on natural scale degree 7 (VII^7 = V^7 of III); the half-diminished seventh chord on scale degree 2; and the fully diminished seventh chord (diminished triad and diminished seventh) on the leading tone. These seventh chords and their designations in both the major and minor modes are listed in Example 1.3. Note the shorthand designation of the diminished seventh chord, °7, and half-diminished seventh chord, °7. The diminished seventh chord often functions in place of the dominant seventh chord, and occasionally the two occur together forming the dominant ninth chord, as shown at the end of Example 1.3.

EXAMPLE 1.3 Seventh Chords in Major and in Minor

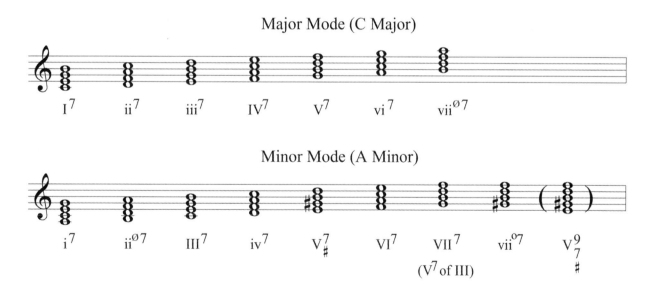

We will not write out all the inversions of all the seventh chords in major and minor. Instead we have shown the inversions of the most common ones, the dominant seventh chord and the diminished seventh chord, in Example 1.4.

EXAMPLE 1.4 Inversions of the Dominant Seventh and Diminished Seventh Chords

Inversions of the dominant seventh chord

Inversions of the diminished seventh chord

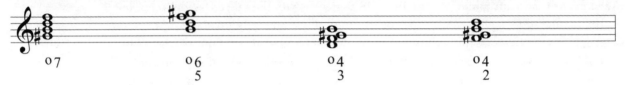

The chordal seventh is a *dissonance* requiring resolution down by step to a note of the following chord. When the resolution does not occur as expected, this is significant. In Example 1.5 we have shown the normal resolution at (a), but at (b) the resolution is transferred to the bass, allowing the top voice to continue its upward motion.[4]

EXAMPLE 1.5 Resolution of the Dissonant Seventh

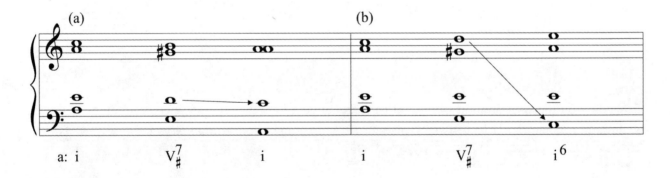

Tonal Functions

A logical way to think of harmonic progression is in terms of three basic functions: tonic, dominant, and preparation for the dominant. As we shall see, a considerable portion of the tonal literature can be understood in terms of these three basic functions. The first two, tonic and dominant, are self-explanatory, while the last requires some clarification. When we speak of preparing the dominant, we mean progressing to the dominant, either by a strong fifth progression, that is, from a supertonic chord in root position, or more frequently by step in the bass and most normally from below, thus supporting the subdominant or the supertonic in first inversion, as shown in Example 1.6 at (a) and (b). Frequently there is a 5–6 linear motion above scale degree 4 in the bass, seemingly creating a harmonic change from IV to ii⁶, but where this change is the result of linear rather than harmonic considerations, we will indicate this change as shown at (c). In this instance, the 5–6 motion avoids parallel perfect fifths between the bass and alto parts. Finally, we also find the root of the dominant harmony approached from a step above, supporting either the submediant or, more often, the subdominant harmony in first inversion, as shown at (d).

EXAMPLE 1.6 Harmonic Functions and Cadences

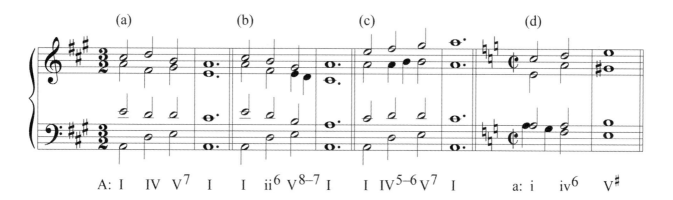

Cadences articulate important points of arrival or division in music. For our present discussion, we need to distinguish two types: the **half cadence** (HC), which ends on the dominant, thus coming to partial rest, and the **authentic cadence**, which ends on the tonic. Depending on the final position of the top part, the authentic cadence is called **perfect** (ending on scale degree 1) or **imperfect** (ending on scale degrees 3 or 5), abbreviated as PAC and IAC respectively. In Example 1.6, the progressions at (a), (b), and (c) all culminate with perfect authentic cadences, while (d) ends with a half cadence. Not represented here is the cadential $^6_4$, a common component in music of the eighteenth and early nineteenth centuries. The cadential $^6_4$ is the result of linear motion—of the passing sixth and fourth on their way to the fifth and third over scale degree 5 in the bass—and thus the resulting chord is not considered as a separate harmony from its resolution. It, along with its resolution, is labeled as V to show its dominant function. This illustrates a very important point, namely, that the labeling of chords should not result from the mechanical application of chord inversion. The collection of notes of the cadential $^6_4$ is the same as the tonic triad, but its function is not tonic, but rather an accented passing motion delaying arrival at the dominant triad. If the $\frac{6}{4}$ chords in Example 1.7 were to be removed, a melodic gap would be created in each case. At (a) the sixth and fourth above the bass, A4 and F4, resolve to the fifth and third leading to a perfect authentic cadence in F major. The second example, in D minor, concludes with a deceptive progression, where VI replaces the expected tonic. The progression at (c) shows a common variant of the normal voice leading; here the fourth still resolves to the third above the bass, but the sixth progresses to the seventh rather than to the fifth. In other words, in (c) the cadential $\frac{6}{4}$ resolves to V^7 rather than to V.

EXAMPLE 1.7 The Cadential $\frac{6}{4}$

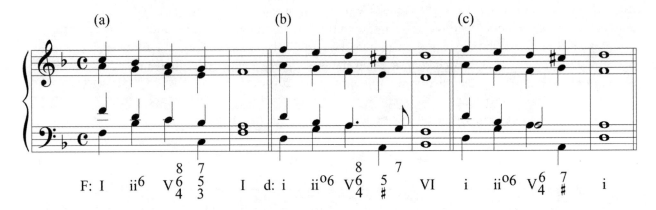

Though brief, the preceding review is sufficient for us to examine three short excerpts from Mozart's piano sonatas. All three examples have the same formal organization. Each consists of two phrases, the first—the **antecedent phrase**—ends on the dominant (half cadence) and the second—the **consequent phrase**—concludes with a perfect authentic cadence. The two phrases are said to have **parallel** construction (as opposed to contrasting), meaning that they open with the same melodic and harmonic material.[5] Together the two phrases form a musical **period**.

The first Mozart excerpt is the opening eight measures of the last movement from his Piano Sonata, K. 545 (Example 1.8). The opening harmony is incomplete, but in retrospect, considering where the phrase leads, the only logical choice is tonic. Furthermore, these eight measures start the final movement of a sonata in C major. The half cadence is prepared by IV^{5-6}, where the change to ii^6 is emphasized by the chromatic passing tone C♯ and the subsequent change of bass note. **Passing tones**, which connect notes belonging to the underlying harmony, have been placed in parentheses and labeled "P." In the second and third measures, these passing tones occur "offbeat," here on the second and fourth sixteenths, but the C♮ in m. 4 falls on the beat, and is thus called an **accented passing tone**. The situation in the consequent phrase is somewhat different. Here the A5 on the second beat of m. 6 and the C♯5 on the following downbeat are not approached by step, a characteristic of the passing tone. Both are **incomplete neighbors** (IN), the first diatonic, the second chromatic.[6]

EXAMPLE 1.8 Mozart, Piano Sonata in C Major, K. 545, III, mm. 1–8

Our second example is the opening period from the third movement of the Sonata, K. 333 (Example 1.9). As in the preceding example, the antecedent phrase leads to a half cadence, in this case involving the cadential $^6_4$, and the consequent phrase completes the motion to the tonic. The G4 (inner part, left hand) on the fourth quarter of m. 1 (and later in m. 5) arises conceptually from an implied F4 and is thus interpreted below as resulting from a linear motion (5–6) above the bass note B♭3. Although we have placed the Roman numeral vi in parentheses below the 6 here, we will not do so later in the text, since the resulting chord is the product of voice leading, not harmony. In m. 3, the melodic notes corresponding to the harmony are displaced by incomplete neighbors (appoggiaturas). In m. 4, D5 is embellished by its upper neighbor before resolving to C5, and the last three eighth notes are passing, leading up to F5. Regarding the harmonic analysis, we have labeled all chords, though the result can be misleading, since this implies that all chords in the succession are equal. They are not. We will return to this example later in the chapter to uncover levels of harmonic organization.

EXAMPLE 1.9 Mozart, Piano Sonata in B♭ Major, K. 333, III, mm. 1–8

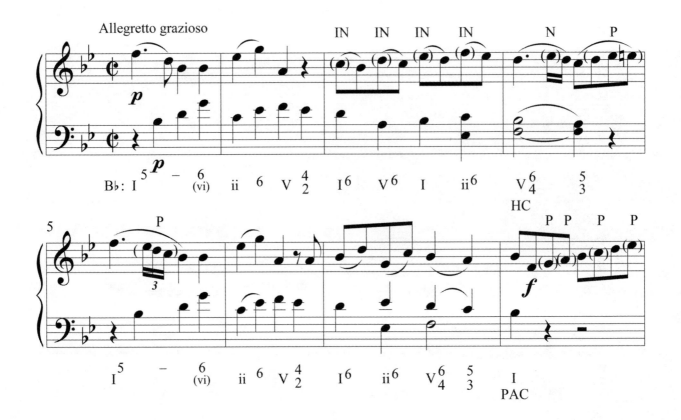

Our third example is the opening period from the third movement of the Sonata, K. 280. An interesting feature of this theme is the exchange of the outer parts of the chords $V^4_3 - I$ (mm. 2–3 and later 10–11) resulting in the progression $V^4_2 - I^6$ (mm. 4–5 and 12–13). The function of the two dominant seventh chords in this progression is to extend tonic harmony through m. 5, which then leads to a half cadence in m. 8. The dominant is prepared by IV^{5-6}, and the actual change to ii is then clarified by the change of bass in m. 7. Once again we have labeled all chords, but here we have shown the progression operating at two levels. The five chords in mm. 1–5 (and later mm. 9–13) prolong the tonic harmony, which is then followed by the cadential progression $IV - ii - V$ and in the consequent phrase $IV - V^{6-5}_{4-3} - I$. Note how this level of organization is articulated by the dynamics: the *forte* dynamic clarifies the connection between the initial I and the I^6 in the fifth measure of each phrase, and the *forte* then continues into the cadential progression.

In examining these three excerpts from Mozart's piano sonatas, we have touched on two new topics, phrase structure and non-chord tones. The first of these will be developed in detail in Chapter 3. For now it is sufficient that you understand what is implied by the terms "phrase" and "period." A phrase is a unit of tonal progression separated from its continuation by a cadence. A period consists of two or more phrases that end with an authentic cadence. Here the periods all consist of two parallel phrases, an antecedent leading to a half cadence and a consequent ending with a perfect authentic cadence.

EXAMPLE 1.10 Mozart, Piano Sonata in F Major, K. 280, III, mm. 1–16

The second topic concerns non-chord tones: passing tones (P), accented and unaccented, chromatic and diatonic; neighbor notes (N); and incomplete neighbor notes (IN), also called appoggiaturas. All these are notes of melodic embellishment, and it is useful to label them in harmonic analyses until distinguishing between chord and non-chord tones becomes automatic. A related phenomenon we have not yet touched on is the suspension, which results from rhythmic displacement rather than melodic embellishment. A **suspension** arises from the extension of a note belonging to one chord into the time-span occupied by a

EXAMPLE 1.11 Bach, *"O Lamm Gottes, unschuldig"* (Chorale No. 165)

subsequent chord, where it becomes a dissonance requiring resolution to the note it has temporarily displaced. So the process involves two chords: 1) the chord preceding the suspension, which contains the chord tone to be suspended; and 2) the chord carrying the suspension and its resolution.

An excellent source for studying the use of melodic embellishment and suspensions, as well as the imaginative use of harmony to articulate a text, are the chorales of J.S. Bach. His setting of "*O Lamm Gottes, unschuldig*" ("O Innocent Lamb of God") is reproduced as Example 1.11. Note that all suspensions, which are marked on the score, resolve down by step to the note they have displaced. The most common types of suspension are those represented here: 9–8, 7–6, and 4–3; these numbers signify the intervals above the bass (i.e., figured-bass numerals). A suspension may be sounded again, as with the first 4–3 suspension, or held over from the previous chord, as with the first 9–8 suspension, both occurring in m. 1. But beware, not all ties signify a suspension, as, for example, in the bass part directly after the repeat; here, the tied F3 is a chord tone and the following E3 is a passing tone. Finally, the 4–3 suspension in m. 4 has an embellished resolution; that is, the resolution of F4 is the E4 on the second quarter note, not the submetrical E4 on the second half of the first quarter.

Common Sequential Patterns

In this section we will examine sequential patterns commonly encountered in the music of the eighteenth and nineteenth centuries. A sequence consists of a repeated voice-leading pattern that connects two important points. From a harmonic perspective, some sequential patterns are circular, that is, they return to the point of origin, while others are progressive, connecting one harmony to another. Most important always are the boundaries, the point of departure and the point of arrival.

The first type of sequence we will examine, the **descending fifth sequence**, is very common. It utilizes chords built on all degrees of the scale, and, when complete, returns harmonically to the point of origin, the tonic. In major keys: I – IV – vii° – iii – vi – ii – V – I. See Example 1.12a, mm. 18–26 from the first movement of Mozart's Piano Sonata, K. 545. This excerpt is in the key of the dominant, G major. In this example, the sequential pattern alternates between first-inversion and root-position triads: I^6 – IV – vii^{o6} – iii – vi^6 – ii – V^6 – I.[7] The sequence extends the initiating tonic harmony and is followed by a confirming perfect authentic cadence. A simplification of the voice leading of this passage is provided in Example 1.12b. Observe that the note values employed in the first four measures of this analytic representation do not correspond to Mozart's written durations. Why have we done this? We perceive a stepwise descending line in the top part resulting from notes struck on successive downbeats, and likewise one in the inner part resulting from those struck on the second half of each measure. The note values, then, represent the durations between successive notes in these lines.[8] As indicated above the top part in Example 1.12b, the sequence supports a descending fifth D6–G5, which is then followed by the cadential pattern ii^6 – V^{6-7}_{4-3} – I. Careful examination of these measures reveals that they support a more encompassing descent of the fifth D6–G5 occurring over the span of the entire phrase. The notes of the descent at this level are circled in Example 1.12b. This example represents a major step in the analytic process, one we do not expect you to

EXAMPLE 1.12a Mozart, Piano Sonata in C Major, K. 545, I, mm. 18–26

EXAMPLE 1.12b Voice-leading simplification of Example 1.12a

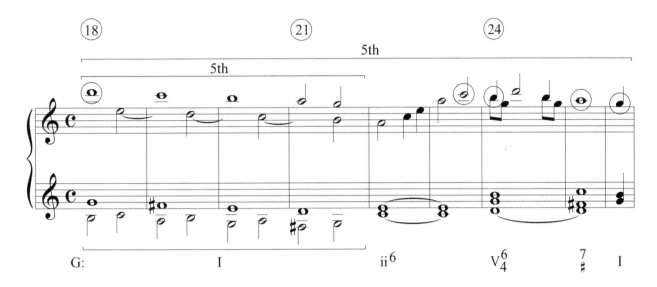

reproduce at this early stage, but one you can follow. We have gone beyond the stage of describing the sequence only in harmonic terms to show its function within the passage as a whole. That is one of the goals of music analysis: to reveal the function(s) of the parts within a larger context.

Our second example is a transitional passage from the first movement of Mozart's Piano Sonata, K. 332 (Example 1.13a). In this excerpt, Mozart changes from the major to the minor mode before initiating a descending fifth sequence, this time utilizing a series of seventh chords in root position.[9] The result is a pattern of alternating 10–7 intervals above the bass, as shown in the simplification of the voice leading of these measures (Example 1.13b). In this instance the goal of the progression is the dominant, and the function of the extension of the dominant is to allow the top part to complete its descent to G4. An important rhythmic feature of this passage is the hemiola pattern indicated by brackets above the score (Example 1.13a, mm. 200–201).[10]

Our next example is the opening section of the Trio from Haydn's String Quartet, op. 20, no. 2 (Example 1.14). Here the descending fifth progression involves alternating root-position triads and seventh chords in first inversion. The sequence connects i (m. 57) to i[6] (m. 64), followed by a passage in octaves leading to V.

The second type of pattern we will examine is referred to in the literature both as a **descending 5–6** and a **descending third sequence**. The first refers to the pattern of intervals above the bass, and the second to the interval between the roots of alternating triads. An example is the opening phrase from Beethoven's Piano Sonata, op. 109 (Example 1.15). The intervallic pattern 5–6 is shown directly below the music and the harmonic analysis below that. The dotted brackets mark the repeated pattern. As in the previous example, the sequence connects I with I[6].

EXAMPLE 1.13a Mozart, Piano Sonata in F Major, K. 332, I, mm. 192–203

EXAMPLE 1.13b Voice-leading simplification of Example 1.13a

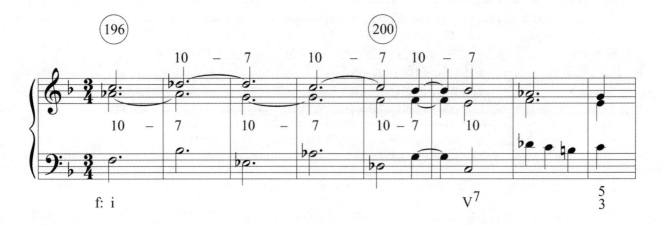

Example 1.14 Haydn, String Quartet, op. 20, no. 2, III, mm. 57–68

EXAMPLE 1.15 Beethoven, Piano Sonata in E Major, op. 109, I, mm. 1–4

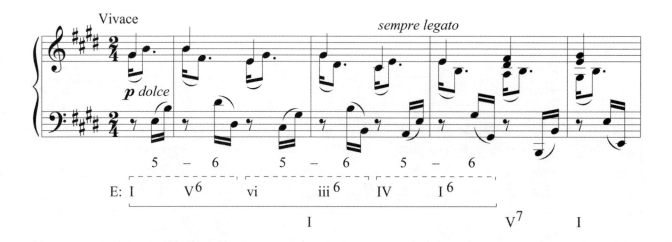

Our third type of pattern is the **ascending 5–6 sequence**, a voice-leading corrective to avoid parallel fifths. We will offer a single example, the opening of Leporello's famous aria "Madamina" from Mozart's *Don Giovanni* (Example 1.16). Here the 5–6 pattern of mm. 3–4 is repeated twice in the next four measures at successive higher steps connecting the initial tonic harmony to its first inversion (m. 8), coinciding with Leporello's arrival at D4. This is shown on the score below the system in Example 1.16. Labeling the intervening chords makes little sense; what is important are the boundaries of the sequence, I . . . I⁶. This is followed by a cadential progression that is repeated in root position leading to a perfect authentic cadence and strong arrival at scale degree 1 in the vocal part.

Passing and Neighboring Chords

In this text we will make a distinction between **passing chords**, those formed by passing notes in either or both of the outer parts, and **neighboring chords**, those formed by neighboring notes in one or both of these parts. While it is important for us to understand chord-to-chord syntax, there is a danger inherent in providing a label for each chord, since this implies that they all have equal status. Yet this is not true, and we have already seen proof of this in our examination of at least two of our examples so far: the opening period from the third movement of Mozart's Piano Sonata, K. 280 (Example 1.10); and mm. 18–26 from the first movement of Mozart's Piano Sonata, K. 545 (Example 1.12). The succession of chords in the consequent phrase (mm. 9–16) from the first of these reads as follows:

$$I - V^4_3 - I - V^4_2 - I^6 - IV - V^{6-5}_{4-3} - I$$

Examination of the opening measures of this phrase reveals that the chord in m. 10 harmonizes the passing note B♭4 between the previous C5 and the following A4, and that the chord in m. 12 harmonizes the passing note G4 between the A4 and following F4. Thus the melodic motion from the initial C5 to the F4 on the downbeat of the fifth measure of

EXAMPLE 1.16 Mozart, "Madamina" from *Don Giovanni*, mm. 1–16

the phrase outlines the tonic triad C5–A4–F4, an **enlargement** of the phrase's opening gesture. The intervening chords are passing. Thus a more accurate picture of the harmonic organization of this phrase is:

$$\underbrace{\text{I} - \text{V}^4_3 - \text{I} - \text{V}^4_2 - \text{I}^6}_{\text{I}} \qquad \text{IV} - \text{V}^{6-5}_{4-3} - \text{I}$$

In this text we will also make a distinction between chord and harmony. The famous Austrian musician Heinrich Schenker (1868–1935) used the German word *Stufe* to designate the latter, by which he meant harmonic scale-step, a harmony that may control several chords in succession.[11] In this example the first five chords are controlled by one harmony, the tonic, and the harmonic succession (not the *chord* succession) is I – IV – V – I. Similarly we have seen that the descending fifth sequence in the second excerpt cited above (Example 1.12) extends a single harmony, the tonic, which is then followed by a standard cadential progression leading to a perfect authentic cadence. We do not mean to dismiss the sequential progression as insignificant, but rather to suggest that there are different levels of harmonic organization in operation. Recognizing these levels is part of the analytic process.

The notion of passing chords is clearly illustrated in the opening measures from the second movement of Beethoven's Piano Sonata, op. 10, no. 1 (Example 1.17). The first sixteen measures of this movement form a musical period, divided into an antecedent phrase leading to the dominant and a consequent phrase concluding with a perfect authentic cadence. The first phrase is divided into two subphrases articulated by the change in melodic material in m. 5. Careful examination of mm. 1–5 reveals that mm. 3–4 are a response to the first two measures; that is, melodically they repeat the gesture of mm. 1–2 a step higher.[12] Looking at the melodic detail of m. 1, we see that the C5 on the second quarter is an incomplete neighbor (appoggiatura) displacing B♭4, which is a neighbor to the A♭4 in mm. 1 and 2. Already we have an interesting conflict between surface design and underlying structure. The descending third C5–B♭4–A♭4 in mm. 1–2, answered by the third a step higher in mm. 3–4, is aurally prominent. Yet this clearly articulated motivic gesture masks the underlying neighbor-note pattern A♭4–B♭4–A♭4 harmonized by the progression $\text{I} - \text{V}^6_5 - \text{I}$. It is clear that the second of these chords is neighboring to the outer two. Likewise, the underlying melodic structure of mm. 3–4 is B♭4–C5–B♭4 harmonized by $\text{V}^6_5 - \text{I} - \text{V}$. In this instance the tonic chord in the middle is neighboring, providing support to the neighbor note C5. The melodic line then progresses via the chromatic passing tone B♮4 to C5 on the downbeat of m. 5. The harmonic analysis below suggests three levels of organization. In the first two measures the controlling harmony is the tonic supporting A♭4, and in the next two measures the controlling harmony is the dominant supporting B♭4, which moves up to C5 supported by tonic harmony in m. 5. The harmonic progression at level 2 is then I – V – I. At the deepest level of organization (level 3), we can see (and hear!) that the middle V chord is passing (it supports the passing tone B♭4 in the ascending third A♭4–B♭4–C5). The tonic harmony spanning mm. 1–5 progresses to the subdominant and eventually to the dominant in m. 8. But what about the tonic harmony at the end of m. 7? We have placed the chords $\text{V}^6_5 - \text{I}$ that occur here in parentheses to show that they are passing between IV and V. Certainly there is not a return to stable harmony here. It is

EXAMPLE 1.17 Beethoven, Piano Sonata in C Minor, op.10, no. 1, II, mm. 1–16

impossible to play this part of the phrase in such a way to make this chord the goal of motion; rather the motion passes through this point to V.

Let us return briefly to the opening phrase from the third movement of Mozart's Piano Sonata, K. 333. When we examined this phrase initially, we labeled all the chords (see Example 1.9). Is there something in the music to suggest different levels of harmonic organization? First we might note that the melodic gesture of m. 2 is an answer to the previous measure, though rhythmically altered and with G5 displacing the C5 that would be there if Mozart had repeated the descending pattern of the opening arpeggio. We hear the second measure as passing, leading to tonic harmony on the downbeat of m. 3. This suggests that all the chords up to the downbeat of m. 3 fall under the tonic scale-step, to use Schenker's term. If we now consider the melodic motion F5 (m. 1) to E♭5 (m. 2), this predicts D5 on the downbeat of m. 3, but this does not follow. Instead, the melodic line begins from B♭4 (actually from the incomplete neighbor temporarily displacing B♭4), the resolution of the A4 (leading tone) from the previous measure, and the expected D5 is not reached until the third quarter over tonic harmony. There is a specific relationship between the first and third quarters of m.3, known as a **voice exchange**, where the notes of the two voices exchange places, here B♭4 over D4 (first quarter) to D5 over B♭3 (third quarter). This is shown in Example 1.18, a simplification of the motivic content and the voice leading of the phrase, by the crossed lines.[13] The harmonic analysis below indicates that all chords through the third quarter of m. 3 fall under the tonic scale-step or harmony, which is followed by ii^6 preparing the dominant at the half cadence. There is a subtle suggestion regarding performance in this interpretation, namely that there could be the slightest separation between the third and fourth beats of this measure, despite the continuous surface pattern. Mozart has articulated this change in harmonic level with the addition of a third voice, starting with the ii^6 harmony.

There is a pattern emerging from our examination of the last two examples, namely that it is the opening tonic harmony of the phrase that is extended by a progression of chords up to the cadential progression: I . . . ii^6 – V – I. Though any harmony can be prolonged in this way, we will see that this is by far the most common pattern.

EXAMPLE 1.18 Voice-leading simplification of Example 1.9

Functions of Individual Chords

The following is a summary of the most common usages or functions of the diatonic chords in both modes.

Tonic

1. The normal point of departure and the eventual goal of tonal motion.

2. The tonic chord, like all chords, can function in a passing or neighboring capacity. See Example 1.17, m. 3 (neighboring) and m. 7 (passing).

Supertonic

1. Most frequently employed as preparation for the dominant. See Example 1.8, mm. 1, 5, and 7; Example 1.9, mm. 2, 3, 6, and 7; Example 1.10, m. 7; Example 1.12a, mm. 22–23; and Example 1.16, mm. 10 and 14.

Mediant

1. In the major mode, the mediant triad is not an independent chord. It does occur:

    a. in a descending fifth sequence (see Example 1.12a, m. 19); and

    b. as a substitute for I^6 (see Example 1.19)

2. In the minor mode, III is a frequent goal of motion.

EXAMPLE 1.19 Substitution of iii for I^6

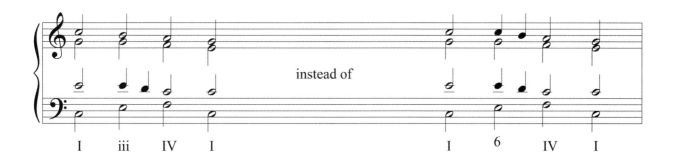

I   iii   IV   I   I   6   IV   I

Subdominant

1. Often used as preparation for the dominant. See Example 1.10, mm. 6 and 14; and Example 1.17, mm. 6–7 and 14.

2. Provides support to the neighbor note in motions involving scale degrees 5–6–5 or 3–4–3. See Example 1.20: Haydn, Chorale St. Antoni, mm. 1–5.

3. The subdominant chord can also occur as a passing chord, as shown in Example 1.21, where it offers temporary consonant support to the passing seventh of the dominant.

EXAMPLE 1.20 Haydn, Chorale St. Antoni, mm. 1–5

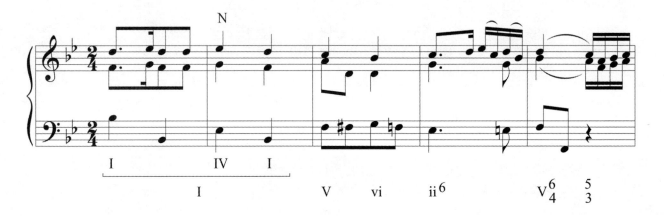

EXAMPLE 1.21 IV⁶ as Passing Chord

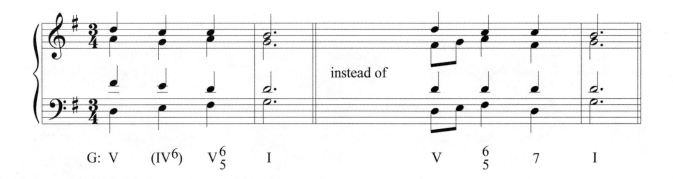

Dominant

1. Frequent goal of motion, e.g., half cadence, or proceeding to the tonic.

2. As a neighboring or passing chord. See Example 1.17, m. 1 (neighboring) and m. 7 (passing).

Submediant

1. The submediant is sometimes employed as a third divider in the descending fifth progression from I to IV or ii⁶: I – vi – IV/ii⁶. See Example 1.8, m. 1.

2. It is also used as a substitute for the tonic after dominant harmony (the "deceptive" progression). See Example 1.22: Chopin, Prelude in B Minor, mm. 15–18. The harmonic analysis of this excerpt is difficult. We have been guided by the fact that m. 16 is an embellished repetition of m. 15. The B4 on the downbeat of m. 16 is thus a suspension displacing the leading tone, and the G4 in the alto part displaces the F♯4, anticipating the submediant chord in the next measure. Note the passage's beautiful shadings of the submediant with its welcome major-mode color: the submediant serves first an illusory sonority at the end of m. 16, then briefly as a harmony in m. 17, and finally as the phrase's tonal goal.

EXAMPLE 1.22 Chopin, Prelude, op. 28, no. 6, mm. 15–18

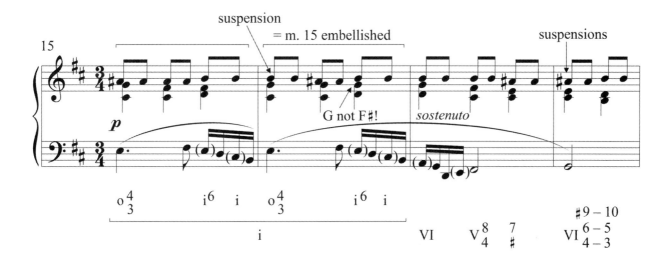

Leading-Tone Triad

1. Most frequently found as a passing chord between I and I⁶: I – vii°⁶ – I⁶.

2. Also occurs as part of a descending fifth sequence. See Example 1.12a, m. 19. VII in the minor mode, the subtonic chord, leads to III as part of a sequence or as its dominant.

SUMMARY OF CONCEPTS AND TERMINOLOGY

We have covered a lot of territory in this chapter, some of it undoubtedly familiar, but other ideas are most likely new. As a summary and an aid in checking your understanding of the main concepts, we offer the following outline.

A. Review the following:

1. All chords (triads and seventh chords), their names, their inversions, and their designations in major and minor keys.

2. Cadences
    a.   half
    b.   authentic, perfect and imperfect
    c.   deceptive

3. Notes of melodic/rhythmic embellishment
    a.   passing tone, accented and unaccented
    b.   neighbor note
    c.   incomplete neighbor (appoggiatura)
    d.   suspension

4. Form
    a.   phrase and period
    b.   antecedent and consequent

B. Make sure you understand these concepts:

1. Tonal functions: tonic, dominant, and dominant preparation

2. Passing and neighboring chords

3. Distinction between chord and harmonic scale-step

SUGGESTED ASSIGNMENTS

Sequences

In all of the following you should try your hand at simple reductions to show the underlying voice leading. Also provide a harmonic analysis for each.

1. Bach, Partita No. 1, Allemande, mm. 24–27. (Note that the key signature does not reflect the actual key of this excerpt.)

2. Bach, Keyboard Suite in A Minor, Giga, mm. 39–45

3. Schubert, Impromptu, op. 90, no. 2, mm. 25–32

4. Bach, French Suite No. 5, Gavotte, mm. 1–4

Periods

1. Mozart, Piano Sonata, K. 331, I, mm. 1–8. What is the chord on the downbeats of mm. 3 and 7? Does it have harmonic meaning?

2. Mozart, Piano Sonata, K. 333, I, mm. 23–38. Note that each of the eight-measure phrases is divided into subphrases of four measures. (Note that the key signature does not reflect the actual key of this excerpt.)

3. Mozart, Piano Sonata, K. 284, II, mm. 1–16. Study levels of harmonic organization and melodic structure. As a guide for your analysis, review our analysis of harmonic levels in Beethoven's Piano Sonata, op. 10, no. 1, II, mm. 1–16 (Example 1.17).

2 Expanding the Diatonic Palette

To contemporary Western ears, a diet of purely diatonic music would soon become boring. It is the expansion of the diatonic palette to include chromatic elements and modulation that provides interest and color to this basic sound world.

Secondary Dominants and Diminished Seventh Chords

The first step to expanding diatonic progression from a harmonic perspective is the inclusion of secondary dominant and diminished seventh chords to the stable triads in the key other than the tonic.[1] In the major mode, $V^{(7)}$ of ii, of iii, of IV, of V, and of vi; and in the minor mode, $V^{(7)}$ of III, of iv, of v, and of VI. The purpose of the secondary dominant is to place emphasis on a chord within the diatonic progression. Consider the two progressions in Example 2.1. The basic progression at (a) is I – ii – V. It is expanded diatonically by the passing chord I^6 on the fourth beat of the first measure, connecting ii and ii^6. Note that there is a voice exchange between the outer parts of these two chords shown by the crossed lines. The progression is further elaborated harmonically by secondary dominant seventh chords leading to ii and later to V. Rather than writing out V^6_5 of ii followed by ii, we have employed a shorthand system: $[V^6_5]$ ii. We will utilize this system where it is convenient throughout this text. The basic progression at (b) is i – iv – V♯ in A minor. This progression is expanded initially by a passing $vii^{o\sharp6}$ connecting i and i^6 and later by a passing $^6_4$ connecting iv and iv^6. In each of these cases there is a voice exchange between the outer parts of the two inversions of the same harmony. The progression is further expanded by the secondary dominant seventh chord of iv.

In Chapter 1 we noted that the diminished seventh chord often substitutes for the dominant, and this applies to secondary chords as well. The diminished seventh chord occurs naturally in the minor mode built on the leading tone, but it occurs in both major and minor as chromatic chords emphasizing stable triads in the key. At (a) and (b) in Example 2.2, we have taken the progressions in Example 2.1 and rewritten them, substituting diminished seventh chords for the secondary dominants. Note the shorthand notation: $[^o7]$. We will notate the inversions of secondary diminished seventh chords in a similar fashion. At (c) we have written out the dominant ninth chord in A minor, since this chord—formed when the dominant seventh and diminished seventh chords occur together—also appears as an applied chord. We will encounter the dominant ninth chord shortly in our examination of the opening section from the second movement of Beethoven's Piano Sonata, op. 31, no. 2.

EXAMPLE 2.1 Expanding Diatonic Progressions with Secondary Dominants

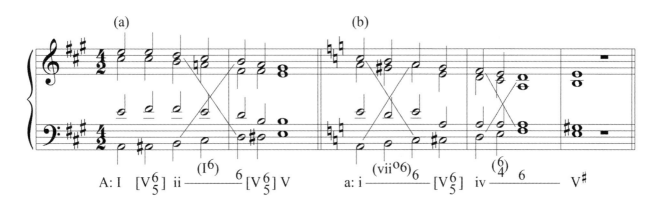

EXAMPLE 2.2 Expanding Diatonic Progressions with Secondary Diminished Sevenths

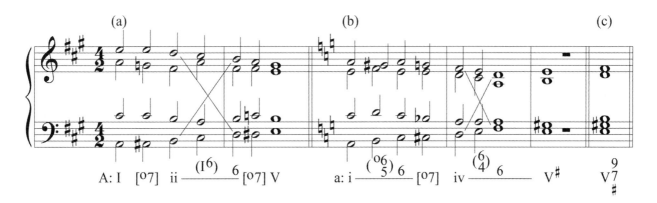

With the addition of secondary dominants and diminished seventh chords, our sound world now contains all twelve pitches, though, of course, not twelve equal pitches. The chromatic elements serve as elaborations of the notes of the diatonic scale, which have their own hierarchy. This is demonstrated by the schemata in Example 2.3. At (a) the top line is an ascending chromatic scale, missing only A♯, where the chromatic elements are harmonized as secondary dominants. At (b) the chromatic scale is now in the lowest voice, and the chromatic elements support secondary diminished seventh chords.

Our first example from music literature is from the first movement of Mozart's Piano Sonata, K. 333 (Example 2.4). This passage is in the key of the dominant, F major. The tonic harmony is stated clearly in the first measure (m. 42), but then in the next two measures we are faced with incomplete chords. Nevertheless, the progression is clear: IV − V − vi with the motion to vi emphasized by its diminished seventh chord.[2] The submediant then leads to a perfect authentic cadence, but melodic closure is avoided at the last minute by delaying the sounding of F5 in m. 46, thus creating forward momentum. The entrance of

EXAMPLE 2.3 Secondary Dominant and Diminished Sevenths in C Major

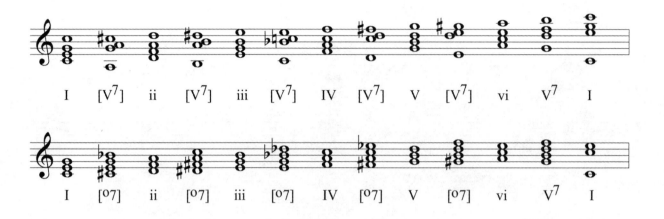

EXAMPLE 2.4 Mozart, Piano Sonata in B♭ Major, K. 333, I, mm. 42–50

E♭5 in the second half of this measure suggests we might be headed once again to the subdominant, but the chromatic change in the bass creates a secondary dominant leading instead to ii. Measure 48 is an answer to m. 47 a step lower, completing the progression to I, which is then followed by a secondary dominant leading to the dominant (V^{6-7}_{4-3}) and closure. This particular variant of this standard cadential pattern—where the sixth is delayed in the top part until the chord has resolved to the true dominant, thus sounding like an incomplete neighbor or appoggiatura—is a hallmark of Mozart's style.

Our second example is a parallel period from the second movement of Beethoven's Piano Sonata, op. 14, no. 1 (Example 2.5). The third and fourth measures of the antecedent phrase present an interesting problem in notating the harmonic progression. The chord in

EXAMPLE 2.5 Beethoven, Piano Sonata in E Major, op. 14, no. 1, II, mm. 33–51

the third measure is the diminished seventh of V: A♯–C♯–(E)–G. Instead of leading to V, what follows is a substitute for V, the diminished seventh chord D♯–F♯–A–C. (The G on the downbeat of the fourth measure is a 7–6 suspension.) So we have two diminished seventh chords in a row.[3] The dilemma is how to indicate most accurately what is occurring in the music. The notation [°7] $^{o4}_3$ makes little sense, so we decided to write out °7 of V to $^{o4}_3$ (substitutes for V), which is accurate and describes the functions of the two chords. The equivalent spot in the consequent phrase is more straightforward. Here C♮ is an incomplete neighbor displacing B; the chord is $^{o4}_3$ of iv leading to iv⁶. This is repeated twice, followed by a voice exchange between the outer parts of the iv⁶ and iv chords, which then leads to a perfect authentic cadence. The underlying progression of this consequent phrase is i – VI – iv⁶ – V – i. In this instance it is not the initial harmony, the tonic, that is prolonged by intervening chords, but the subdominant.

Our third example, the opening phrase from the second movement of Beethoven's Piano Sonata, op. 10, no. 3, also makes extensive use of diminished seventh chords (Example 2.6). The diminished seventh chord on the downbeat of m. 3 is extended by passing $^6_4$ chords connecting °7 to $^{o6}_5$ and back to °7 on the downbeat of m. 4. The expected resolution of this chord is to the tonic, but instead it leads directly to V^4_2 of iv. As a result, the leading tone C♯ does not resolve to D, but rather falls by semitone to C♮, the seventh of the secondary dominant. The subdominant is then further emphasized by [V^6_5] iv. Though not indicated on the score, note the relationship between iv⁶ and iv: a voice exchange between the outer voices (G4 over B♭2 to B♭4 over G2). As we have seen, this is a very common means of prolonging a single harmony. The subdominant leads to a $^{o4}_3$ chord. Once again this chord

EXAMPLE 2.6 Beethoven, Piano Sonata in D Major, op. 10, no. 3, II, mm. 1–9

EXAMPLE 2.7 Beethoven, Piano Sonata in D Minor, op. 31, no. 2, II, mm. 1–17

does not resolve to a tonic harmony (i⁶), but rather the bass progresses up this time by semitone to G♯ supporting °7 of V. It would seem, then, that the function of this $^{o}_{3}^{4}$ in m. 6 is not really harmonic, but linear, offering support for E5 as it reaches up to F5 in m. 7.

   Our final example in this section, the opening period from the second movement of Beethoven's Piano Sonata, op. 31, no. 2, also makes extensive use of secondary dominant and diminished seventh chords (Example 2.7). The first of these, $^{o}_{5}^{6}$ of ii⁶ occurs on the third beat of m. 6. The following ii⁶ is delayed until the second beat of m. 7 by suspensions in the top and "tenor" voices. This is followed by a passing $^{6}_{4}$ connecting ii⁶ to ii$^{4}_{3}$, and the introduction of the E♮ transforms the latter into V$^{4}_{3}$ of the following dominant at the half cadence in m. 8, which is decorated by suspensions in the inner voices. In the consequent phrase we have a very clear example of a dominant ninth chord, where the ninth, G♭, is heard as the chromatic upper neighbor of F (note the motion G♭–F at the end of m. 12). The dominant is subsequently prolonged by a motion to vi, where this G♭ is now respelled as F♯ supporting the °7 of vi (mm. 14–15).

Chromaticized Sequences

Sequences frequently include chromatic elements, including secondary dominants. We will begin by examining two examples of **chromatic fifth sequences**. The first (Example 2.8), written in a Baroque imitative style, requires little explanation. It utilizes secondary dominant seventh chords to elaborate a simple diatonic progression of descending fifths in C minor. The second example, a transition passage from Chopin's Mazurka, op. 68, no. 4, is far more complex (Example 2.9a). Here the underlying progression is elaborated by chromatic passing tones and suspensions, so we have enclosed the chords in boxes to make it easier to follow the discussion. From the opening G major chord (V of V in F minor), the music progresses by a series of secondary dominant seventh chords ($D^7 - G^7 - C^7 - F^7 - B\flat^7 - E\flat^7$) until m. 37, where the pattern changes[4] and the chords progress down by chromatic steps in parallel motion leading to the cadential $^6_4$. A representation of the underlying voice leading of this complex passage is provided in Example 2.9b.[5] As shown below the system, the intervening seventh chords connect V of V (m. 31) to V (m. 40), which is subsequently extended until its resolution to the tonic at the conclusion of the following phrase.

EXAMPLE 2.8 Descending Fifth Sequence with Secondary Dominants

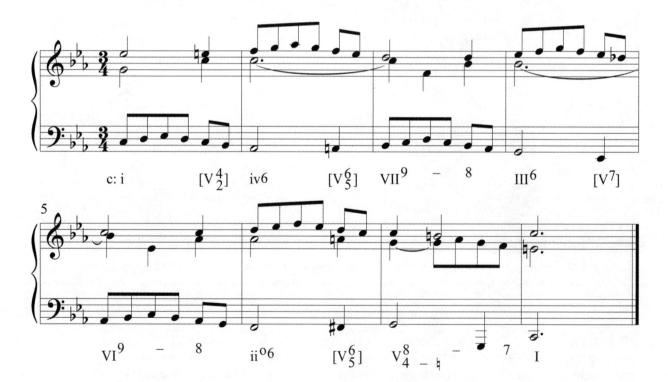

EXAMPLE 2.9a Chopin, Mazurka in F Minor, op. 68, no. 4, mm. 31– 40

EXAMPLE 2.9b Voice-leading representation of Example 2.9a

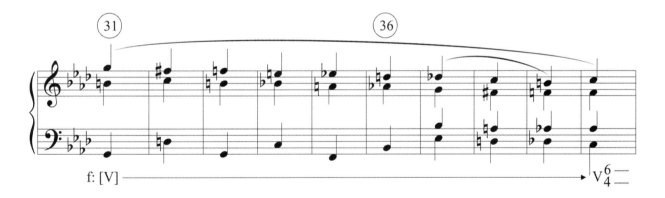

Next we will examine two examples of **chromatic ascending 5–6 sequences**. The first of these is found in mm. 19–21 of the allemande from Bach's Keyboard Partita No. 4 in D Major (Example 2.10a). This passage leads from the subdominant to the tonic in the key of the dominant, A major. The 5–6 sequence and the chromatic notes creating secondary dominant $\frac{6}{5}$ chords are very clear in the left-hand part. However the right-hand part is complex, and for this reason we have provided a simplification that removes all suspensions and passing tones in the right-hand part (Example 2.10b). A two-level harmonic analysis is provided below the simplified score. Though the chord-to-chord harmonic syntax makes perfect sense, it is important to keep in mind that the purpose of a sequence is to lead from the point of initiation (IV) to the goal (I), here through the dominant.

EXAMPLE 2.10a Bach, Partita No. 4 in D Major, Allemande, mm. 19–21

EXAMPLE 2.10b Voice-leading simplification of Example 2.10a

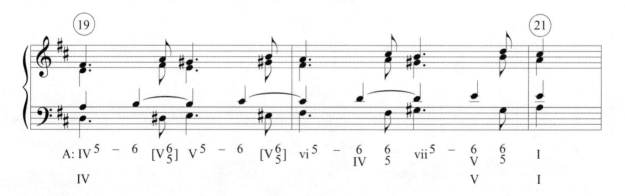

The second example of this type of sequence comes from the second movement of Beethoven's Piano Sonata, op. 7 (Example 2.11a). Again the 5–6 sequence is clear in the left-hand part (mm. 17–18), whereas the right-hand part is a bit more complex. A detailed harmonic analysis is provided below the score, showing the elaboration of an ascending diatonic step progression by secondary dominants. Especially important in this regard is the diminished seventh chord of vi (*sf*) in m. 18, which supports F5, the upper neighbor of E5. Looking ahead you will see that we have placed parentheses around mm. 20–23. This parenthetical insertion, which delays arrival at the tonic harmony, expands the length of the phrase from six to ten measures. This and other types of phrase expansion will be discussed in detail in Chapter 3. A simplification of the voice leading is provided in Example 2.11b. Here it is possible to see the sequence's underlying voice leading and how it fits into the phrase as a whole. The outer voices of the sequence proceed in ascending parallel tenths

EXAMPLE 2.11a Beethoven, Piano Sonata in E♭ Major, op. 7, II, mm. 15–24

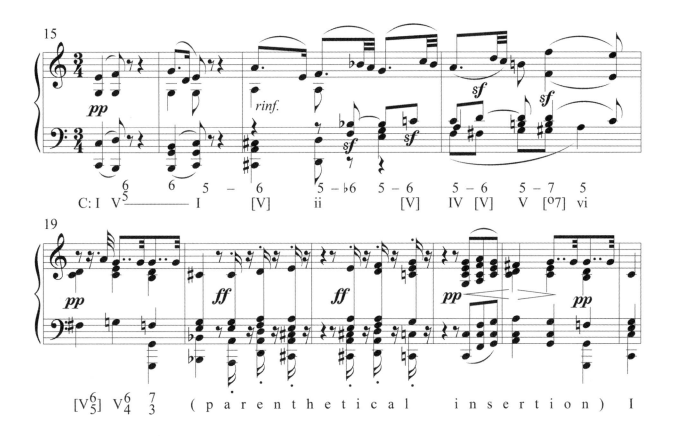

EXAMPLE 2.11b Voice-leading simplification of Example 2.11a

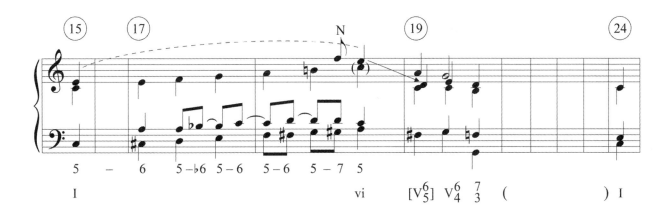

EXAMPLE 2.12a Beethoven, Piano Sonata in C Major, op. 53, I, mm. 1–9

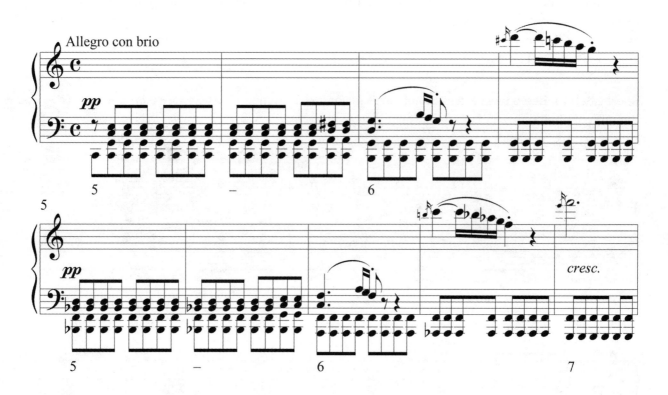

EXAMPLE 2.12b Voice-leading representation of Example 2.12a

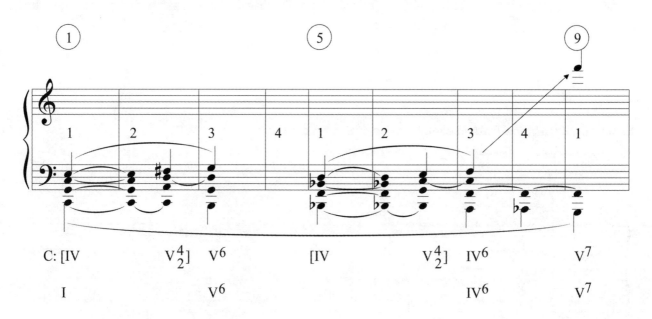

connecting E4 over C3 (I) to C5 over A3 (vi), while the inner line proceeds by 5–6 motions.[6] Above this, E5 is introduced by its upper neighbor, and we have connected this to the point of origin, E4. As shown by the arrow, the top line is then transferred down to the original octave position, temporarily covered by A4–G4. Once again we have a situation where it is possible to label all chords in the sequence, but most important are the point of initiation (I) and the goal of the motion (vi). This level of harmonic organization is indicated below Example 2.11b.

We turn now to the **chromatic descending 5–6 sequence** with an example from the opening of Beethoven's "Waldstein" Sonata, op. 53. The repeated 5–6 pattern is marked beneath the score (Example 2.12a). A cursory examination of the bass line reveals that it is a chromatic descending tetrachord leading from tonic to dominant (V^7). A closer examination reveals that these measures are organized in two groups of four, where the fourth measure is a kind of response to the third in the higher octave; that is, mm. 5–8 are a slightly modified restatement of mm. 1–4 a step lower. Harmonically the first group progresses from I to V^6, the second leads to IV^6 and then to V^7. Thus the overall progression is $I - V^6 - IV^6 - V^7$, as shown at the lowest level below the representation of the voice leading in Example 2.12b.[7] The issue here is how to represent the logic of the chord-to-chord progression. It might occur to you to label the B♭ chord in mm. 5–6 as ♭VII, but that does not indicate how it functions as leading to IV^6 in m. 7. A better description is that it functions in relation to the subdominant as IV of IV leading to V_2^4 of IV. We represent this through expansion of the square brackets: $[IV - V_2^4]\,IV^6$. Looking back at mm. 1–4, we can see that the opening tonic also functions in retrospect as a subdominant in relation to V^6.

A similar situation is found in mm. 15–21 from the opening movement of Schubert's String Quartet, D. 887 (Example 2.13). Once again the bass is a descending chromatic tetrachord leading from tonic to dominant. And mm. 17–18 are an answer to mm. 15–16 a step lower, so V^6 (m. 16) is answered by IV^6 (m. 18). The third statement, beginning from the E♭ chord, is altered, leading through a passing $^6_4$ on the downbeat of m. 20 to IV,

EXAMPLE 2.13 Schubert, String Quartet in G Major, D. 887, I, mm. 15–21

EXAMPLE 2.14 Mozart, Piano Sonata in F Major, K. 280, I, mm. 14–26

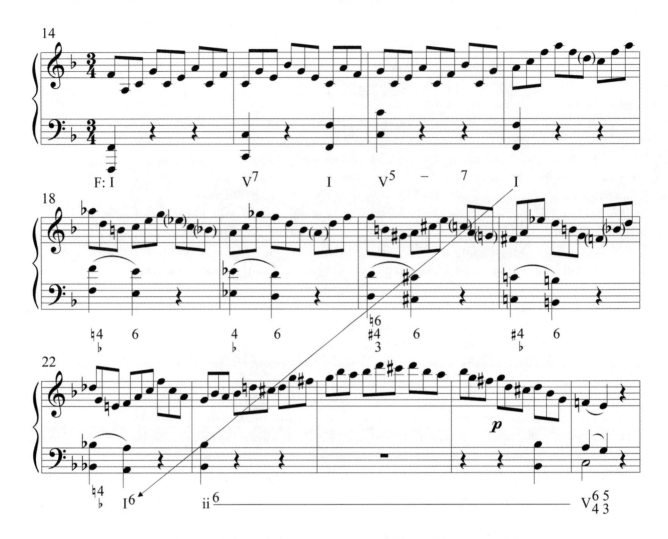

thus extending the subdominant until it resolves to the dominant, decorated by a 4–3 suspension, in m. 21. In Beethoven's op. 53 we were able to ascribe harmonic function to each chord between the terminal points, but here the chords in mm. 17 and 19 do not have harmonic function. They are solely the product of repetition of the 5–6 pattern at successively lower steps.

This last example illustrates an important point, namely, that we cannot—nor should we attempt to—ascribe harmonic function to chords that result purely from linear considerations. In the preceding examples we have indicated chord-to-chord harmonic syntax along with deeper levels of harmonic organization as long as doing so has provided further insight into the logic of a passage. But there are clearly some instances where labeling every chord not only can be meaningless, but can be misleading. This is illustrated by examining the sequential passage in Example 2.14, the transition to the second theme from the first movement of Mozart's Piano Sonata, K. 280. The tonic harmony is established in mm. 14–17. Beginning in m. 18 there is a repeated descending pattern of $^{o4}_{3}$ chords leading to first-inversion triads. If we were to label these triads, the result would be V⁶ – IV⁶ – III⁶ – II⁶ – I⁶, each preceded by its $^{o4}_{3}$ chord. This is a meaningless string of symbols from the point of view of harmonic logic. What is important here is that this repeated descending pattern connects I (m. 17) to I⁶ (m. 22), indicated by the arrow in Example 2.14. This is a good illustration of the distinction we have made before between chord and harmony (harmonic scale-step). The harmony controlling this passage is the tonic. Providing the intervening chords, those between I and I⁶, with Roman numerals would ascribe to them harmonic status, where their real function is passing.

A more complex example of passing chords—in this case not a sequence—is provided in Example 2.15. It is the opening phrase of the development section from the first movement of Mozart's Piano Sonata, K. 333. This phrase is in the key of the dominant, F major. It opens with the tonic harmony and proceeds to the passing chord vii^{o6} (or V$^{4}_{3}$ if you count the grace note C), which is repeated in the lower octave in the third measure. The diatonic continuation would normally be to I⁶, but instead Mozart writes a secondary diminished seventh chord directing the motion more strongly to the ii⁶ chord in the next measure.⁸ So far, so good. It is the next chord that is potentially a problem. Its notes say it is V⁷, but its function is not to lead to the tonic. Rather it is a passing chord connecting ii⁶ to the $^{o6}_{5}$ of V, similar to the way vii^{o6} had previously connected I to the $^{o6}_{5}$ of ii⁶. The "real" dominant comes in the seventh measure of the phrase. Labeling the chord in the second half of the fifth measure as V⁷, at least without indicating its passing function, would give a distorted picture of the harmonic logic of this phrase.

EXAMPLE 2.15 Mozart, Piano Sonata in B♭ Major, K. 333, I, mm. 64–71

The purpose of these last two examples is to demonstrate that the interpretation of the harmonic organization of a passage is not a mechanical, automatic process. You should always consider the larger picture first, that is, to see and hear where a passage is leading before deciding how to label the details. There is a very significant difference between chord and harmony. All harmonies are chords, but not all chords are harmonies.

Diatonic Modulation

Modulation—change of tonal center—occurs in various ways and in varying strengths. Regarding the latter, we will make a distinction in this text between a transient modulation, where there is a temporary shift of tonal center, and a true modulation that is carefully prepared and confirmed by a cadence. We will also refer to the new key in relation to the tonic, for example, a modulation to the key of the dominant, G major. Such a statement carries much more information than saying simply that the piece has modulated to G major. We are concerned here primarily with the tonal style in which a piece or movement begins and ends in the same key, though possibly with a change of mode, and it is important to describe internal changes of key in relation to this tonic.

Though modulation can occur from any key to any other key, our concern in this chapter is diatonic modulation, which is limited to those keys whose tonic triads are stable triads in the original key. Mode—major or minor—depends on the quality of the triad in the original key. Thus, from C major we modulate to D minor (ii), E minor (iii), F major (IV), G major (V) and A minor (vi); and from A minor we modulate to C major (III), D minor (iv), E minor (v), F major (VI) and G major (VII).

At a minimum, a tonicization or a passing modulation requires the dominant of the new key and at least temporary continuation in that key. True change of key also requires confirmation by a cadence in the new key. The smoothest modulations are often those where there is a **pivot**, a chord that functions in both the original and the new key, most frequently a chord preparing the new dominant. We identify pivot chords in retrospect, since we are not aware that a modulation is about to take place until after this point, when the dominant of the new key is sounded. A list of frequently encountered pivots is provided in Figure 2.1. We will provide examples of the most common modulations, and, where appropriate, indicate the pivots.

Modulation from an Initial Major Key

I to V

1. Bach, Prelude in D Major (*WTC* I), mm. 1–6 (Example 2.16). Pivot: I^{5-6} becomes ii^6. This is an interesting passage to examine from the perspective of near, but not exact, sequential repetition. For example, note that the right-hand pattern in the second half of m. 1 is repeated with minor alteration in the first half of m. 2, and that the right-hand pattern in m. 3 is repeated a third lower, again with minor alteration, in m. 5. In both instances, the changes are the direct result of differences in the supporting harmonies. Note also that the G♯5 on the downbeat of m. 4 is not resolved in that octave within this initial phrase, a sure sign that Bach will return to that register shortly.

Major Mode		Pivot
I	to ii	ii/i (read: ii becomes i) or IV/III
	to iii	vi/iv or I/VI
	to IV	ii/vi or IV/I
	to V	vi/ii or I/IV
	to vi	ii/iv or IV/VI or vi/i
Minor Mode		
I	to III	iv/ii or VI/IV or i/vi
	to iv	iv/i or VI/III
	to v	i/iv or III/VI
	to VI	iv/vi or VI/I
	to VII	i/ii or III/IV

FIGURE 2.1 Common Pivots in Modulations

EXAMPLE 2.16 Bach, Prelude in D Major (*WTC* I), mm. 1–6

2. Beethoven, Piano Sonata, op. 31, no. 1, I, mm. 1–11 (Example 2.17). Pivot: vi becomes ii. The opening phrase, with its staggered entrances between the hands and the sudden dynamic outburst, sets the mood for this playful movement.

EXAMPLE 2.17 Beethoven, Piano Sonata in G Major, op. 31, no. 1, I, mm. 1–11

3. Haydn, String Quartet, op. 77, no. 2, Menuetto, mm. 1–12 (Example 2.18). As in the preceding example, the pivot is vi/ii (actually vi^6/ii^6). However, vi^6 is not an independent harmony here, but arises from I$^{5-6}$, in this instance elaborated by the intervening chromatic passing tone C♯, which is emphasized by the marking *sf*.

I to IV

Schumann, *Dichterliebe*, no. 4, mm. 1–8 (Example 2.19). There are a couple of unusual features of the harmonic syntax of these eight measures. First, the progression leads in a normal way to the dominant in m. 4, but there, instead of returning to I, the accompaniment insists on ii. This harmony, the supertonic, becomes the pivot in the next measure in the modulation to IV: ii becomes vi. This is followed by a secondary dominant in $\frac{4}{2}$ position leading to IV^6 in the new key. From there the progression continues through a passing $\frac{6}{4}$ to ii$^6_5$. The expected continuation is to the cadential $\frac{6}{4}$, but instead Schumann interjects I^6 – IV (*forte*) before the perfect authentic cadence in the new key. We have placed this I^6 – IV in parentheses and below we have shown the normative progression. So why might Schumann do this? It preserves the parallel motion between voice and bass, and at the same time emphasizes the words "*ganz und gar*," which mean totally or completely.

EXAMPLE 2.18 Haydn, String Quartet in F Major, op. 77, no. 2, III, mm. 1–12

EXAMPLE 2.19 Schumann, *Dichterliebe*, no. 4, mm. 1–8

A Summary Example: Bach, French Suite No. 5, Gavotte (Example 2.20)

The form of this engaging stately Gavotte is binary; it is divided into two parts, each of which is repeated. The first part consists of a period divided into two parallel phrases, the second of which modulates to the dominant. The second part comprises two periods, each divided into two phrases. The first phrase ends on a half cadence in the key of the submediant, and the second phrase completes the modulation to vi. The final period is organized similarly, with the first phrase ending on the dominant and the final phrase completing the return to the tonic. Each of the periods ends with a perfect authentic cadence.

EXAMPLE 2.20 Bach, French Suite No. 5 in G Major, Gavotte

A cursory examination of the Gavotte reveals the frequent recurrence of a three-note motive, repetitions of which are marked on the score by brackets. The initial phrase opens with two statements of this idea harmonized by the descending 5–6 sequence. The second phrase opens with a modified statement of the motive leading to V_2^4 in the new key of V. We have indicated the previous tonic harmony as the pivot in the modulation to V: I/IV. And we have circled the bass note G3 on the downbeats of mm. 5 and 6, the seventh of the dominant in the new key. Our expectation is that this dissonance will resolve down by step at the change of harmony, but instead the resolution is temporarily transferred to the top part (F♯5) in mm. 6–7. Note, however, that our expectation is satisfied by the sounding of the F♯ in the bass on the second quarter note of m. 7 (I^6 in the new key).

The second part opens with the inversion of the motive. Temporarily we have returned to the tonic key (note the consistent use of C♮ rather than C♯), and it is from this key that Bach prepares the modulation to the submediant (E minor). The pivot chord is IV/VI followed by $iv^{5–6}$ $V^{\sharp}$ in the new key. The dominant is subsequently prolonged throughout the next phrase until the final cadence in mm. 15–16 confirming the modulation. This prolongation of the dominant consists of a modified statement of the opening right-hand part now in the lower part, above which Bach has added counterpoint extending the eighth-note motion of the preceding phrase, broken only at the cadence. The final period then opens with another statement of the inverted motive in the right-hand part as the bass picks up the eighth-note motion, which this time continues through the phrase division until the final cadence.

Following our earlier practice, we have placed all non-chord tones in parentheses, but because they are so numerous we have not labeled them. The one exception is the appearance of a type not yet mentioned, the **anticipation** of the final G5 in the top part.

Modulation from an Initial Minor Key

i to III

1. Bach, Prelude in C♯ Minor (*WTC* I), mm. 1–8 (Example 2.21). The first four measures of this prelude establish the main key and the main motivic idea, which alternates between the top part and an inner voice (left hand). The $^6_4$ chords on the last quarter note of mm. 1 and 2 are neighboring, and the tonic chord on the last quarter of m. 3 is passing between V_5^6 and V. The continuation, beginning in m. 5, is a sequence by descending fifths alternating between $^4_2$ and $^6_5$ chords. The pivot in the modulation to III (E major) is shown as VI_2^4/IV_2^4 at the outset of the descending fifth sequence.[9] Arrival at the new key is marked by repetition of the main motive.

2. Mozart, Piano Sonata, K. 310, I, mm. 9–16 (Example 2.22). These measures are the consequent phrase (modulating consequent) of a period. The goal of this phrase is the dominant in the new key (III). The pivot in the modulation is shown as $VI^{5–6}/IV^{5–6}$, which is followed by a secondary dominant leading to ii and then V in the new key. In this phrase the tonic is initially embellished by $^{\circ}7$ over a tonic pedal (mm. 9–11). An important motivic

EXAMPLE 2.21 Bach, Prelude in C♯ Minor (*WTC* I), mm. 1–8

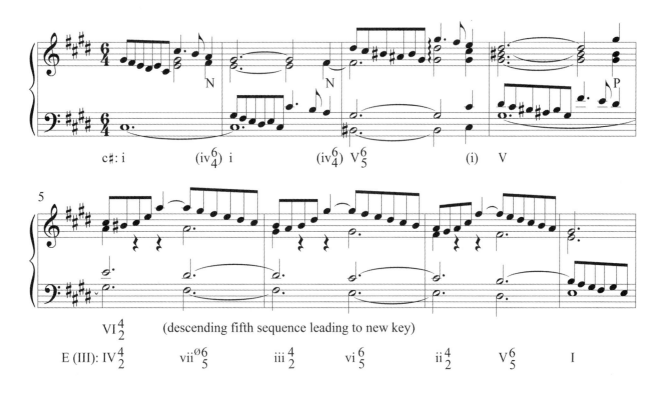

EXAMPLE 2.22 Mozart, Piano Sonata in A Minor, K. 310, I, mm. 9–16

component of these measures—as well as the antecedent phrase—is the decoration of E5 by its upper and lower neighbors (F5 and D♯5). If we skip ahead to the measure marked *calando*, we see that Mozart has cleverly built reference to this motivic idea into the latter part of the phrase leading to the dominant of III. By delaying the entrance of F♮5, D♯5, and E5, we hear the last of these sounded one final time in reference to an A minor chord, now heard as vi in the new key rather than tonic.

3. Beethoven, Piano Sonata in C Minor, op. 13, I, mm. 1–5 (Example 2.23). This is an interesting passage to examine with respect to passing chords. First, the $^6_4$ in m. 1 is a passing chord between i and i^6, then in m. 2 the root-position dominant is passing between $^{o4}_2$ and $^{o4}_3$; and finally this same progression occurs twice in relation to V. In each of these cases, there is a voice exchange between the outer voices, shown in Example 2.23 by the crossed lines. The pivot in the modulation to III (E♭) is iv^6/ii^6, in this case emphasized by its secondary dominant. The extensive use of diminished seventh chords in this introductory passage contributes to the "Pathétique" quality of this movement.[10]

EXAMPLE 2.23 Beethoven, Piano Sonata in C Minor, op. 13, I, mm. 1–5

i to v

1. Beethoven, Piano Sonata in D Major, op. 10, no. 3, I, mm. 23–30 (Example 2.24). The pivot in the modulation to v (F♯ minor) is i^6/iv^6.

EXAMPLE 2.24 Beethoven, Piano Sonata in D Major, op. 10, no. 3, I, mm. 23–30

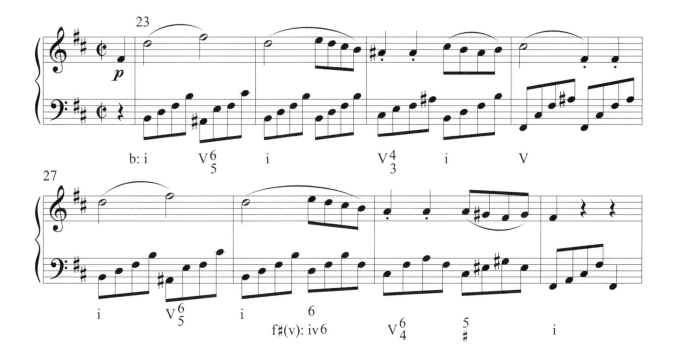

2. Bach, Prelude in E♭ Minor (*WTC* I), mm. 1–16 (Example 2.25). The first four measures establish the main key by the progression $I - iv_4^6 - vii^o - i$ (an alternate to the more common $i - ii_2^{o4} - V_5^6 - i$). This is followed by the progression $i - VI - iv - V - i$, where VI and iv are introduced by their secondary dominants. The pivot for the modulation to v (B♭ minor) is i/iv. The new key is subsequently confirmed by a strong cadence in mm. 15–16.

EXAMPLE 2.25 Bach, Prelude in E♭ Minor (*WTC* I), mm. 1–16

A Summary Example: Bach, French Suite No. 2, Menuet (Example 2.26)

This is an excellent example with which to conclude this chapter, since it illustrates many of the ideas expressed so far, but also points the way toward new territory we will be discussing as we get deeper into music analysis. We begin by examining the movement's formal organization and overall tonal structure. This movement, like the gavotte discussed earlier (Example 2.20), is in binary form, and we have outlined its main formal divisions and subdivisions on the score (Example 2.26). The first part consists of an eight-measure period that modulates to III (E♭). It is divided into two phrases, the first ending on the dominant and the second modulating to III. The pivot in the modulation is i^{5-6}/IV^6.[11] The two phrases are marked "forephrase" and "afterphrase," a correct if somewhat awkward translation of the German terms *Vorsatz* and *Nachsatz*.[12] The second part opens with a period that is similar in certain respects to the opening one. The forephrase leads from tonic to dominant in the new key, and the afterphrase modulates to another new key. In this case there is no pivot, but rather the bass note E♭ of m. 9 is led via the chromatic passing tone E♮ in mm. 13–14 to F in m. 15, after which the modulation is confirmed by the perfect authentic cadence in mm. 15–16. Heard in relation to E♭ (III), this is a modulation to its supertonic, but, in relation to the original key, it is a modulation to iv. The next eight measures are a descending fifth sequence connecting the subdominant to the dominant. We might expect a return to the tonic at this point, but instead the forephrase of the final eight measures extends the dominant, the tonic coming only at the beginning of the afterphrase, which concludes with a perfect authentic cadence on the tonic. The overall tonal organization, then, is i – III (m. 8) – iv (m. 16) – V (m. 24) – i (m. 32).

The discussion above tells us a good deal about this short movement, but, in fact, it has much more to tell us if we look more closely. To this end we have prepared a simplification of the voice leading with additional analytical notations (Example 2.27). If we were to ask ten different music analysts to prepare a simplified representation of the score, we would probably get ten slightly different results depending on decisions about how much to include or exclude, but they would all agree in principle. The point is this: there is no "right" solution, but several "right" ones; however, there are clearly "wrong" ones, where there is a misreading of the harmony or voice leading. We will not explain every measure, but rather we will talk through the decisions made in the opening phrase. Later on, beginning in m. 17, a conscious decision was made to include less detail than earlier.

In the first measure, the motivic gesture in the right-hand part masks an underlying stepwise motion in quarter notes moving in contrary motion to the bass. The relationship between the voices is a voice exchange, where the middle of the three notes is passing. In the second measure, a modified statement of the motive in eighth notes is taken by the left-hand part, masking a motion in parallel tenths with the top part leading back to tonic harmony supporting E♭5 on the downbeat of m. 3. In the third measure E♭5 is decorated by a turn figure before progressing to D5 and on down to B♮4 supported by the dominant in m. 4. Once again the eighth-note motion in m. 4 covers an underlying quarter-note progression in the top part, which forms a voice exchange with the lower part. We have indicated the motion in parallel tenths in mm. 2–3 between the staves in Example 2.27, and above mm. 2–4 we have indicated that these measures should be compared to mm. 17–24. The latter engages a new topic, that of **motivic parallelism**, a topic we will touch on here and

EXAMPLE 2.26 Bach, French Suite No. 2 in C Minor, Menuet

EXAMPLE 2.27 Voice-leading simplification of Example 2.26

there, as appropriate, in later chapters. In this instance, the motion in parallel tenths in mm. 2–3, beginning from A♭5 over F4 and leading to E♭5 over C4, is expanded by the sequence beginning in m. 17, where each 10 falls every other measure, the pattern breaking at E♭5 over C3 in m. 23. If this parallel is not convincing at first, compare the continuation (mm. 23–24) to mm. 3–4. The arrow from the E♭5 in m. 23 to the D3 two measures later indicates that the line, clearly articulated by the eighth-note motive, continues in the lower part. Once the parallel between mm. 2–4 and 17–24 is pointed out, this aspect of the composition's fabric becomes clear. If we were to scan this short movement for additional statements of this motivic idea A♭–G–F–(E♭), we would find that it occurs numerous times in a variety of contexts. See mm. 5–6 (inner voice), 15–16 (top voice), 25–26 (inner voice), 29–30 (inner voice), and 30–31 (top voice), where the descent to closure occurs. Less obvious, perhaps, are references to this idea in mm. 10–11 (right hand) and 12 (left hand). One goal of this text is to make you aware of relationships of this sort so you can uncover them in your own study of music.

In this chapter we have employed two types of reductions, which we have referred to as simplifications and representations of the voice leading. In the first type, note values represent relative durations once notes of melodic and rhythmic embellishment have been removed. See Examples 2.10b, 2.11b, and 2.27. You should use the last of these as a model in preparing the assignments suggested below. In the second type, we are interested only in representing the underlying voice leading, as in Examples 2.9b and 2.12b, where note values do not represent duration. A fuller explanation of these two types of reductions is provided in the Appendix.

SUGGESTED ASSIGNMENTS

Secondary Dominants and Diminished Seventh Chords

1. Beethoven, Piano Sonata, op.14, no. 2, II, mm. 1–20. Note the unusual resolution of the B♭4 in m. 7. What gives rise to this? Where is its resolution?

Modulation

We suggest you prepare analyses of one or both of the following movements by Bach: Menuet from French Suite No. 3 (a) and the Sarabande from French Suite No. 1 (b). Follow these steps:

1. On the score identify the major formal divisions (periods) and their subdivisions into phrases, identifying the relationship between phrases (e.g., antecedent-consequent, forephrase-afterphrase). Indicate the harmonic goals of phrases and, where appropriate, indicate the pivot of a modulation.

2. Prepare a simplification of the voice leading by removing all notes of melodic embellishment and rhythmic displacement. You may find this difficult at first, so the instructor may want to begin this as an in-class project. After completing this step, consider specific relationships between voices, like motion in parallel tenths or voice exchange, and indicate below your reduced score levels of harmonic organization.

(a) Bach, Menuet from French Suite No. 3

(b) Bach, Sarabande from French Suite No. 1

3   Phrase Design

Up to this point our focus has been largely on understanding the principles that direct the harmonic organization of the music of the eighteenth and nineteenth centuries. In this chapter, we begin our study of formal organization. First, we consider what constitutes a musical phrase and discuss the most common ways that phrases are constructed and combined. Then we consider how phrases can be expanded. The chapter concludes with an analysis of a complete piece by Haydn that comically plays with our expectations about phrase design. Although the main purpose of this chapter is to establish formal principles in advance of our study of longer pieces in Part II of this book, even within this chapter we will see how composers both worked within a set of norms for phrase construction and also stepped outside these norms, balancing the need for familiarity with the pleasure of surprise, the goal of comprehensibility with the passion of expression.[1]

Phrase Design

What is a phrase?

The term "phrase" is one that all musicians use frequently, often without giving a second thought to what constitutes a musical phrase. There is a shared sense among musicians that "phrase" designates a segment of music that belongs together and that conveys motion—a feeling of "beginning – middle – end." Where musicians' conceptions of "phrase" differ is typically in the length of musical passage referred to. In the intensity of a rehearsal or coaching, many things are often called "phrases"—from units of perhaps two measures to sixteen or more measures. And, it is certainly true that skilled performers provide a sense of shape both to short spans of music and to longer ones at the same time. The most inspiring performances ensure that local shaping never interferes with the projection of larger-scale musical spans. This is one of the reasons why music analysts have become increasingly precise in our usage of the term phrase, reserving it for the larger spans that have a true capacity for "beginning – middle – end."

In the repertoire under consideration in this book, musical phrases come in a variety of lengths, but four measures and eight measures are the most common. Length does not determine what constitutes a musical phrase, but it is helpful to remember that a true musical phrase hardly ever has a length shorter than four measures. Phrases are defined by cadences: if there has been no tonal motion leading to a cadence, there has been no phrase. Thus, our discussion of phrase design must begin with a review of cadences.

Although cadences are classified in terms of their harmonic content, they arise from a combination of harmonic, melodic, and rhythmic factors. Cadences are formed only by a very small number of harmonic progressions, but the mere presence of one of these harmonic progressions does not automatically indicate the presence of a cadence. The harmonic progression must be wedded to a degree of completion in the melody. Often, there is also a reduction in rhythmic activity at the cadence, but this is not always the case, especially in music of the early eighteenth century, such as much of Bach. Remember, however, that a cadence rarely occurs less than four measures away from adjacent cadences.

There are two principal types of cadences: those that end on tonic harmony and those that end on dominant harmony. The former, referred to as **authentic cadences**, move from a root-position V (or V^7) to a root-position I. Both the V and I chords must be in root position for an authentic cadence to occur. Cadences that end on the dominant are referred to by a variety of interchangeable names: half, inauthentic, and semicadence; we will refer to them as **half cadences** (HC). In a half cadence, there is only a restriction on the ultimate chord, which must be V in root position.[2] The preceding chord is often one with predominant function (such as IV, ii^6, or V^6_5 of V), but this need not be the case. Some writers on music also describe "deceptive" and "plagal" cadences, corresponding to the harmonic motions V (or V^7) – vi and IV – I respectively. As will become clear below, these progressions hardly ever articulate the level of form corresponding to the musical phrase and thus rarely constitute cadences. Most often, a V – vi progression delays arrival at the harmonic goal, necessitating another run at closing the phrase—a motion that achieves an authentic cadence. When IV – I occurs at the end of a melodic unit, its function is almost always post-cadential: it comes after a V – I progression that actually brought closure to the phrase with an authentic cadence.

It is useful to distinguish between an authentic cadence where the upper line ends on $\hat{1}$ and one where the upper line remains on $\hat{3}$ or $\hat{5}$.[3] The former, referred to as a **perfect authentic cadence** (PAC), has a greater degree of finality than the latter, the **imperfect authentic cadence** (IAC). Thus, in degree of finality, there is an increase from half cadence to imperfect authentic cadence to perfect authentic cadence. Certain types of cadences are used in particular locations within pieces to provide the appropriate degree of closure.

Phrase Construction and Combination—Part 1: The Period

In Chapter 1, we already introduced an important type of phrase organization: the **parallel period**, which consists of an **antecedent phrase** and a **consequent phrase**. We discussed three examples from Mozart's piano sonatas (Examples 1.8, 1.9, and 1.10), and we reproduce the second of these here as Example 3.1. Two phrases constitute a musical period if the first ends with a weaker cadence (HC or IAC) and the second ends with a stronger cadence (IAC or PAC) and it makes sense to group the two phrases together into a larger formal entity. By far, the most common cadential pairing is HC – PAC, as seen in Example 3.1. The term "parallel" refers to the deployment of the same melodic material at the beginnings of the antecedent and consequent phrases. The vast majority of periods are parallel. A period where the consequent does not begin with the same material as the antecedent is termed a **contrasting period**, and we will provide an example of this later (see Example 3.2).

EXAMPLE 3.1 Mozart, Piano Sonata in B♭ major, K. 333, III, mm. 1–8

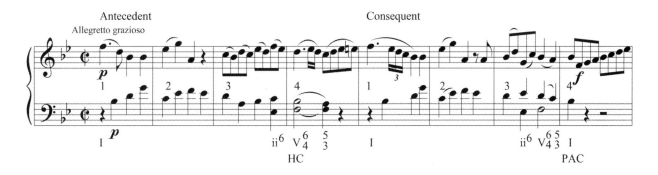

Note that in Example 3.1 the two phrases are of equal length. This is what usually happens in a period, and when this is not the case it is almost always because the consequent is *longer* than the antecedent. We will explore the topic of phrase expansion later in this chapter. The most common length for a period is eight measures (4 + 4), but other lengths are found, especially sixteen measures (8 + 8). Within each of the phrases in a period there is often a binary division, that is, a subdivision of the phrase into two-measure subphrases. In Example 3.1 this is particularly clear given the rest near the end of the second measure and the highly contrasting rhythm and melodic contour of mm. 3–4 compared to mm. 1–2.

If we list only the initial and final harmonies of each phrase in Example 3.1, our analysis would be I – V for the antecedent and I – I for the consequent. Since it is possible to have cadential pairings other than HC – PAC, other tonal plans are possible. The four tonal plans below account for nearly all period designs:

Antecedent phrase			*Consequent phrase*			
I	–	V (HC)	I	–	I (PAC)	interrupted
I	–	V (HC)	X	–	I (PAC)	continuous
I	–	V (HC)	I	–	X (PAC)	progressive
I	–	I (IAC)	I	–	I (PAC)	sectional

A full description of the organization of Example 3.1, then, would be "parallel interrupted period." We use the term **interrupted** because of the stoppage of the harmonic motion at the dominant, after which the consequent begins again with tonic harmony. Often, there is an accompanying melodic interruption as well, whereby the melody descends to $\hat{2}$ at the end of the antecedent (the C in m. 4 of Example 3.1) and, after beginning again at its original pitch, descends to $\hat{1}$ at the end of the consequent (the B♭ at the start of m. 8).

We now offer an example of each of the other tonal plans listed above. In continuous and progressive periods, the antecedent phrase still ends on V, but either the beginning or the end of the consequent does not present the initial tonic harmony. In a **continuous** period, the consequent phrase begins with a non-tonic harmony, almost always the dominant or the supertonic. In the initial eight measures of the minuet from Beethoven's Piano Sonata, op. 22, the consequent phrase picks up with the dominant harmony from the end of the antecedent (Example 3.2). Unlike our other examples, the consequent phrase does not begin with the same material as the antecedent; thus, this is a **contrasting** period. The turn figure with which the consequent begins does derive from the antecedent, but not from the beginning of the phrase. When we are making the distinction between parallel and contrasting periods we are comparing the *beginnings* of phrases. In a contrasting period, the consequent often has a motivic connection to some portion of the antecedent, just not to the beginning. The minuet from Beethoven's Piano Sonata, op. 10, no. 3 (Example 3.3) begins with a parallel **continuous** period, but here the harmony at the start of the consequent is supertonic (not dominant). Note that this period spans sixteen measures (8 + 8). Of course, this period does not take twice as long to perform as the previous one given its faster tempo (observe the absence of any subdivisions smaller than the quarter note).

EXAMPLE 3.2 Beethoven, Piano Sonata in B♭ major, op. 22, III, mm. 1–8

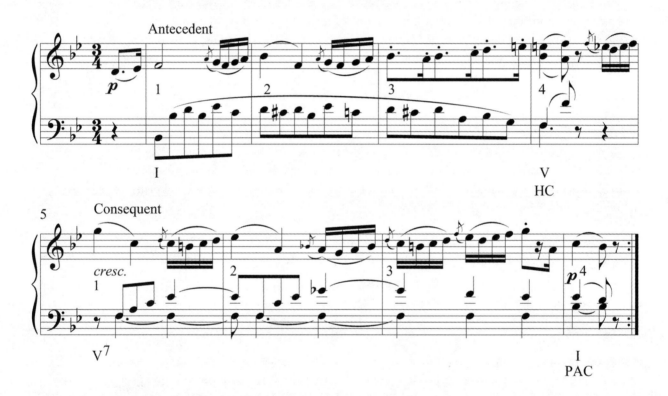

A **progressive** period involves modulation during the consequent phrase. In theory, the modulation could be to any key, but in practice the modulation is usually to the dominant (in the case of major mode) or to the relative major (in the case of minor mode). Instead of the term "progressive," some authors refer to this organization as a "period with modulating consequent." An example is the opening eight measures of the finale of Haydn's Piano Sonata No. 34 in E minor (Example 3.4). The consequent preserves the first measure of the antecedent before the pivot chord (m. 6: iv⁶/ii⁶) takes the period to a PAC in the relative major.

EXAMPLE 3.3 Beethoven, Piano Sonata in D Major, op. 10, no. 3, III, mm. 1–16

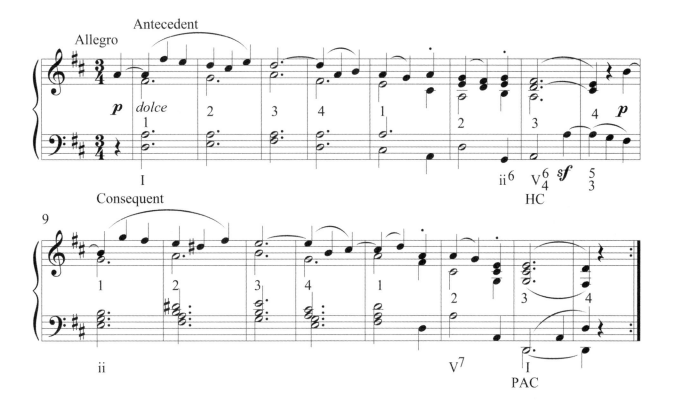

EXAMPLE 3.4 Haydn, Piano Sonata in E Minor, Hob. XVI/34, III, mm. 1–8

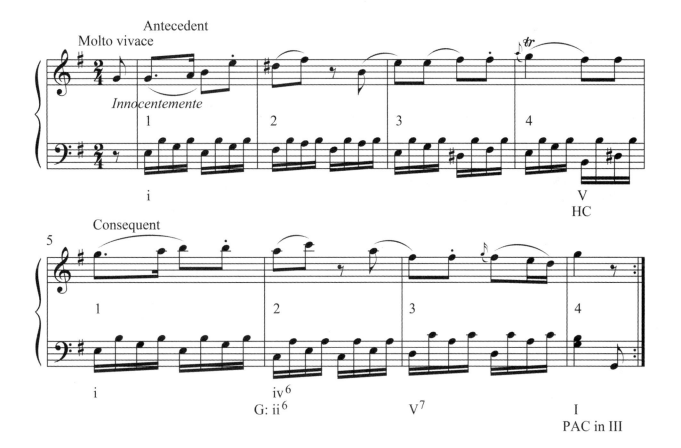

EXAMPLE 3.5 Mozart, Piano Sonata in B♭ major, K. 281, I, mm. 1–8

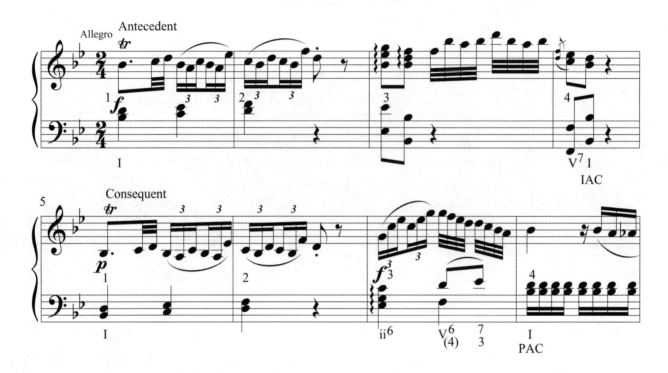

The final tonal plan, the **sectional** period, differs from all of the others in that its first phrase is closed. Mozart's Piano Sonata, K. 281, opens with a parallel **sectional** period due to the tonic harmony at the end of the antecedent phrase (Example 3.5). Note that the cadence in m. 4 is an IAC since $\hat{3}$ (D) occurs in the melody.

Phrase Construction and Combination—Part 2: The Sentence

A period is a design involving *two* phrases. We turn now to a common way in which an individual phrase can be organized: sentence design.[4] In a musical sentence, a **basic idea** is stated and immediately repeated, and then the phrase continues to a cadence. We will refer to the statement of the basic idea and its repetition as a **presentation** and the remainder of the phrase as a **continuation**. The continuation is typically the same length as the presentation; when this is not the case it is almost always because the continuation is *longer* than the presentation. Most often, a musical sentence consists of eight measures: a two-measure basic idea, its repetition, and a four-measure continuation. However, sentences of sixteen measures (4 + 4 + 8) and, in slower tempos, of four measures (1 + 1 + 2) are by no means unusual.

As with period design, a sentence can have various tonal plans. It is useful to identify three different tonal plans for presentations. First, the repetition of the basic idea can be **exact**, meaning that it expresses the same harmony as the initial statement. (This harmony is almost always tonic harmony.) Second, the repetition of the basic idea can be a **response** to the initial statement, meaning that it exchanges dominant harmony for the tonic harmony of the original statement. This can occur in two ways. If the basic idea expresses only tonic harmony, then the response will express only dominant harmony; if the basic idea progresses I – V, then the response goes V – I. Bear in mind that even when these harmonies occur in root position they do not have a cadential function: a basic idea and its repetition do not form a melodic unit that is sufficiently complete to constitute a musical phrase. Third, the repetition of the basic idea can be **sequential**, meaning that it transposes the initial statement of the basic idea to another harmony (other than the dominant); this other harmony is usually supertonic (and thus this type of presentation is not characteristic of sentences in the minor mode).

The continuation typically brings a feeling of intensification. This quality often arises from a shortening of the melodic subphrases. In a sentence with a two-measure basic idea, the continuation often begins with a pair of one-measure segments before a two-measure unit leads to the cadence. This shortening of melodic units generally results from a literal fragmentation of the presentation's basic idea, but the continuation need not have a tight thematic connection to the presentation. Other features commonly found in a continuation include an increase in harmonic rhythm, a speeding up of surface rhythm, and the use of sequence.

A quintessential example of a musical sentence is the opening of Beethoven's Piano Sonata, op. 2, no. 1 (Example 3.6). The presentation is of the response type, since the basic

EXAMPLE 3.6 Beethoven, Piano Sonata in F Minor, op. 2, no. 1, I, mm. 1–8

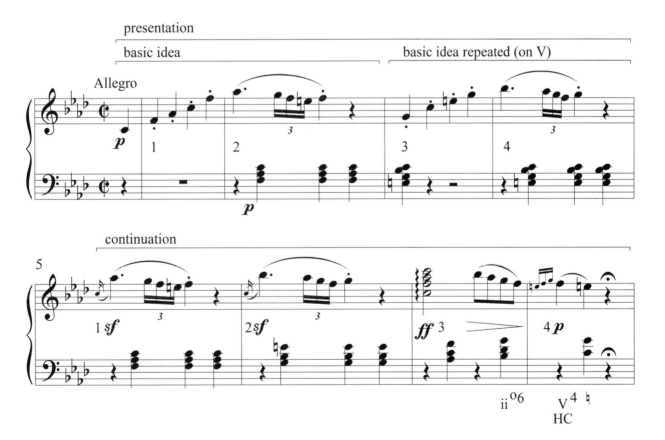

idea expresses tonic harmony, while the repetition expresses dominant harmony. The start of the continuation brings a return to tonic harmony. In Chapters 1 and 2, we frequently mentioned that harmony operates on different levels. When one looks at the overall tonal structure of a sentence, it is almost always the case that the local chord changes within the presentation participate in a prolongation of the initial tonic harmony that lasts at least until the start of the continuation. In Beethoven's sentence, note that the first two measures of the continuation present a fragment—the second half—of the basic idea. There is thus both a shortening of subphrase length and a clear motivic connection to the presentation. In addition, the harmonic rhythm accelerates to one chord per measure in mm. 5–6 and then to two chords per measure in m. 7. A very similar construction occurs near the start of Beethoven's Fifth Symphony, except that the sentence spans sixteen, rather than eight, measures (Example 3.7). We will provide examples of presentations with exact repetition and with sequential repetition later in this chapter (see Examples 3.11 and 3.15 respectively).

EXAMPLE 3.7 Beethoven, Symphony No. 5, op. 67, I, mm. 6–21

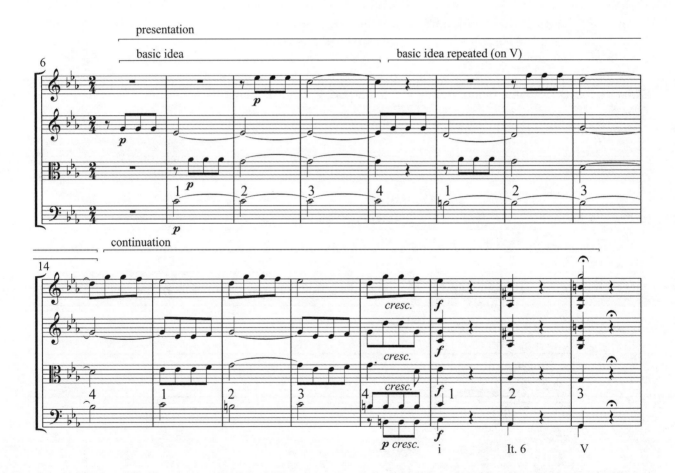

Phrase Construction and Combination—Part 3: Larger Period Design

We now turn to a larger design based on the concept of the period, namely a period where the antecedent and consequent phrases are each in sentence design. Since the most common length for a sentence is eight measures, the most common length for a period comprised of two sentences is sixteen measures. The opening of the slow movement from Beethoven's Piano Sonata, op. 10, no. 1, which was studied in Chapter 1 (Example 1.17), provides a good illustration; we reproduce Example 1.17 as Example 3.8. As noted in Chapter 1, there

EXAMPLE 3.8 Beethoven, Piano Sonata in C Minor, op. 10, no. 1, II, mm. 1–16

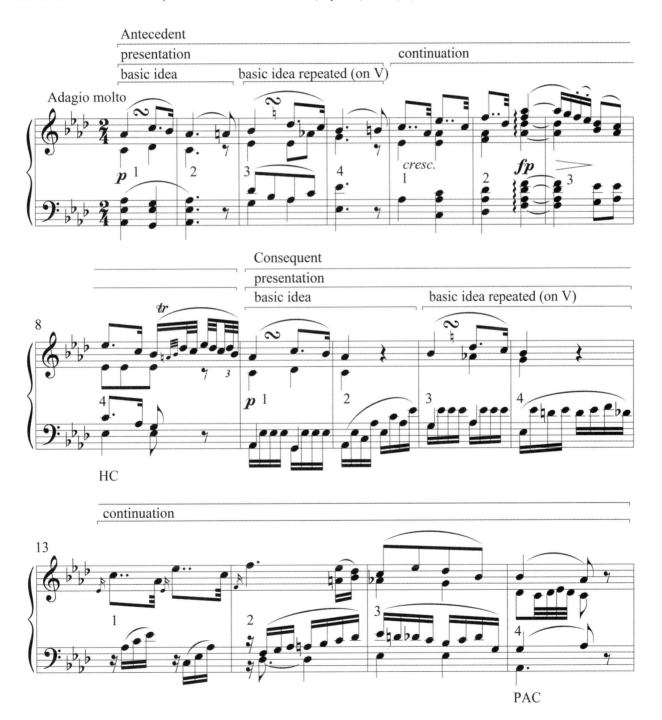

is an eight-measure antecedent leading to the dominant and an eight-measure consequent ending with a PAC. Looking more closely at the antecedent, we observe a basic idea in mm. 1–2 that is repeated over dominant harmony in mm. 3–4. Thus, like our previous two examples, the presentation is of the response type. At the start of the continuation (m. 5), there is a sense of acceleration since the new double-dotted melodic figure is stated on three successive beats in contrast to the slower repetition of mm. 1–2 in mm. 3–4. Recognizing that mm. 1–8 deploy melodic material in sentence design helps us realize immediately that the root-position dominant in m. 4 does not end the phrase by articulating a HC. The melodic structure is not sufficiently complete for a cadence to occur at this point.

We have only discussed the most common types of phrase organization. Not every phrase can be described as a sentence design or understood as part of a musical period. Some phrases are simply phrases. Being aware of the most common ways of organizing the melodic content of a phrase, however, expedites determining where phrases begin and end. As we will see, it also enables us to recognize when a composer writes a phrase that is modeled on a common phrase design but departs from it in some way. Such departures have structural and expressive significance.

Phrase Elision and Hypermeter

Phrase Elision

In all of the examples up to this point, every phrase ends before the subsequent phrase begins. This is not always the case. Sometimes the final event of a phrase coincides with the start of the next phrase. The slow movement of Beethoven's Piano Trio, op. 1, no. 2 (Example 3.9) provides an example. The first phrase is in sentence design; mm. 1–4 constitute a statement-response presentation of the I – V, V – I type (rather than the simpler I, V type seen thus far). The continuation does not achieve its cadence within four measures; the tonal motion does not stop on the V^7 chord at the end of m. 8. The V^7 chord resolves to the E major harmony in m. 9, which coincides precisely with the start of the melody in the violin. We will refer to this as **phrase elision**; some writers use the equivalent term **phrase overlap**. Phrase elision helps to maintain musical flow and prevent the music from becoming excessively segmented.

Another instance of phrase elision occurs near the start of Haydn's Symphony No. 104; Example 3.10a provides the orchestral score, while Example 3.10b gives a piano reduction with analytic annotations.[5] After the eight-measure antecedent, one expects an eight-measure consequent leading to a PAC. Tonic harmony does arrive eight measures after the start of the consequent, but the dynamics are suddenly *fortissimo* and winds, brass, and timpani join the strings in a jolting orchestral *tutti*. The subsequent music continues in this new dynamic and texture; in other words, the cadential arrival elides with the next phrase.

We will return to both the Haydn symphony and the Beethoven trio below and explore a bit further why the Haydn feels quite different from the Beethoven even though both exhibit the same phenomenon of phrase elision.

EXAMPLE 3.9 Beethoven, Piano Trio in G Major, op. 1, no. 2, II, mm. 1–9

EXAMPLE 3.10a Haydn, Symphony No. 104, I, mm. 17–33

EXAMPLE 3.10b Annotated piano reduction of Example 3.10a

Hypermeter

On the examples in this chapter, we have been including Arabic numerals: 1 2 3 4. It probably appeared that they were simply an aid in counting measures, but they actually have a deeper significance. Turn back to the excerpt we studied from Beethoven's Fifth Symphony (Example 3.7), and try to conduct it. Beethoven's metronome marking is ♩ = 108, meaning that each measure lasts just over half a second. Clearly, it is not possible to conduct the quarter notes in Beethoven's notated $\frac{2}{4}$ meter. Instead, the pulse that a conductor would beat in this movement corresponds to the notated measure. A conductor would beat a quadruple pattern (i.e., the conducting gestures for $\frac{4}{4}$ meter) across four-measure units. Thus, the "1 2 3 4" annotations on the score represent a type of meter—not just a counting of numbers of measures. All of the measures marked "1" have a strength or metric accent in the same way that the first beat in a $\frac{4}{4}$ measure does. In the music of the eighteenth and nineteenth centuries, meter—like harmony— operates on multiple levels. Meter that operates above the level of the notated meter is referred to as **hypermeter**. In the case of Beethoven's Fifth the hypermeter actually corresponds to the spontaneously *perceived* meter of the listener; often, the notated meter is the perceived meter and hypermeter is perceptible only when one specifically focuses on its slower pulses. We will use the term hypermeter, though, for any meter above the level of the notated measure, regardless of whether it is the perceived meter or a perceptible meter.

In discussing hypermeter, analysts adapt terminology used in discussing meter. Just as measure refers to a cyclical grouping of beats within a meter, the term **hypermeasure** refers to the analogous grouping within a hypermeter. Thus, a four-measure unit labeled as "1 2 3 4" would constitute a hypermeasure within a quadruple hypermeter. The start of a hypermeasure is a **hypermetric downbeat**—just as the first beat of a measure is a down-beat—or in abridged form, **hyperdownbeat**. The subsequent beats in a hypermeasure can be designated as "second (or third, or fourth) **hypermetric beat**" or more succinctly "**hyperbeat** 2 (or 3, or 4)."

Not all hypermeter is quadruple, but this is by far the most common scenario. Extended passages with triple hypermeter are rare. A famous instance occurs in the scherzo of Beethoven's Ninth Symphony, and the composer specifically tells the conductor "*ritmo di tre battute.*" As in the Fifth Symphony, this very fast movement is a piece where the perceived meter (and the meter given by the conductor's gestures) is actually the hypermeter. The explicit indication of triple hypermeter in this passage is helpful, since elsewhere the music proceeds in quadruple hypermeter (which Beethoven indicates as "*ritmo di quattro battute*"). Some pieces have duple hypermeter—that is, a simple alternation of strong and weak measures rather than the "strong–weak–medium–weak" feeling of quadruple hypermeter. However, as we will see below, it is possible to have an underlying quadruple hypermeter even when the music does not literally proceed in four-measure units throughout. Therefore, it is important not to infer duple hypermeter without considering the possibility of quadruple hypermeter.

Except for a very few pieces like the scherzo from Beethoven's Ninth, hypermeter is not explicitly notated in the score. This is different from pitch or rhythm or meter at the level of the notated meter. What, then, creates our feeling of hypermeter? How can we discern hypermeter when looking at a score? Hypermeter is closely related to phrase and subphrase design. Phrases (and large subphrases) generally begin at or slightly before hypermetric downbeats. In addition, when musical material is repeated, it retains its original hypermetric identity as much as possible. The onset of an event that is sustained for a relatively long time—a pitch, a harmony, a texture—can also be indicative of a hypermetric downbeat. Thus, the sense of "beginning" is associated with hypermetric downbeats. As we shall see, when events with strongly initiatory quality occur unexpectedly close to, or far from, one another, there is often a contraction, or expansion, within the hypermeter.

We return now to the examples of phrase elision from the Beethoven trio and the Haydn symphony. In the Beethoven trio (Example 3.9), the elision keeps the hypermeter periodic. Since the first phrase does not end until the downbeat of m. 9, only by launching the new phrase at that downbeat can the quadruple hypermeter continue without disruption. In the Haydn symphony (Example 3.10), on the other hand, the elision introduces an irregularity in the hypermeter. A measure that we expected to be hypermetrically weak—hyperbeat 4—is made to function as a hypermetric downbeat for the following phrase. In Example 3.10b, notice that the hypermetric analysis of the measure containing the elision is 4 = 1. Just as the tonic harmony at the start of this measure both concludes a phrase and launches the next one, hypermetrically this downbeat both provides the last hyperbeat of the preceding phrase and the hypermetric downbeat for the following one. When a measure has two hypermetric functions, we refer to this as a **hypermetric reinterpretation**.[6] The hypermetric reinterpretation is another reason why this measure has such a jolting effect, besides the shock of the *fortissimo* and entrance of winds, brass, and timpani. By far, the most common hypermetric reinterpretation is 4 = 1, but it is certainly possible for a new hypermetric downbeat to intrude even further into a preceding hypermeasure (e.g., 3 = 1 in a quadruple hypermeter). As we have seen, phrase elision may or may not involve hypermetric reinterpretation. Hypermetric reinterpretation, though, almost always involves elision, if not elision of two phrases then elision of two subphrases.

It is difficult to make generalizations about where elision tends to occur. One piece of advice: If a pair of phrases that begin similarly can be placed in an antecedent-consequent relationship (i.e., a HC at the end of the first phrase), this is almost always the best analysis (rather than an authentic cadence at the end of the first phrase elided to the start of the second phrase). Glance back at Examples 3.1 and 3.8. In both cases there are some short notes that provide rhythmic continuity between the end of the antecedent and the start of the consequent. The underlying structure, though, is the arrival on the V triad; the melodic embellishment provides some momentum towards the next downbeat but does not continue the phrase to the next downbeat.

Phrase Expansion

The phrases in all of our examples thus far have been either four, eight, or sixteen measures in length. While these are the most common lengths, phrases of many other lengths occur. When they do, it is usually possible to understand how they relate to a four-measure, eight-measure, or sixteen-measure model. Generally, phrases of irregular length are longer, not shorter, than the "normative" model to which they may be related. Thus, this section is titled "Phrase Expansion," although phrase contraction occasionally takes place. We will discuss several techniques by which phrases can be expanded. In addition, we will consider the hypermetric consequences of phrase expansion.

External Phrase Expansions

Phrase expansions can be divided into two types: those that are external to the phrase and those that are internal. An external expansion is one that occurs before the real beginning of a phrase or that extends a phrase after its cadence. In the analytic literature, one encounters a variety of terms to denote an expansion before the beginning of a phrase, including introduction, vamp, and prefix. Similarly, multiple terms exist for expansions after the cadence, including post-cadential expansion, codetta (for an extension of an authentic cadence), standing-on-the-dominant (for an extension of a half cadence), and suffix. We prefer the terms introduction and post-cadential expansion (or extension) to refer to the two types of external expansion.

The slow movement of Beethoven's String Quartet, op. 135, demonstrates both types of external expansion (Example 3.11). The underlying phrase is an eight-measure sentence (mm. 3–10): mm. 3–6 constitute a presentation with exact repetition and mm. 7–10 a continuation leading to a PAC on the second beat of m. 10. Note the shortening of melodic subphrases from two measures to one measure when the continuation begins, as well as the quickening of the harmonic rhythm and the use of sequence. Before this sentence begins, there is a two-measure introduction that unfolds the tonic harmony; this is an external expansion. After the PAC in m. 10, there is a two-measure external expansion. The cello imitates the first violin's cadential figure A♭–F–E♭–D♭, which returns to the first violin in the next measure. Harmonically, mm. 11–12 prolong the tonic harmony from the second beat of m. 10 until the downbeat of m. 13, whereupon an ornamented repetition of the eight-measure sentence begins in a higher register. The first twelve measures are thus best understood as an expanded eight-measure phrase.

What are the hypermetric consequences of these phrase expansions? When there is a significant amount of expansion present, it is often useful to distinguish between a **surface hypermeter** and an **underlying hypermeter**. In the Beethoven string quartet, there is a continuous duple hypermeter throughout the entire excerpt; the odd-numbered measures are hypermetrically stronger than the even-numbered ones. This constitutes the surface hypermeter of the passage. If we take the phrase expansions into account, we can understand an underlying quadruple hypermeter in mm. 3–10. Measures that do not participate in the underlying hypermeter can be designated with "———" in the hypermetric analysis to indicate that they expand another hyperbeat or by placing parentheses in the hypermetric analysis. In this excerpt, the surface and underlying hypermeters have a straightforward relationship; measures that are hypermetrically strong (or weak) in the underlying hypermeter possess the same relative hypermetric strength in the surface hypermeter. As we will see below, the relationship between surface and underlying hypermeters can be more complex.

We turn now to a phrase studied near the end of Chapter 2 (Example 2.22), the second phrase of Mozart's Piano Sonata, K. 310 (Example 3.12). As discussed in the last chapter, the phrase modulates from A minor to C major, ending with a half cadence. The phrase is an expanded eight-measure sentence; note the acceleration in harmonic rhythm in the fifth measure. The shortening of melodic units is less obvious, but observe the handling of the descending slurred two-note idea. It occurs in the second and fourth measures of the presentation, and it occurs three times in close succession at the start of the continuation. The goal dominant arrives at the phrase's eighth measure (m. 16) and is extended for seven

EXAMPLE 3.11 Beethoven, String Quartet in F Major, op. 135, II, mm. 1–14

measures (mm. 16–22). The relationship between this post-cadential expansion and the underlying phrase differs from that in the Beethoven string quartet. The expansion does not simply repeat the cadential gesture; rather it enters boldly with a new left-hand texture and a return of the dotted-note motive from the start of the phrase. There is thus some initiatory quality within the expansion, and the expansion itself proceeds in two-measure melodic units with a change in melodic content and rhythmic texture at its fifth measure (m. 20). In the underlying hypermeter, the final hyperbeat coincides with the arrival of the dominant at m. 16, and the post-cadential expansion delays the next hyperbeat until the subsequent phrase begins in m. 23. The expansion projects its own surface hypermeter, reinterpreting hyperbeat 4 in the underlying hypermeter as hyperbeat 1 in its surface hypermeter. Thus, the downbeat of m. 16, which is hypermetrically weak in the underlying hypermeter, is a hypermetric downbeat in the expansion's surface hypermeter. Distinguishing underlying and surface hypermeters recognizes the two qualities of musical time operative in this passage: the expansion is rhythmically energetic but ultimately does not advance the tonal story of the music.

Example 3.12 Mozart, Piano Sonata in A Minor, K. 310, I, mm. 9–23

Internal Phrase Expansions

Phrases can be expanded internally through several techniques, including repetition, composed-out deceleration, parenthetical insertion, and cadential evasion. We will demonstrate each of these techniques, either acting individually or in combination.

Consider the opening of Beethoven's Piano Sonata, op. 2, no. 3 (Example 3.13). Measures 1–8 consist of an eight-measure sentence with statement-response presentation and a continuation that begins with fragmentation of the presentation's basic idea. The cadence in m. 8 is an IAC. Beethoven repeats the entire continuation (with the melody placed in the bass), leading to a PAC at the downbeat of m. 13. The cadence elides with the beginning of the next phrase, an elision that maintains the quadruple hypermeter. Taken as a whole, the true cadence of the phrase is the PAC—not the IAC—and thus we can consider the expansion as internal to a phrase spanning mm. 1–13. Strictly, there is also a composed-out deceleration involved. Notice that in m. 8 the dominant harmony lasts only two beats, whereas in the repetition of the continuation dominant harmony governs mm. 11–12. This delay allows the goal tonic harmony to arrive on a downbeat, which in addition to the melodic closure on $\hat{1}$, gives the cadence greater impact than the third-beat cadence of m. 8.

EXAMPLE 3.13 Beethoven, Piano Sonata in C Major, op. 2, no. 3, I, mm. 1–13

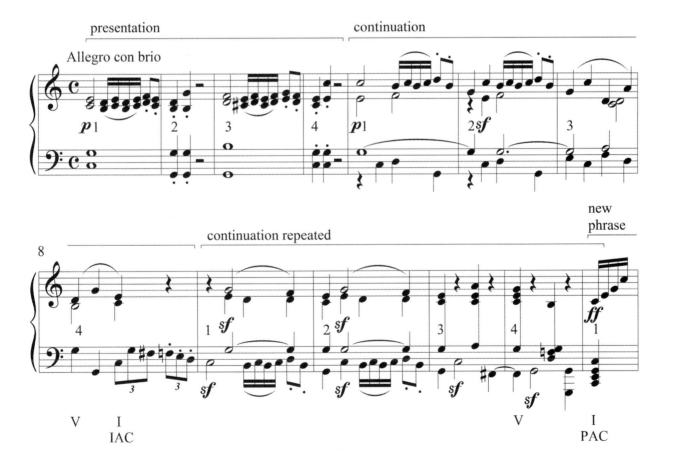

Extremely similar is the start of the second movement of the same sonata (Example 3.14). This movement opens with a four-measure antecedent phrase leading to the dominant. The antecedent is itself in sentence design, an instance of a four-measure sentence (note the *Adagio* tempo). The consequent phrase, also in sentence design, begins on the supertonic—as often happens in a continuous period—and reaches an IAC in the middle of m. 8. Beethoven repeats the continuation (with the left and right hands exchanging material) to attain a PAC at the downbeat of m. 11, which elides with the start of the next phrase. As in the first movement of this sonata, the repeat of the continuation is slightly lengthened so that the

EXAMPLE 3.14 Beethoven, Piano Sonata in C Major, op. 2, no. 3, II, mm. 1–11

EXAMPLE 3.15 Mozart, Piano Sonata in C Major, K. 309, III, mm. 1–19

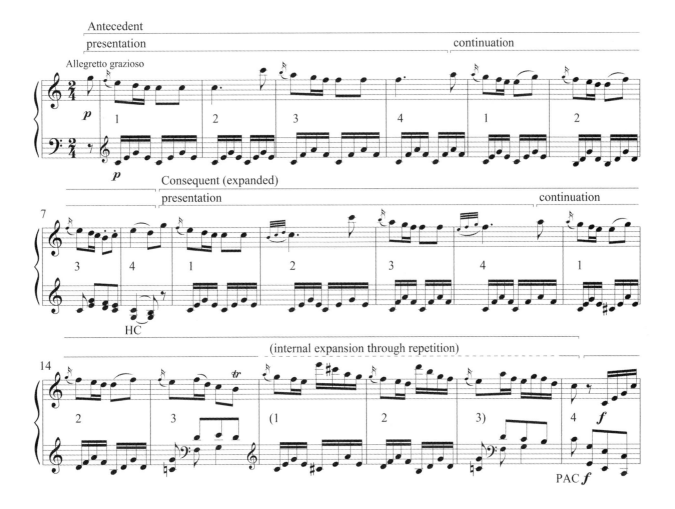

tonic harmony arrives on a downbeat rather than in the middle of a measure. Our careful study of phrase design in the initial themes of these two movements has revealed a striking similarity in construction, despite their vastly different moods.

Expansion can result from repetition that occurs earlier in a phrase. Slightly earlier is the repetition in the second phrase of the finale from Mozart's Piano Sonata, K. 309 (Example 3.15). Based on eight-measure sentence design, this phrase is on the brink of a PAC when the first three measures of the continuation are repeated with slight variation. Instead of eighth notes expressing a rising third (as in mm. 13–14), sixteenth notes fill in falling sixths (mm. 16–17).

Mozart's Clarinet Quintet, K. 581, provides a fascinating instance of phrase expansion in its minuet movement. The second trio of that movement begins with the parallel period given in Example 3.16.[7] This period is striking in several regards. First, the antecedent ends with V^7 – vi; the deceptive progression actually serves in a cadential capacity here. Second, note that the consequent returns the clarinet melody and upper strings exactly but places C♯ rather than A in the cello, substituting first-inversion for root-position tonic harmony.

EXAMPLE 3.16 Mozart, Clarinet Quintet, K. 581, III, Trio II, mm. 1–12

Third, and most importantly for our present discussion, the consequent phrase has four measures of internal expansion (mm. 7–10). In the antecedent $ii^6_5 - V^7$ occurs in mm. 2–3; in the consequent ii^6 begins, as expected, in m. 6 but is reiterated for an additional four measures until the dominant arrives at m. 11. Notice that on the last beat of m. 10 the clarinet returns to the exact same pitches it had on the last beat of m. 2 (shown by the dotted bracket on the score). This makes the return from the digressive measures particularly smooth, as does the clarinet's touching on F♯5 at the downbeat of m. 10, as this was the clarinet's last pitch before the expansion began. Since the expansion consists of four measures and the underlying hypermeter is quadruple, the surface hypermeter continues without interruption during the expansion (i.e., 3 4 1 2 in mm. 7–10).

It is perfectly clear that Mozart's consequent phrase has been expanded and exactly where this has occurred. Less obvious is whether the expansion arises through repetition or parenthetical insertion. The first violin echoes the clarinet's melody—giving the impression of expansion through repetition—but the expansion has an abruptly new texture and accompaniment pattern (or lack thereof), which suggests a parenthetical insertion. Agreeing on the primary technique that generates this expansion is of much less importance than recognizing the presence of expansion.[8]

A straightforward example of parenthetical insertion occurs in the minuet from Haydn's String Quartet, op. 74, no. 1 (Example 3.17). The phrase is headed for a PAC at the downbeat of its eighth measure when three measures of highly contrasting material intrude. The *sforzandi*, introduction of triplets, and the two-beat grouping of material (in contrast to the prevailing triple meter) all distinguish the insertion from the surrounding music. This expansion is quite similar to the one we studied in the C major piano sonata by Mozart (Example 3.15), except that there the three extra measures repeated material that had occurred earlier in the phrase. In the Haydn, note that there is also a brief external expansion as the concluding tonic harmony is extended by a measure.

The only one of the four techniques of internal phrase expansion listed above that we have not seen is cadential evasion. There are various ways that the resolution of a root-position dominant can be evaded, but the most common are through the deceptive progression (to the submediant) or a descending bass line that leads from V through V^4_2 to first-inversion tonic harmony. The former progression occurs in the second phrase of the finale of Beethoven's Violin Sonata, op. 24 (Example 3.18). The first two phrases constitute a parallel interrupted period with each phrase in sentence design. In the seventh measure of the consequent (m. 15), a PAC seems imminent but at the end of the measure the bass moves up to vi instead, necessitating another run at the cadence, which is achieved two measures later.

The slow movement of Mozart's String Quartet, K. 589, provides an explicit example of cadential evasion with V^4_2. Example 3.19 gives the movement's initial four phrases. In the first two phrases (mm. 1–4 and 5–8), the cello soars above the other strings, which results in the viola supplying the bass line. These two phrases form a contrasting interrupted period. Starting in m. 9, the first violin takes the melody and leads a repeat of the preceding two phrases. The first phrase is repeated exactly in mm. 9–12, but the second phrase is expanded by two measures. At the end of its third measure (m. 15), the cello steps down from B♭ to A♭, and two additional measures are required to attain a PAC (whose tonic harmony elides with the start of the next phrase). Mozart's *mfp* indication beautifully marks the expansion, as does the first violin's momentary touching of the high E♭6.

EXAMPLE 3.17 Haydn, String Quartet in C Major, op. 74, no. 1, III, mm.49–60

EXAMPLE 3.18 Beethoven, Violin Sonata in F Major, op. 24, IV, mm. 1–18

EXAMPLE 3.19 Mozart, String Quartet in B♭ Major, K. 589, II, mm. 1–18

It is crucial to bear in mind that a minority of deceptive progressions or $V_2^4 - I^6$ progressions generate a phrase expansion. More often, these progressions partake in the progression that makes up the underlying phrase. Context plays a critical role in determining whether or not a phrase expansion has occurred. Sometimes the decision is easy, as in the previous example, where a version of the phrase occurs first without expansion and then with expansion. In period structures, an expansion of the consequent is readily detected as well, since the antecedent sets up a definite expectation for the length of the consequent. Similarly, with sentence design, the length of the presentation specifies the normative length for the continuation. Sometimes, though, the music offers no such model to assist in our analytic decision-making. In these cases, the lengths of surrounding phrases still play an important role. If all of the surrounding phrases proceed in four-measure units (or multiples thereof), then a phrase with a non-quadruple-based length is much more likely to be an expanded phrase than if there are other nearby phrases with unusual lengths. A five-measure phrase without any expansion rarely occurs, but when it does it would almost surely be close to (likely adjacent to) another phrase of five measures (or at the very least, a phrase with a non-duple length).

We close our discussion of phrase expansion with one example of phrase contraction. The second movement of Schubert's Piano Sonata, D. 664, opens with a parallel sectional period where the first phrase consists of seven measures and the second consists of eight (Example 3.20). A close look at the first phrase reveals that it begins with a four-measure statement-response presentation. The continuation starts in typical fashion by repeating a one-measure fragment of the basic idea. The cadence, however, is achieved in a single measure. The conclusion of the phrase feels early not only because of the contracted phrase length but also due to the suddenly faster harmonic rhythm in m. 7 that arises from the passing bass motion inserted between $\hat{5}$ and $\hat{1}$. Note that our hypermetric analysis indicates "1 2 3" for the continuation; the hypermeasure simply ends after hyperbeat 3. The next measure functions only as a hypermetric downbeat for the following phrase; it in no way continues the preceding hypermeasure (i.e., the hypermetric analysis 4 = 1 would be inappropriate for m. 8). The consequent phrase is a normative eight-measure sentence. The movement's first sonority is an interesting one. Given the slow tempo, we do hear a first-inversion B minor triad for some duration, but ultimately we understand the B as an embellishment of the ensuing A (a 6–5 motion above the bass). This motive completely dominates the melodic structure of these phrases, but its reach extends into the harmony too. The passing bass motion in mm. 6–7, which was noted above, enables a B minor sonority to occur on the downbeat of m. 7. In the consequent the presentation is sequential rather than statement-response, and the sequence is to the submediant (mm. 10–11). The B minor harmony extends into the first measure of the continuation, which results in mm. 8–13 proceeding from I to I^6 via a three-measure vi chord!

EXAMPLE 3.20 Schubert, Piano Sonata in A Major, D. 664, II, mm. 1–15

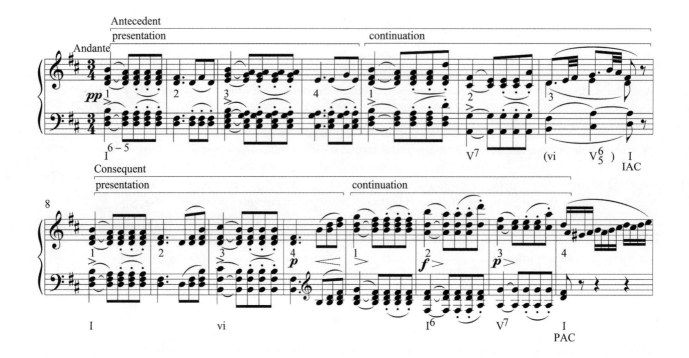

A SUMMARY ANALYSIS (HAYDN)

As a conclusion to this chapter, we will examine the minuet from Haydn's String Quartet, op. 64, no. 6 (Example 3.21). Not only does this analysis allow us to review several of the chapter's main concepts, but it also demonstrates some of the challenges that can arise in studying phrase expansion and hypermeter. The analysis of phrase expansion and hypermeter sometimes admits the possibility of multiple good interpretations.

The minuet consists of two repeated parts with a return of the opening material midway through the second part (mm. 21ff.), a form known as rounded binary form and that will be presented in detail in Chapter 5. The first part of this minuet consists of two phrases that form a parallel progressive period modulating to the dominant. Each of these phrases is six measures long, and our hypermetric analysis treats them as real six-measure phrases—not as expanded four-measure phrases (or as contracted eight-measure phrases). It would, of course, be possible to recompose mm. 1–12 as two four-measure phrases, a possibility demonstrated in Example 3.22. However, these phrases seem quite short, and the recomposition removes their most distinctive feature, namely the accented dissonant chord in the third measure of each phrase. A further argument in support of our hypermetric reading is the fact that there are two adjacent phrases of the same length. As noted earlier, when an irregular phrase length recurs, it is much easier to hear the seeming irregularity as normative. Finally, bear in mind that the hypermetric analysis 1 2 3 4 5 6 implies a regular alternation of strong and weak measures; that is, hyperbeats 1, 3, and 5 are stronger than hyperbeats 2, 4, and 6. It is notable that in these six-measure phrases, there is a slowing of rhythmic activity in the fourth measure. In each case, though, the harmony cannot serve as a cadential goal: IV in the first phrase and a V^6_5 of B♭ in the second phrase. While it is harmonically clear that the fourth measures are not cadential arrivals, the melody's rhythmic slowing draws attention to the lack of cadential articulation and the unusual length of the phrases.

At the start of the minuet's second part, Haydn works with the eighth-note figure played by violin I at the approach to the preceding cadence (mm. 11–12). This is a good example of **linkage technique**, which entails beginning a new phrase with the melodic figure that closed the preceding phrase. After two repetitions that continue the dominant harmony, the figure moves through a descending fifth sequence that returns the music to the tonic key of E♭ major. This eight-measure phrase leads to a half cadence in the tonic at m. 20.

In m. 21, the opening music returns but reworked to avoid modulation. The goal of this material is now the PAC in E♭ major at m. 32. Thus, we again have a twelve-measure span (mm. 21–32), but it is treated very differently than the first twelve measures of the minuet. Instead of two phrases that form a period, there is a single phrase. Further, the hypermeter, which is strongly articulated through rests and the change in dynamics, is now quadruple. On the score, we have shown mm. 21–32 as a twelve-measure phrase that consists of three hypermeasures. Another possibility, indicated above the score, would be to consider the *piano* measures (mm. 25–28) as a parenthetical expansion within an underlying eight-measure phrase. A parenthetical interpretation would be motivated by the sudden changes in dynamics and the rests that separate these measures from their surroundings. In addition, there is a clear harmonic connection between the preceding IV harmony (m. 24) and the ii⁶ harmony (m. 30) that is the first consonant sonority in the subsequent *forte* music. On the other hand, the *piano* measures trace an almost chromatic stepwise ascent from the C5 above the IV harmony (m. 24) to the F5 above the ii⁶ harmony (m. 30). This

EXAMPLE 3.21 Haydn, String Quartet in E♭ major, op. 64, no. 6, III, mm. 1–36

EXAMPLE 3.21 *continued*

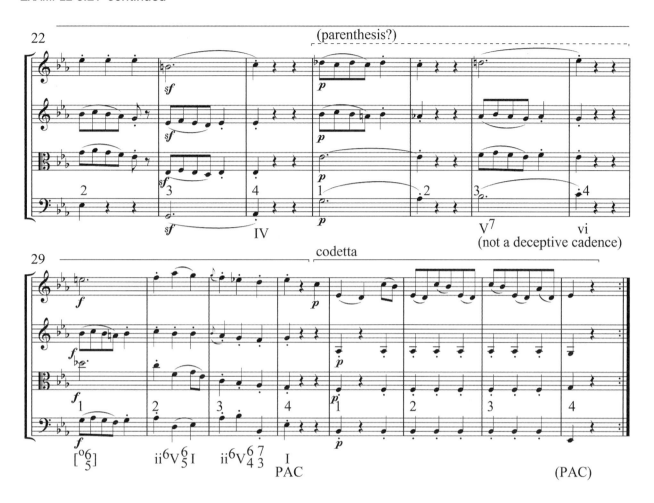

EXAMPLE 3.22 Eight-measure recomposition of mm. 1–12 of Example 3.21

melodic connection cuts across the rests and sharp dynamic changes to support hearing the *piano* measures as integral to the phrase. While either of these interpretations is defensible, a third interpretation would not be. It would not be satisfactory to consider the vi chord in m. 28 as the goal of a deceptive cadence; mm. 21–32 must be considered as a single phrase and not as two phrases. Neither mm. 21–28 nor mm. 29–32 is at the same formal level as mm. 1–6 and mm. 7–12. Regardless of whether one interprets mm. 21–32 as an expanded eight-measure phrase or as a true twelve-measure phrase, one notes the presence of quadruple hypermeter and the momentum of a relatively long phrase leading to the PAC. Compared to mm. 1–12, the reworking of the thematic material resolves the six-measure lengths and provides a phrase that seems more balanced and satisfying. A beautiful detail is Haydn's incorporation of the same chromatic chord in m. 29 as in m. 9; it has a slightly different function—in m. 9 as part of the modulation to the dominant, in m. 29 as an applied diminished seventh of ii^6—but the reuse of this striking sonority provides a compelling connection amidst the very significant amount of thematic reworking that has occurred.

The minuet ends with a short four-measure unit that consists solely of a cadential gesture. When we study complete pieces in Part II of this text, we will see that this type of passage frequently occurs at the end of a piece after the "big" PAC, and we will refer to such passages as codettas. Note that this codetta is based on the cadential figure from the minuet's first phrase (m. 5). This was an element of the opening phrase that had never returned subsequently. Thus, although the codetta is not needed to bring tonal closure to the minuet (the PAC at m. 32 does that), it provides the valuable service of ensuring that every thematic element of the opening phrase recurs somewhere else in the minuet.

Many of the concepts outlined in this chapter may be entirely new, as introductory theory courses and textbooks necessarily focus largely, if not entirely, on chord construction and usage. Therefore, it might be interesting to know that all of the concepts discussed here were written about—using different terminology—in the eighteenth century. Material that is especially similar to our discussion can be found in the composition handbooks authored by Heinrich Christoph Koch between 1782 and 1793. While the music of composers such as Haydn, Mozart, and Beethoven provides the best evidence of the utility of intensive study of phrase design and hypermeter, there is historical justification to do so as well. In this chapter, we have restricted ourselves almost entirely to the music of these three composers because phrase design is more crisply articulated in their music than in the music of earlier composers (especially Bach) and later ones. In Part II of this book, we will analyze phrase design and hypermeter across a broader range of composers, especially later ones.

SUGGESTED ASSIGNMENTS

In all of the following, you should identify where phrases begin and end and what types of cadences occur. Then, consider if the phrases can be described in terms of sentence and/or period structures. Finally, look for phrase elision and phrase expansion, and consider their implications for hypermeter.

1. Mozart, Piano Sonata, K. 279, III, mm. 1–10

2. Mozart, Piano Sonata, K. 576, I, mm. 1–8

3.   Mozart, Piano Sonata, K. 283, I, mm. 1–16

4.   Beethoven, Piano Sonata, op. 31, no. 3, II, mm. 1–9

5.   Mozart, Piano Sonata, K. 457, I, mm. 23–63

6.   Mozart, Piano Trio, K. 502, I, mm. 1–12

7.   Haydn, String Quartet, op. 33, no. 2, II, mm. 1–26

mm. 25–34 = mm. 1–10

8.   Mozart, Piano Sonata, K. 311, I, mm. 1–16

4 Further Expansion of the Harmonic Palette

In Chapter 2 we explored extension of the diatonic realm by means of secondary dominant and diminished seventh chords and by modulation to what are generally referred to as "closely related" keys, namely, those keys whose tonic chords are stable triads within the original key. Here we will consider additional means of expanding the harmonic realm: 1) modal mixture; 2) chromatic chords; and 3) modulation to non-diatonic keys.

Modal Mixture

Modal mixture involves the borrowing of elements from the parallel mode, for example, the use of notes or chords from C minor within the context of C major, or the opposite, thus altering the quality but not the function of the chord in question. Most often the term refers to the former, that is, to borrowing from the parallel minor. In its simplest form, modal mixture involves the borrowing of a single note, most often $\flat\hat{3}$ or $\flat\hat{6}$, from the minor mode. The first of these is expressed frequently as a change in the tonic harmony. Of the many examples in the literature, we offer two, the first from Schubert's String Quartet, D. 887. The quartet opens with a clear statement of I/i leading to V in the fourth measure. See Example 4.1a. As shown by the Arabic numerals between the viola and cello parts, the fifth measure, which has the character of a distant echo, extends the initial four-measure gesture and is thus considered as an extension of the hypermetric unit. These five measures are then repeated a fifth higher. Not shown here is the opening of the recapitulation, beginning in m. 278, where Schubert reverses the mixture: i/I. At the close of the movement (Example 4.1b), Schubert makes final reference to this modal duality. Here the duple/quadruple hypermeter is clearly expressed.

   A slightly more complex example of mixture occurs in the opening of Brahms's Third Symphony, a piano reduction of which is provided in Example 4.2. Here the opening tonic harmony (F) is initially embellished by a diminished seventh chord utilizing $\flat\hat{3}$ (A♭). The major tonic chord is then restated in m. 3 coinciding with the initial statement of the motive marked with a bracket,[1] but in the fourth measure $\flat\hat{3}$ is once again introduced, this time as a coloration of the tonic harmony. The process of borrowing from the minor mode continues in the fifth measure with the introduction of $\flat\hat{6}$ (D♭), which is cancelled by the D♮ in the next measure as part of the embellishing diminished seventh chord, the same one we heard in the second measure, which now functions as $^{o}4\atop3$ of V leading to V⁶. Within these initial measures we have two modal inflections, $\hat{3}/\flat\hat{3}$ (A/A♭) and $\flat\hat{6}/\natural\hat{6}$ (D♭/D♮).

EXAMPLE 4.1a Schubert, String Quartet in G Major, D. 887, I, mm. 1–10

EXAMPLE 4.1b Schubert, String Quartet in G Major, D. 887, I, mm. 437–444

EXAMPLE 4.2 Brahms, Symphony No. 3, op. 90, I, mm. 1–7

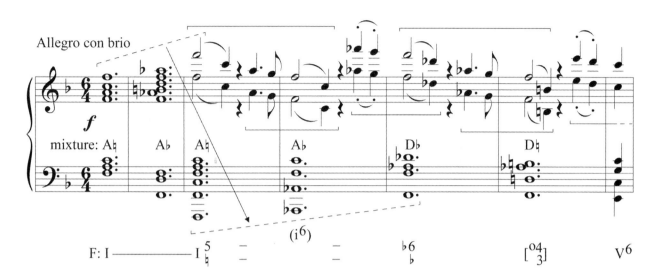

The use of ♭$\hat{6}$/♮$\hat{6}$ is clearly expressed in mm. 49–50 of our next example, Schubert's famous song, "Du bist die Ruh" (Example 4.3a). Schubert's setting of the final verse of this Rückert poem expands this modal inflection into the harmonic realm. The simultaneous introduction of ♭$\hat{3}$ (G♭) and ♭$\hat{6}$ (C♭) in m. 55 creates the ♭VI chord in first inversion, which is subsequently prolonged by its dominant. The ♭VI chord then leads to V in m. 58, which in turn resolves to the tonic in m. 59, but instead of a stable tonic, it is I$^{♭7}$ leading on to the subdominant at the climax of the phrase. The simplification of the score in Example 4.3b shows the function of ♭VI within the tonic scale-step. Corresponding to the prolongation of the tonic harmony in mm. 54–59 is the unfolding of the melodic sixth B♭4–G5, indicated by the slur in Example 4.3b. This sixth is answered by the octave skip A♭5–A♭4 over subdominant harmony, after which the melodic line continues its descent to closure, supported by dominant leading to tonic. At the deepest level of organization the harmonic progression is I – IV – V$^{6-5}_{4-3}$ – I supporting the descending fifth B♭4–E♭4, the notes of which are circled in Example 4.3b. Modal mixture is employed here within the tonic scale-step, which is transformed from stable harmony into the dominant seventh leading to IV.

The topic of modal mixture is extensive if we consider all possibilities, so we will limit our review to mixture of elements from the parallel minor mode in a major key. The chords involved are indicated in Figure 4.1. The first column lists the diatonic chords in the major mode, and the middle column shows the chords (and their constituent scale degrees) borrowed from the parallel minor. We have used boldface for **♭III** and **♭VI**, which involve double mixture (two borrowed tones), since among the chords borrowed from the parallel minor they serve most frequently as goals of modulation. The right column lists chords resulting from compound mixture, that is, from two stages of mixture. The first stage involves change from the diatonic chord (e.g., iii) to the one borrowed from the minor mode (♭III), and the second involves modal change (♭III to ♭iii).

EXAMPLE 4.3a Schubert, "Du bist die Ruh," mm. 48–65

EXAMPLE 4.3b Voice-leading simplification of Example 4.3a

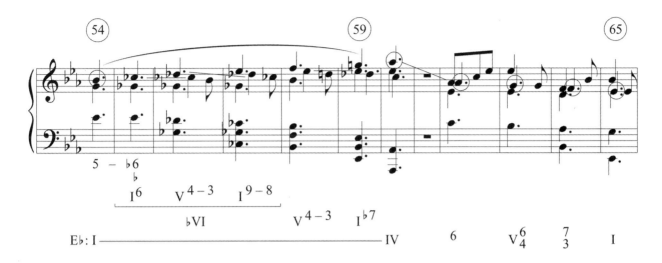

FIGURE 4.1 Modal Mixture (major key)

We will conclude this section with two passages from Schubert's *Moment musicale,* op. 94, no. 2. The first is the consequent phrase from the opening section of this work and the first measure of the following section (Example 4.4). The first borrowing from the minor mode occurs in m. 12, where the minor tonic chord appears as a neighboring chord to the dominant. The introduction of C♭ prepares the following diminished seventh chord of V, which leads to the half cadence in m. 14. This is followed by [°7] IV and a confirmation of the modulation to the subdominant. In the process, the chromatic passing tone B♭♭ in the bass (iv⁶ in the key of IV) anticipates the key of the B section, ♭vii, enharmonically written as F♯ minor rather than G♭ minor. This is an example of compound mixture: A♭ major to G♭ minor, which is a modal alteration of G♭ major. The subdominant, the goal of the initial modulation, becomes V of the new key.

EXAMPLE 4.4 Schubert, *Moment musicale,* op. 94, no. 2, mm. 9–18

The first six measures of the second passage, reproduced as Example 4.5, are the same as the opening of the previous example. Here, however, we have a parenthetical excursion to ♭III (C♭) rather than a modulation to IV.[2] This passage is difficult to sort out, so we will talk through the harmony. In part the difficulty results from deciding how best to indicate what is taking place musically. For instance, the chord on the downbeat of m. 42 appears

EXAMPLE 4.5 Schubert, *Moment musicale*, op. 94, no. 2, mm. 36–47

to be V$^4_3$ of V in C♭, but it never really functions in that capacity. Instead it has been labeled as an altered supertonic with raised third, which, following the chromatic voice exchange indicated on the score, becomes IV in the local key.[3] Note the exchange of F and F♭, $\hat{6}$ and ♭$\hat{6}$ in the original key, within this measure. A final reference to this exchange occurs in the alto voice in m. 46 as the phrase heads toward closure in A♭. Meanwhile the return to A♭ has been accomplished by the sudden return to the dominant, now in six-five position, which had been abandoned in m. 41. Note the registral connection in the bass between the two dominant chords.[4] This return to the original key is made smoother by the overlap between the digression to C♭ and the re-establishment of the original key, which is not shown in the harmonic analysis. But you should be aware that the progression V$^6_5$ – I in mm. 44–45 is also heard as [V$^6_5$] VI in C♭ (♭III).

Two Important Chromatic Chords: The Neapolitan Sixth and the Augmented Sixth

The two chords under consideration here, the Neapolitan Sixth and the Augmented Sixth, are derived from the minor mode, though both occur in the major as well as minor mode. The first of these is the major triad built on the lowered second degree of the scale with the third of the chord, scale degree 4, in the bass: F–A♭–D♭ in C minor. It is used in place of the subdominant or supertonic as preparation for the dominant. In its voice leading, the lowered second scale degree descends to the leading tone (supported by dominant harmony), passing almost always through scale degree 1. We offer two examples, the first from the nineteenth song in Schubert's famous cycle, *Die schöne Müllerin* (Example 4.6). Note that ♭$\hat{2}$, the A♭4 in m. 8, passes through G4 to F♯4, harmonized by the dominant, in the next measure. The harmonic progression in mm. 8–10 is ♭II^6 – V – i.

EXAMPLE 4.6 Schubert, "Der Müller und der Bach," mm. 1–10

The voice leading in our second example, taken from Mozart's D minor Fantasy, is a bit more complex (Example 4.7). The Neapolitan sixth chord is stated forcefully in the second half of m. 52 and subsequently elaborated by the ascending arpeggiation to B♭5. The lowered second scale degree, E♭5, descends first to D5 as part of the arpeggiated [°7] V and then as the fourth above the bass in the cadential $^6_4$ before progressing to C♯4 via octave transfer as part of the V^7. The notes involved in the underlying melodic progression E♭5–D5–C♯4 are circled on the score.

The second of our two chords being considered here is the augmented sixth chord. Actually we are talking about three slightly different versions of the same basic chord. These three, known as the Italian, French, and German augmented sixth chords, are shown in Example 4.8 in the key of A minor. The basic chord, the Italian augmented sixth, is derived from iv^6 with the sixth raised, creating the interval of an augmented sixth with the bass ($\hat{6}$ in the minor mode or ♭$\hat{6}$ in the major mode). The interval of an augmented sixth expands in contrary motion to the octave of V. The French version of this basic chord adds the fourth above the bass, and the German version adds the fifth, normally requiring the intervening six-four over the dominant to avoid parallel fifths. As shown below the system, two of these chords, the Italian and the German, are derived from the subdominant, while the root of the French is ii. Technically this is correct, though in fact they are all slightly different versions (with slightly different sounds) of the same basic harmony. For this reason we will not designate them by Roman numeral in this text, but by the labels It. 6, Fr. 6, and Ger. 6.

EXAMPLE 4.7 Mozart, Fantasy in D Minor, K. 397, mm. 45–54

EXAMPLE 4.8 Augmented Sixth Chords

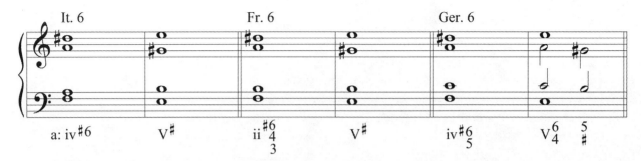

Below we offer examples of each type with minimal commentary. In several of these examples, the augmented sixth chord is preceded by a diatonic chord or secondary dominant having the same function, namely, to lead to the dominant.

EXAMPLE 4.9 Italian Augmented Sixth Chords

(a) Beethoven, Piano Sonata in C Minor, op. 10, no. 1, III, mm. 1–4

(a) Beethoven, Piano Sonata in C Minor, op. 10, no. 1, III, mm. 1–4. A very clear example of an Italian augmented sixth chord that is melodically embellished before its resolution.

(b) Beethoven, Piano Sonata in F♯ Major, op. 78, II, mm. 1–4

(b) Beethoven, Piano Sonata in F♯ Major, op. 78, II, mm. 1–4. This movement opens in an unusual way with an augmented sixth chord resolving to V. Note the local prolongation of the supertonic harmony in m. 3 by voice exchange between the outer parts. The chord in the last eighth of that measure is the half-diminished seventh chord of the following dominant.[5]

EXAMPLE 4.10 French Augmented Sixth Chords

(a) Schubert, "Der Wegweiser," mm. 1–5

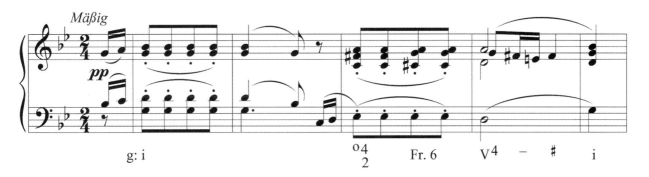

(a) Schubert, "Der Wegweiser," mm. 1–5. In this instance the French augmented sixth chord is introduced by $^o{}^4_2$. Note the elaborated resolution of the 4–3 suspension in m. 4.

(b) Beethoven, Piano Trio in B♭ Major, op. 97, III, mm. 1–8

(b) Beethoven, Piano Trio in B♭ Major, op. 97, III, mm. 1–8. Here the opening tonic harmony is prolonged by a voice exchange between the outer parts, which is subsequently reversed leading to $ii^6 - V$, the latter introduced by its half-diminished seventh chord. The second half of the phrase opens with I^6, which is the pivot for the modulation to V. This IV^6 chord in the new key leads to the French sixth on the third beat of m. 5, which strengthens the motion to the dominant and establishment of the new key. The following cadential $^6_4$ is not a requirement of the voice leading, but of a metric consideration—to create a balance with the initial four-measure unit.

EXAMPLE 4.11 German Augmented Sixth Chords

(a) Beethoven, Piano Sonata in C♯ Minor, op. 27, no. 2, III, mm. 1–9

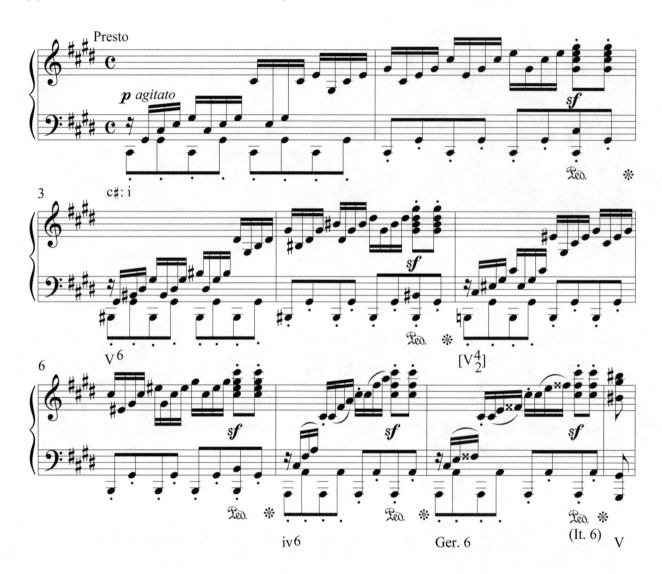

(a) Beethoven, Piano Sonata in C♯ Minor, op. 27, no. 2, III, mm. 1–9. An example of the German sixth introduced by a descending chromatic bass line supporting the progression I – V^6 – [V$^4_2$] – iv^6 – Ger. 6 – V♯. Here one can clearly see and hear the derivation of the augmented sixth chord from iv^6. Note that the German sixth chord does not lead to an intervening $^6_4$, a choice made possible by the omission of the fifth above the bass just before the resolution to V.

EXAMPLE **4.11** *continued*

(b) Beethoven, Piano Sonata in F Minor, op. 2, no. 1, I, mm. 140–152

(b) Beethoven, Piano Sonata in F Minor, op. 2, no. 1, I, mm. 140–152. Here the Ger. 6 resolves in textbook fashion through a cadential $^6_4$. The latter part of the phrase is an extended sequence by descending fifth that alternates $^6_5$ chords and triads and leads to a perfect authentic cadence.

(c) Beethoven, Piano Sonata in F Minor, op. 57, II, mm. 1–8

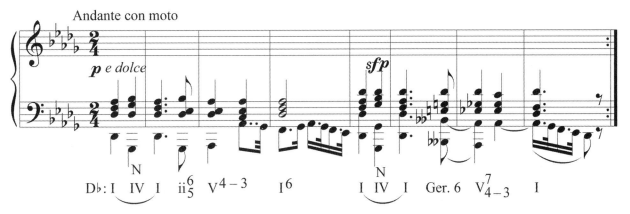

(c) Beethoven, Piano Sonata in F Minor, op. 57, II, mm. 1–8. As indicated by the analysis below the music, the I – IV – I progression that opens both the forephrase and afterphrase prolongs I. The subdominant is a neighboring chord. The German augmented sixth chord introduced on the last eighth of m. 6 looks odd because Beethoven has written the F♭ as E♮.[6] As a result the following progression to the dominant without an intervening $^6_4$ may look fine, but in fact this does not correct the sounding parallel fifths.

Analysis (Beethoven)

A very clear example of modal mixture—specifically of the interaction of $\flat\hat{6}/\natural\hat{6}$ as well as $\flat\hat{3}/\natural\hat{3}$—occurs in the opening movement of Beethoven's *Lebewohl* [Farewell] Sonata, op. 81a. We will examine its first twenty-one measures in some detail. The score with analytic additions is provided in Example 4.12, and a representation of voice leading is provided in Example 4.13.

When listening to this passage, one is struck immediately by the avoidance of the tonic harmony, except in passing, until m. 21. The first statement of the *Lebewohl* motive, G4–F4–E♭4, is harmonized by vi, and the repeat of this idea in mm. 7–8 by ♭VI.[7] This establishes a polarity between C♮ and C♭ that becomes a primary motivic component of this movement. Notice how Beethoven avoids tonic on the downbeat of m. 7 by harmonizing G4 with a diminished seventh chord, which forces this important point of articulation to become passing within a dominant seventh chord that finds its resolution instead to ♭VI. Observe also that the *Lebewohl* motive descends from G4 and that the melodic goal in m. 21, where we get our first stable tonic harmony, is G5. Furthermore, the return to G4 in m. 7 is through its upper neighbor A♭4, and the establishment of G5 in m. 21 is likewise accomplished through its upper neighbor A♭5, first stated in mm. 15–17 harmonized by iv^6/IV^6 and later as seventh of the dominant in m. 20. To summarize, Beethoven has established G4/G5 as the focal pitch, and to highlight its importance we have notated it in Example 4.13 (our representation of the structure of this passage) with a half note. The primary motive of this passage is G4–F4–E♭4, the statements of which are highlighted in Example 4.13 by brackets. Especially important is the interaction between C♮, expressed initially as the bass of vi and later as the bass of IV^6 (m. 16), and C♭, expressed as ♭VI in mm. 8–9 and later as the bass of iv^6 (m. 15). As noted above, the interaction of C/C♭ becomes a primary motivic idea later in the movement. Finally, from the perspective of voice leading, A♭, the upper neighbor, is important as the means by which G is established as the focal pitch associated with tonic harmony.

Let's now look at this passage in even greater detail. We hear the harmonization of the opening statement of the *Lebewohl* motive as I – V – vi and the following material in mm. 3–4 in relation to vi (C minor). The local harmonic progression is shown between the staves in Example 4.12. This material forms a basic four-measure phrase, and Beethoven could have returned directly to the restatement of the *Lebewohl* motive via a dominant seventh chord on the last eighth of m. 4. Instead he repeats m. 4 an octave higher with the added change of B♮5 to B♭5 on the last eighth in anticipation of the change of harmony on the next downbeat. This addition to the basic phrase prepares the return to that register and eventual establishment of G5 in m. 21. As shown in the box at the end of the top system of Example 4.13, the upper neighbor note A♭4 that returns to G4 is approached via a descending chromatic third from C5, which is temporarily broken by the repetition of the initial part of this motion in the upper register.

The progression in C♭ (♭VI) beginning in m. 8 is a bit more complex. First ♭VI is prolonged by its V$^4_3$ until E♭5 is established as a tenth above the bass note C♭ on the third eighth note of m. 9. This is the initial point of a sequential descending progression by step (based on a descending fifth pattern) connecting ♭VI and iv. The underlying motion in parallel tenths is shown by the curved lines on the score (Example 4.12), and the underlying voice leading is shown in Example 4.13. This is followed immediately by a passing i^6 chord leading to

119   *Further Expansion of the Harmonic Palette*

EXAMPLE 4.12 Beethoven, Piano Sonata in E♭ Major, op. 81a, I, mm. 1–21

EXAMPLE 4.13 Voice-leading representation of Example 4.12

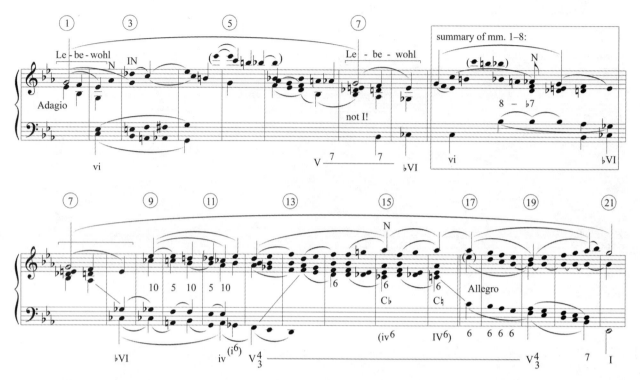

V_3^4 on the downbeat of m. 12. Considered in the larger context, this dominant does not find its resolution until m. 21. But first Beethoven must progress from the inner voice tone D♮5 up to the seventh of the chord, A♭5. He does this, but redirects the harmony to provide temporary stable support for the A♭5, first by iv^6, then IV^6, allowing him to make reference once again to the important interchange between C♭ and C♮. Once this is accomplished, the top voice descends via a series of parallel $^6_3$ chords back to V_3^4 and then ascends once again to A♭5. This time A♭5 is harmonized as seventh of the dominant, resolving to G5/I in the next measure.

Modulation

In this section we will examine modulations to keys borrowed from the parallel minor, notably ♭III and ♭VI, and two examples in the major mode of modulation to iii/III. We will then examine the role of the German augmented sixth chord in enharmonic modulation by half-step, a favorite device of nineteenth-century composers, as well as the use of chains of descending thirds. These are a sampling of the range of chromatic and enharmonic modulations composers devised.

Modulation to keys borrowed from the minor mode are easily achieved by changing first to the parallel mode, for example, from A major to A minor, and then modulating to a key associated with the minor key. There are countless examples of this procedure in the Classical literature, one of which occurs in the minuet of Haydn's Symphony No. 103 (Example 4.14).

EXAMPLE 4.14 Haydn, Symphony No. 103, III, mm. 1–27

EXAMPLE 4.14 *continued*

EXAMPLE 4.14 *continued*

EXAMPLE 4.14 *continued*

The first part of this movement consists of two contrasting four-measure phrases, the first ending on the tonic and the second ending with a half cadence. The second phrase is extended for two measures by echoes in two registers of the falling fifth from the phrase's cadence. Immediately following the repeat, the mode changes to minor, and in the next eight-measure phrase Haydn modulates to III of E♭ minor (♭III of E♭ major). As shown below the score, the pivot in the modulation is VI/IV. The music then returns to E♭ minor for an imitative passage based on the minuet's opening motive, which leads to a Ger. 6 resolving to V (mm. 24–25), which is then repeated. (Note: The German sixth does not lead to an intervening $^6_4$, since the fifth above the bass, stated by the clarinets,[8] is no longer present as the chord resolves to V.) The dominant is subsequently extended for another four measures before the return to the opening material.

Two very different passages involving modulation to ♭VI can be found in Beethoven's Piano Sonata, op. 7. The first occurs in mm. 43–86 of the third movement (Example 4.15). This section opens with an eight-measure antecedent phrase that ends with a half cadence. The consequent phrase, which is greatly expanded, switches to the minor mode, progressing deceptively to ♭VI (VI in E♭ minor) in the fourth measure (m. 54). As in the Haydn example, the motion to ♭VI is prepared by the change to the parallel minor. What follows is an extended excursion—actually a parenthetical insertion—into the realm of ♭VI (mm. 54–69). Confirmation of C♭ as the new tonic is accomplished by the progression beginning in m. 58, which is repeated and expanded immediately following, leading to the It. 6 in m. 68. The derivation of this chord from the minor subdominant (m. 66) is emphasized by the chromatic voice exchange between the two chords: C♭5/A♭3 to A♮4/C♭4. Arrival at the augmented sixth chord returns us to the realm of the tonic, thus ending the excursion to ♭VI. Before leaving this passage you should examine carefully the harmony and voice leading, an analysis of which is provided below the music.

Initially one might expect the repetition of B♭ in mm. 70–71 to represent a cadential $^6_4$ following the augmented sixth chord, but it soon becomes apparent that this is really a tonic harmony, which is extended, first as a $^6_4$ and then later as a root-position chord until the climax of this passage is reached in m. 79 following the long *crescendo*. Here in m. 79, D♭ is added to the chord, transforming tonic into [V^6_5] IV. This whole passage beginning in m. 70 is a complex extension of a single passing chord, the tonic, connecting ♭VI and IV. The means by which this extension is accomplished is shown as the exchange of parts— represented by two different types of brackets in Example 4.15—between the right-hand and left-hand parts, first over a B♭ pedal and then over E♭. In the latter case these exchanges involve chromatic alteration in the embellishing pitches. So much time and energy has elapsed in connecting ♭VI and its extension to IV that Beethoven does not allow the subdominant to complete its motion through the dominant to a perfect authentic cadence immediately, but instead extends this passage further by twice avoiding closure to the tonic by means of deceptive progressions (mm. 82 and 84).

If we take a final survey of this passage, we see an eight-measure antecedent and a greatly expanded consequent that encompasses all of mm. 51–86! This phrase is extended first by the excursion to ♭VI, second by the extension of the passing tonic harmony leading to IV, and finally by twice avoiding closure to the tonic through deceptive progressions. The function of ♭VI in this extraordinary passage is to participate as middle member of the descending arpeggiation from tonic to subdominant, I – ♭VI – IV, which then leads through V to I.

EXAMPLE 4.15 Beethoven, Piano Sonata in E♭ Major, op. 7, III, mm. 43–86

A more direct approach to ♭VI occurs in the second movement of this sonata. The last few measures of its opening section, ending with a perfect authentic cadence in the tonic (C major), is provided at the beginning of Example 4.16. It is followed immediately by the introduction of ♭VI. A change of key of this type, where the tonics of the old and new keys have a single note in common, in this case C, and where the change is direct, is referred to as a **common-tone modulation**. So, here we are suddenly in A♭ major, which is then confirmed as the new key by the progression in mm. 25–28. This is followed by a progression leading to iv (F minor). In the process of confirming F as the new tonic, we encounter an interesting chord with B♮ as the lowest note on the second eighth note of m. 31. If this B♮ had occurred in an inner voice above D♭, the chord would be a French augmented sixth in "normal" position, that is, built above scale degree 6 of F minor. Instead it is inverted, so that the interval of an augmented sixth has become a diminished third. This change does not alter its function. It leads to a perfect authentic cadence confirming the modulation to F minor.

So far the larger progression is similar to what we discovered in this sonata's third movement: I – ♭VI – iv, except here the subdominant is minor, not major, and it does not progress directly to V. Instead the progression by descending thirds continues to D♭, where we have a varied restatement of the earlier four-measure idea in A♭. That is, the progression from F to D♭ imitates the earlier progression from C to A♭. In relation to F minor, this is a progression to VI, but in relation to our original tonic C, D♭ is ♭II. Overall, then, Beethoven has extended the descending third pattern to the chord on ♭II: I – ♭VI – iv – ♭II, and we might expect him to treat this ♭II as a Neapolitan. Instead, Beethoven begins to repeat the four-measure idea from mm. 25–28 a fourth higher. The change in pattern comes in the third measure, where the harmony continues sequentially to [$^{o6}_{5}$] iii^6 instead of V^7 – I in D♭. This F minor chord (iii^6) becomes the pivot (iv^6), which is subsequently altered chromatically to become the German augmented sixth chord leading to the dominant in the original key. This progression leading to V of the original key is abrupt, no doubt one reason why an extended retransition follows this tonal arrival, giving the listener time to readjust his/her orientation.

The next two examples involve modulation to the mediant in the major mode. The first of these, Schubert's "Nachtgesang," is a diatonic modulation from E♭ major to G minor (Example 4.17). What places discussion of this song here is the pivot: IV^6 in E♭, which is emphasized by its dominant, is then treated as ♭II^6 in G minor (iii). The second example, taken from the slow movement of Beethoven's Fifth Symphony, is the famous passage leading from A♭ major (I) to C major (III). See Example 4.18. The passage begins with an ascending figure of a third leading to C5, then to E♭5. The third statement reaches up to G♭5 as the bass progresses chromatically from A♭ to A♮. Our expectation is that this diminished seventh chord will lead to ii (with G♭5 resolving to F5), but in the seventh measure of this phrase the bass returns once again to A♭ in the lower octave. In terms of sound, this chord is I$^{♭7}$ (V^7 of IV), and we might expect it to lead to the subdominant, but Beethoven has rewritten the G♭ as F♯, changing its spelling to the German sixth in C. The chord does not lead us to IV, but resolves to the V$^{6-5}_{4-3}$$^{8-7}$ to I in C (III) for the triumphant statement of this theme, now complete with brass.[9]

EXAMPLE 4.16 Beethoven, Piano Sonata in E♭ Major, op. 7, II, mm. 22–37

EXAMPLE 4.17 Schubert, "Nachtgesang," mm. 1–8

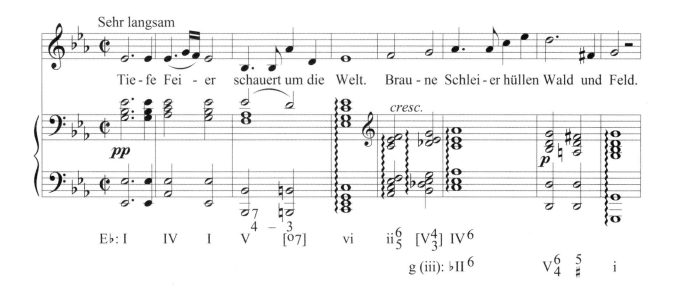

EXAMPLE 4.18 Beethoven, Symphony No. 5, II, mm. 23–31

This last example highlights an important feature of the German augmented sixth chord, namely that it has the same sound as a dominant seventh chord and thus can be used as a source of **enharmonic modulation**. This interchange between pre-dominant and dominant function became part of the harmonic language of the nineteenth century and thus deserves our careful attention. Example 4.19 shows three scenarios, the last a variant of the second one. At (a) the second chord is a Ger. 6 in A minor, a pre-dominant chord that would normally lead to V in that key. Instead the D$\sharp$ has been treated as an E$\flat$, allowing the chord to function as V^7 in B$\flat$ major, a half-step above the original key. At (b) the major tonic chord with added seventh, potentially V^7 of IV, is treated as a Ger. 6 leading to V – I in C$\sharp$ (III$\sharp$ in the original key). This is analogous to the situation encountered in the Beethoven example above. The situation at (c) is a less common variant of (b). Here V^7 in A minor is treated as a Ger. 6 in A$\flat$, a half-step lower. Examples of these three scenarios are provided below.

Example 4.20, taken from Beethoven's *Rondo a capriccio*, op. 129, provides a very clear example of the scenario given at (a) above. Here Beethoven carefully prepares the introduction of the German sixth chord in m. 165, first by changing to the parallel minor mode (mm. 162–163) and then by introducing the C$\sharp$ as part of the $[^{o6}_{5}]$ V in m. 164. The initial appearance of the augmented sixth chord resolves as expected to the dominant, but in its next appearance (m. 168), the C$\sharp$ is rewritten as D$\flat$, and this same chord (now respelled) functions as a dominant seventh leading us to A$\flat$, a half-step above the point of origin.

An example of the scenario given at (b) above, where $I^{\flat 7}$ functions both as a German sixth and as V^7 of IV, occurs in the first movement of Beethoven's Horn Sonata, op. 17 (Example 4.21). The first appearance of the chord in question occurs in mm. 136–137, where the chord is spelled as an augmented sixth chord resolving to the dominant in A minor. This modulation from F major (I) to A minor (iii) is then repeated. Then, in m. 146, we hear this same chord again (*ff*), this time spelled with E$\flat$ rather than D$\sharp$, now functioning as $[V^7]$ IV.

Finally, an example of the third scenario occurs at the end of the A$\flat$ fugal section from the final movement of Beethoven's Piano Sonata, op. 110 (Example 4.22). The fugue ends with the arpeggiation of V^7, the seventh of which (D$\flat$) is subsequently treated as if it were C$\sharp$, the augmented sixth above E$\flat$. This D$\flat$/C$\sharp$ leads up to D5 as part of the cadential $^6_4$ in G minor. The following treatment of this $^6_4$ is unusual. Instead of resolving to $^5_3$, the $^6_4$ leads directly though arpeggiation to the new tonic in root position.

EXAMPLE 4.19 Enharmonic Modulations with German Augmented Sixths

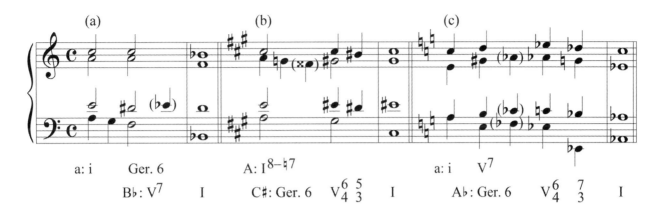

EXAMPLE 4.20 Beethoven, *Rondo a capriccio*, op. 129, mm. 158–171

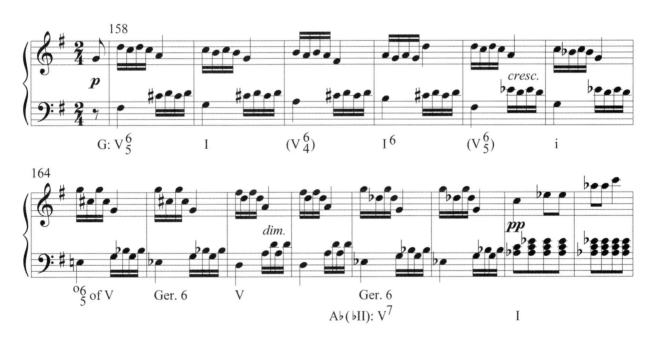

EXAMPLE 4.21 Beethoven, Horn Sonata in F Major, op. 17, I, mm. 134–149

EXAMPLE 4.22 Beethoven, Piano Sonata in A♭ Major, op. 110, III, mm. 111–115

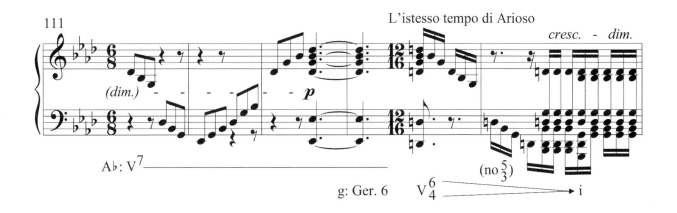

Schubert's *Moment musicale,* op. 94, no. 6, provides an interesting study of the augmented sixth chord. The excerpt provided in Example 4.23 features the return of the opening A♭ major material (designated as a′ on Example 4.23 at the upbeat to m. 54) as well as the preceding retransitional passage (mm. 40–53). The F♭ major chord at the beginning of the excerpt is ♭VI, and the return to A♭ is accomplished via the It. 6 leading to V,[10] which is extended to the end of m. 45. The tonic is then decorated by a 5–6 motion introducing F5, which is suspended over the following dominant with G3 in the bass. This F5 then descends chromatically to D♭5, the seventh of the dominant, in preparation for the return. The following eight-measure phrase is a repetition of the antecedent phrase from the opening of the piece. Examine the harmony of this phrase and the provided analysis of it carefully. The chord in m. 54 is not iv^7, as it may at first appear, but rather the C5 is a suspension displacing B♭4 as root of the following ii$^6_5$. Likewise the chord in m. 56 is not vi$^6_4$, but rather F5 is a suspension prepared by the preceding half-diminished seventh chord momentarily displacing the E♭5 as fifth of I^6. In the latter half of the phrase the controlling harmony is the dominant. As shown by the slurs added below the harmonic analysis of this passage, the chords on the third beats of mm. 58 and 59 are passing.

The consequent phrase, beginning with the upbeat to m. 62, opens with notes borrowed from the parallel minor, F♭ ($♭\hat{6}$) and also the chromatic passing tone C♭ ($♭\hat{3}$). This gesture is then repeated. What follows is an E major-minor $^4_2$ chord, enharmonically the notes of the German augmented sixth chord (F♭–A♭–C♭–D♮), but with D♮ in the bass. It is not going to function here as a German sixth, but rather as V$^4_2$ of ♭II, rewritten enharmonically by Schubert as an A major rather than a B♭♭ major chord. This passage looks complicated, but, in fact, the sound is as follows: $[V^4_2] - ♭II^6 \ldots V^{♭6-5}_{4-3} - i$. Here Schubert has realized the potential of this versatile augmented sixth chord, which earlier had resolved to the dominant in A♭, to function now as V^7 of the Neapolitan (♭II).

As a final example in this section on modulation we will examine a passage taken from the second movement of Schubert's "Unfinished" Symphony in B minor (D. 759). The main key of the movement is E major, but the section we have selected is in C♯ minor (vi). See Example 4.24, a reduction of the orchestral score of mm. 66–83. A feature of the accompaniment in the opening measures of this passage is the decoration of G♯4 by its upper

EXAMPLE 4.23 Schubert, *Moment musicale*, op. 94, no. 6, mm. 40–77

neighbor A4 as the clarinet melody ascends to A5. In m. 72, with a prominent change of dynamic (*f*), the harmony changes to V^6_5 of ♮II, to which it resolves in the next measure while the clarinet sustains A5. In the next few measures, as the clarinet begins its descent, the harmony moves toward F major, III of D minor (♮ii) or ♮III of D major (♮II), but at the last moment the progression pulls back to a D minor chord (♮ii) via a deceptive progression. As shown below the lower staff, the controlling harmony in these measures is ♮II/ii, and the suggestion of F major is embellishing. (However, if you examine the entire movement you will discover that this brief suggestion of F major foreshadows the dramatic emphasis on F major, ♮II in E major, in mm. 252–253.) The clarinet's return to the passage's opening third (C♯5–E5) in m. 77 is harmonized by V^7 of ♮II (D). Here, however, the seventh of the chord, G♮4, is changed to F𝄪4, transforming its spelling as well as its function into a German augmented sixth, which leads us back to C♯ minor, which at the last minute changes to the parallel major. Here, in this passage, we have a very clear example of the dual function of the German augmented sixth chord as dominant of ♮II and as leading to the dominant in the local tonic.

EXAMPLE 4.24 Schubert, Symphony in B Minor ("Unfinished"), D. 759, II, mm. 66–83

SUGGESTED ASSIGNMENTS

Chromatic Harmony

1. Schumann, Waltz, op. 124, no. 4

2. Mozart, Piano Sonata, K. 284, I, mm. 11–17

3.   Mozart, Piano Quartet, K. 478, III, mm. 330–351

340

346
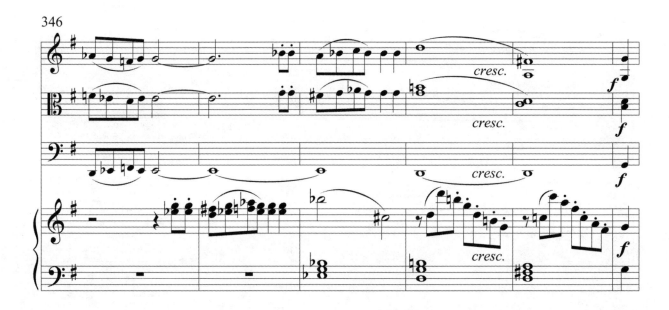

4.   Beethoven, Piano Sonata, op. 57, I, mm. 1–16

5. Beethoven, Piano Sonata, op. 13, III, mm. 193–210

Chromatic Modulation

1. Schubert, "Unfinished" Symphony, D. 759, II, mm. 96–111. How does Schubert modulate from C♯ minor to D major?

2. Schubert, Piano Sonata, D. 845, I, mm. 1–26. Determine the harmonic progression, paying particular attention to mm. 20–23.

3. Haydn, String Quartet, op. 76, no. 6, Fantasia, mm. 9–16 and 31–39. This movement is a study in modulation. The excerpt at (a) modulates from B major (I) to C♯ minor (ii). How does Haydn accomplish this? What is the chord on the third beat of m. 14? The excerpt at (b) returns to B major from B♭ major. Note the mixture of sharps and flats in mm. 35–36, where you must use your ear, not your eyes, to determine the progression.

4. Beethoven, Piano Sonata, op. 90, II, mm. 114–126. Determine the harmonic progression, paying particular attention to mm. 120–121. What is the function of the $\frac{6}{4}$ chord on the downbeat of m. 121? What is the relationship between the chords on the second halves of mm. 120 and 121? (Hint: To answer this question you will have to respell the chord on the second half of m. 121.)

5. Chopin, Nocturne, op. 27, no. 1, mm. 41–52. Determine the harmonic progression, paying particular attention to mm. 45–52. What are the harmonies in m. 45 and on the last beat of m. 48?

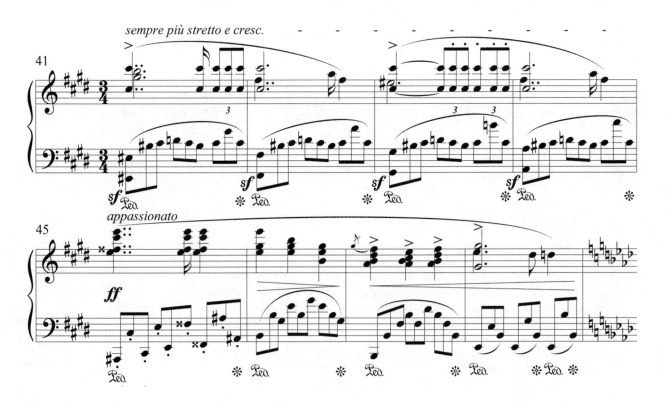

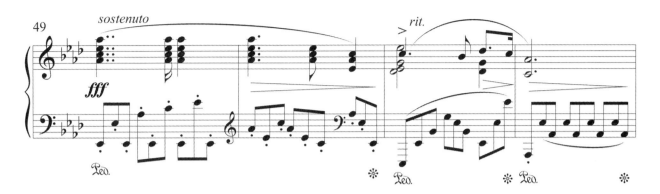

6. Schubert, Piano Sonata, D. 960, I, mm. 1–48. An important feature of this movement is the emphasis given to ♭VI, first hinted at in m. 8 in the bass. Provide a detailed harmonic analysis of each section; then consider the large-scale harmonic plan. An interesting issue to consider is the role of the section beginning in m. 20 in relation to the eventual goal of the passage given (m. 48). Stated somewhat differently, what is the role of the return to B♭ major prior to the modulation to F♯ minor?

PART II

Analysis

5 Binary and Rounded Binary Forms

Beginning with this chapter, we shift exclusively to the analysis of complete pieces. This chapter focuses on movements in binary, or two-part, form. There are two types of binary forms: those without a return of the opening music in the tonic key in the second part (**binary** or **simple binary**) and those with such a return (**rounded binary**). The former type of binary form is commonly found in dance-inspired pieces from the early eighteenth century. It is the usual form of movements in, for example, Bach's cello and keyboard suites and his violin partitas. Although examples of binary form can be found throughout the eighteenth century, rounded binary became the predominant type by the time of Haydn, Mozart, and Beethoven.[1] Rounded binary form is the standard form for Classical minuets (and their trios) and, in the nineteenth century, for scherzos (and their trios). We will briefly review two examples of binary forms from Bach's keyboard suites studied in Chapter 2 and one example of rounded binary form from a Haydn string quartet studied in Chapter 3. We will devote most of this chapter to the handling of rounded binary form in a minuet–trio movement from a symphony by Haydn and in two scherzo–trio movements from piano sonatas by Beethoven and Brahms.

Binary Form

Binary forms consist of two parts, which are nearly always repeated (with repeat signs rather than varied repetition).[2] Tonally, we can make a basic distinction between binary forms that close on the initial tonic harmony at the end of the first part (**sectional binary**) and those that do not (**continuous binary**). Continuous binary is somewhat more common than sectional binary.[3] In the major mode, the first part of a continuous binary piece invariably moves to the dominant. In the minor mode, the modulation is usually to the relative major, but the minor dominant is occasionally found instead; either way, the modulation is confirmed with a perfect authentic cadence. The tonal structure of the start of the second part is much more variable. Most often, there is a tonicization (with cadential confirmation) of a closely related key, usually the subdominant or the submediant. This portion of the form can instead feature very brief digressions to one or more closely related keys without cadential confirmation, or it can even be in the tonic key (perhaps with emphasis on dominant, rather than tonic, harmony). Regardless of the tonal structure of the start of the second part, at some point the tonic key returns and is cadentially confirmed. Due to the relative brevity of most binary-form pieces, it is not infrequent for there to be only one

Continuous binary (major mode)	‖:A	:‖:B	:‖
	I	V X	I
		(PAC)	(PAC)

Continuous binary (minor mode)	‖:A	:‖:B	:‖
	i	III* X	i
		(PAC)	(PAC)
	* sometimes v		

Sectional binary (major mode)	‖:A	:‖:B	:‖
	I	I X	I
		(PAC)	(PAC)

FIGURE 5.1 Basic Models of Binary Form

cadence in the tonic key during the second part—the perfect authentic cadence at the very end. Figure 5.1 summarizes the basic tonal plans for continuous and sectional binary forms.

In Chapter 2 we studied two binary-form pieces by Bach, one in G major and one in C minor. Both involved modulation in the first part: G major to D major and C minor to E♭ major respectively. We will briefly review each of these pieces in light of our general comments on binary form. The piece in G major was the gavotte from the French Suite No. 5 (Example 2.20). The first part consists of two phrases that combine into a parallel progressive period ending with a PAC in the dominant in m. 8. The second part consists of four phrases that combine into two periods. The first period begins back in the tonic key but ends with a PAC in the submediant (m. 16), a key often emphasized at this point in binary form. Note that the start of the second part begins with a melodic inversion of the gavotte's initial three notes. In Bach's binary forms, there is usually a direct thematic connection between the start of the first part and the start of the second part; sometimes, there is melodic inversion involved, as here, but in other cases the initial melodic material reappears in its original version but transposed to a new key. Observe also the shifting of the main melodic material into the left-hand part in mm. 12–14; this, too, is commonly found in the second parts of Bach's binary forms for keyboard. The gavotte's concluding period modulates back to G major, ending with a PAC. The start of the last phrase (mm. 20–21) bears a strong melodic similarity to the gavotte's opening, but notice that the harmonic support here is dominant, not tonic. There is some recall of the opening material after the return to the tonic key—more exposed recall than there is in many binary pieces—but it does not provide the feeling of "beginning again" that defines rounded binary form.

The binary piece in C minor from Chapter 2 was the minuet from the French Suite No. 2 (Example 2.26). Again, the first part consists of an eight-measure progressive period, although its two phrases are thematically contrasting rather than parallel (and the modulation is to the relative major, not the dominant). Unlike the gavotte, the start of the second part remains in the key from the end of the first part. Notice the direct thematic correspondence between the first measure of the first and second parts; these measures are related by exact transposition (rather than melodic inversion as in the gavotte). Like the gavotte, the first two phrases of the second part, lead to a PAC in a new key, this time the subdominant. The minuet's second part is eight measures longer than the gavotte's, principally as a result of the descending fifth sequence in mm. 17–24 that leads back to the tonic key. Very occasionally, the two parts of a binary form are of equal length, but nearly always the second part is longer, sometimes much longer. The minuet's final phrase bears some similarity to the first part (compare especially m. 29 with m. 5), but again there is no moment of "beginning again" as one finds in rounded binary form. As in the gavotte, the only PAC in the tonic key occurs in the final measure of the minuet.

There is one thematic relationship often found in Bach's binary forms that doesn't happen to occur in either the gavotte or the minuet. In many continuous binary pieces there is a direct relationship between the final two (or so) measures of the first part and the corresponding ones in the second part. Giving these two cadences the same melodic content (but transposed) contributes a further sense of unity to the piece. Some authors refer to binary forms with this "cadential rhyme" as **balanced binary**.

We examined the motivic design of these two pieces, especially the minuet, in some detail in Chapter 2. It was clear that both pieces redeploy their initial materials in multiple guises, sometimes through repetition, transposition, or simple embellishment, but other times through enlargements that create hidden motivic parallelisms. Binary forms are predicated upon thematic unity much more than thematic contrast (compared to a form like ternary or rondo). A central component of any analysis of a binary piece must be a thorough assessment of its handling of motivic materials at various levels of design.

Rounded Binary Form

In rounded binary form, there is a return of the initial thematic material in the tonic key in the middle of the second part. Usually, this return is preceded by an arrival on the dominant of the home key—in other words by a half cadence. Occasionally, this arrival on the dominant is extended for a few measures as a brief **retransition** before the thematic return. The amount of the initial thematic material that returns varies. Since there is no modulation in the first part of sectional rounded binary, it is possible for the entire first part to return without— or with minimal—modification. In continuous rounded binary, the modulation in the first part necessitates recomposition, at least from the point corresponding to the initial modulation, though often the exact thematic restatement breaks off even earlier. The important point to remember is that it is the return of the *opening* measures of the first part in the *tonic* key that creates rounded binary form; the second part of a simple binary form may incorporate a tonic return of another portion of the first part or a non-tonic return of the opening measures. Figure 5.2 summarizes the basic outlines of continuous and sectional rounded binary forms.

The diagrams in Figure 5.2 might give the impression that rounded binary form is, in some way, a three-part form due to the A B A′ thematic labels. Keep in mind, first of all,

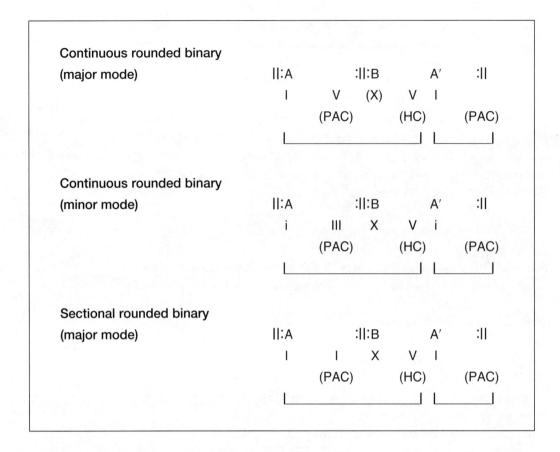

FIGURE 5.2 Basic Models of Rounded Binary Form

that in the eighteenth century the form nearly always consists of two repeated sections; only in the nineteenth century do composers sometimes omit the repeat of the second part, but by then the usage of rounded binary form for certain types of movement had become an established convention. Second, although it is traditional to use the letter B to designate the start of the second part in rounded binary form (just as it is traditional to use B for the entire second part of binary form), there is no strong thematic contrast here. The outset of the second part of rounded binary form nearly always elaborates upon the thematic material from A. When the thematic connection between B and A is less clear, it is usually because B is very short. It happens not infrequently in major-mode continuous rounded binary that B consists only of a few measures based entirely around the dominant, transforming it from its own key area back into V of the tonic key. Thus, when B is less thematically dependent on A, it is generally very evident that it does not constitute an independent formal unit. After we examine ternary form in Chapter 8, it will be perfectly clear why rounded binary form is not a ternary form, despite the traditional usage of the labels A B A′.

To this point, we have not particularly distinguished between the typical tonal structures of binary forms and those of rounded binary forms. This is completely appropriate for the first part and the start of the second part of these forms. However, because of the return of the opening material in the tonic in the second part, rounded binary form projects a two-part tonal structure. The first branch leads from the initial tonic to the dominant arrival, midway through the second part, that prepares the thematic return. The tonal structure then starts over with tonic harmony, which is subsequently confirmed with a perfect authentic cadence at the end. These tonal divisions are shown by the brackets beneath the diagrams in Figure 5.2; note that this two-part tonal structure does not align with the two-part formal design. Occasionally, binary form has similarly clear rearticulation of tonic harmony midway through the second part that balances a prior I – V motion, but in general binary form gives the impression of a single tonal arch. Recall, for example, the i – III – iv – V – i motion that spanned the C minor minuet. We will consider the interaction of tonal structure and formal design more closely in our discussion of sonata form in Chapter 6, as this issue becomes more significant in that larger form, which is an outgrowth of rounded binary form.

At the end of Chapter 3, we studied the minuet (but not the trio) from Haydn's String Quartet in E♭ Major, op. 64, no. 6. The score is available in Example 3.21, and we provide a voice-leading representation here as Example 5.1. As we would expect in a Classical minuet, the form is rounded binary; the tonal type is the more common continuous structure with modulation to the dominant during the first part. The first part consists of a parallel progressive period, which is an exceedingly common design for this portion of a binary or rounded binary form. The second part continues the dominant for a couple of measures before launching a descending fifth sequence that returns to the tonic key. Note, however, that the goal of this phrase is a half cadence in m. 20. Thus, even though there is a return to the tonic key around mm. 16–17, there is no rearticulation of the tonic harmony at a high level of structure. The E♭ major harmony on the third beat of m. 18 is a passing harmony within a broader span of predominant harmony (mm. 17–19). This brief, metrically unaccented chord harmonizes the melodic passing tone G5 within the descending fifth C6–F5 that frames the predominant harmonic function within the phrase. The local nature of the harmonic motions within these measures is further projected by the dropping out of the cello; the cello sounds B♭2 at the perfect authentic cadence in m. 12 and again in m. 15, and the true bass register of the cello comes back only with the E♭3 at the thematic return (m. 21). In longer pieces, the connection between the dominant harmony at the end of the first part and the one that sets up the thematic return will seem more abstract. Even with greater separation between these arrivals and more elaborate intervening material, however, this deeper harmonic connection is still understood. In the Haydn, there is a clear corresponding melodic connection; the F5 in the first violin can be heard extending across the PAC in m. 12 as well as the HC in m. 20. (And, in fact, one can trace a stepwise octave descent between these two points in the first violin line—with a registral adjustment in m. 16 that will permit the concluding F to sound in its original register.)

The thematic return during the second part was discussed at length in Chapter 3 due to the reworking of phrase length and hypermeter. It is in the fourth measure of the thematic return where modifications begin to occur, and tonal closure is provided with the PAC in m. 32. The minuet concludes with a four-measure **codetta**, a brief passage consisting of repeated cadential gestures that takes place after tonal closure has been attained. A codetta is not uncommon at the end of a rounded binary form. (It *is* uncommon to find a codetta at the end of a binary form.)

EXAMPLE 5.1 Voice-leading representation of Haydn, String Quartet, op. 64, no. 6, III, mm. 1–32

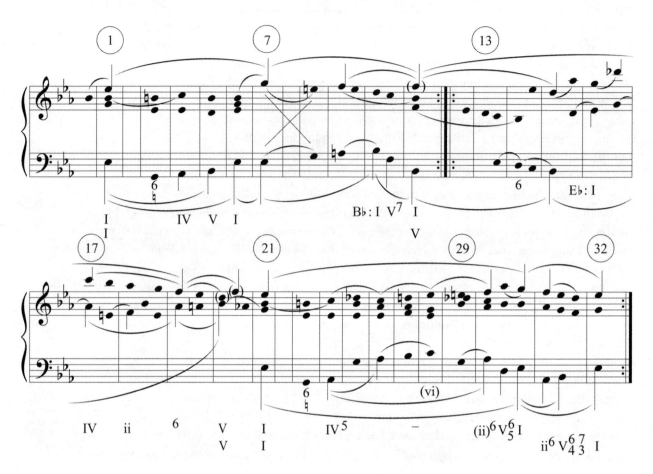

With our survey of the basic principles of binary and rounded binary form complete, we turn now to the analyses that are this chapter's main focus. We will first examine the minuet–trio movement from Haydn's Symphony No. 101 in D Major, another Haydn movement where the treatment of phrase design and hypermeter is especially notable. We will then proceed to the scherzo–trio movements from Beethoven's Piano Sonata in A♭ Major, op. 26, and Brahms's Piano Sonata in F Minor, op. 5. Both of these depart somewhat from the norms for the tonal structure of rounded binary form.

Haydn, Symphony No. 101 in D Major ("Clock"), III

Haydn's Symphony No. 101 is a large-scale work written for the composer's second trip to London in 1794–95. An annotated score of its minuet appears in Example 5.2. The minuet's first part begins with a period (specifically, a parallel progressive period), but it spans twenty measures and is followed by additional material confirming the key of the dominant. The period's eight-measure antecedent is in sentence design. In the repetition of the basic idea (mm. 3–4) notice that the upper-voice pitches from mm. 1–2 occur in the bass line (bracketed on the score). This is not particularly salient, since throughout mm. 2–7 the bass simply moves in parallel tenths with the melody, but Haydn develops this feature later. The chromatic descent at the end of the phrase (marked by a dotted bracket) seems like an innocuous way to descend to scale degree 2 at the half cadence, but it too provides significant material for subsequent development.

The twelve-measure consequent is expanded internally. The modulation to the dominant occurs during the repetition of the basic idea (mm. 11–12). Instead of peaking around A5, as in the first phrase, the melodic motion continues up to E6. Since this is already the sixth measure of the phrase, it is not hard to imagine why Haydn might have decided to expand the phrase in order to descend convincingly for the melodic cadence. The expansion results from a four-measure stasis on I^6 of the new key (mm. 14–17), an expansion that is quite apparent because it is based on repetition. The I^6 alternates with its neighboring V^4_2, except in the fourth measure of the expansion where the I^6 persists throughout the entire measure. This permits the bass motion to D to fall on the subsequent downbeat, where it supports ii^6 as the cadential progression begins to take shape. Notice also that in the last measure of the expansion the final melodic tone consonant with the I^6 harmony is E5; in other words, the expansion transfers E6 down to E5. From this point there is an embellished descent through the fifth E5–A4 to melodic closure in m. 20; these pitches are circled in the first violin part. We show two levels of hypermeter on the score. Most important is the underlying hypermeter, which corresponds to the basic phrase, but we also note that the expansion, given its length, could produce a momentary surface hypermeter of its own.

The remainder of the first part confirms the modulation to the dominant and in a sense could be considered an expansion. It does, however, present a complete phrase, which is repeated, and has a distinct melody and interesting dialogue of *sforzandi* between upper and lower instruments. This is why we have labeled mm. 20–23 (and mm. 23–26) as a closing phrase. The junctures between these phrases require comment. In our hypermetric analysis, we show no reinterpretation at the start of the closing phrase, but we do show a reinterpretation (4 = 1) at the start of its repetition. Yet, the two locations are very similar. In both cases, we understand the presence of phrase overlap; the syncopated and accented pitch that launches the closing phrase "should have" occurred on the downbeat—it has been displaced by a beat. (Note that the clarinets, which double the melody in the closing phrase, do enter on the downbeat of m. 20.) Recall from our discussion in Chapter 3 that phrase overlap may or may not generate a hypermetric reinterpretation; sometimes overlap is necessary to preserve periodic hypermeter. The latter is the case at m. 20, where the consequent phrase's concluding harmony spills over onto the downbeat of m. 20 rather than entering during the eighth measure of the basic phrase. The closing theme is precisely four measures long, which means that when its repetition begins in m. 23 the overlap does induce a hypermetric reinterpretation. The repetition of the closing phrase is extended with a couple of measures that feature rapid chord alternations. After the expanded consequent, there is a feeling of acceleration throughout the remainder of the first part. The closing phrases are short (four measures) and further energized by the syncopations and *sforzandi*, and this is followed by the dizzying repetitions within the final extension (mm. 26–28). These rhythmic features give the first part a powerful sweep.

EXAMPLE 5.2 Haydn, Symphony No. 101 in D Major ("Clock"), III, mm. 1–80

EXAMPLE 5.2 *continued*

EXAMPLE 5.2 *continued*

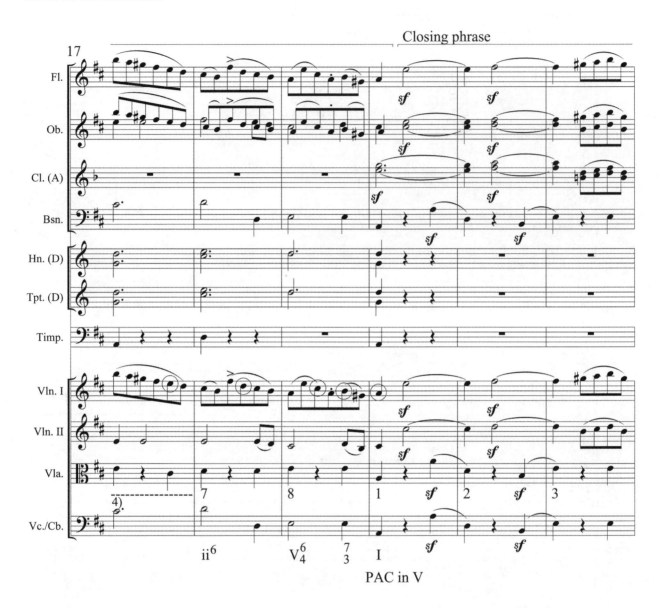

EXAMPLE 5.2 *continued*

EXAMPLE 5.2 *continued*

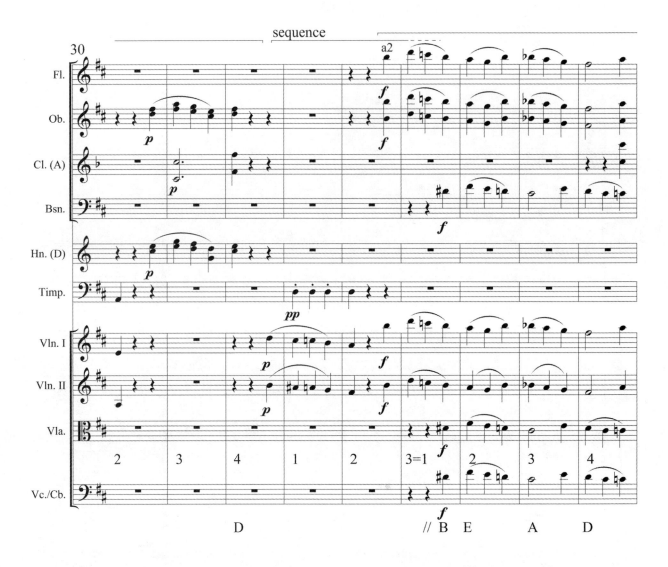

EXAMPLE 5.2 *continued*

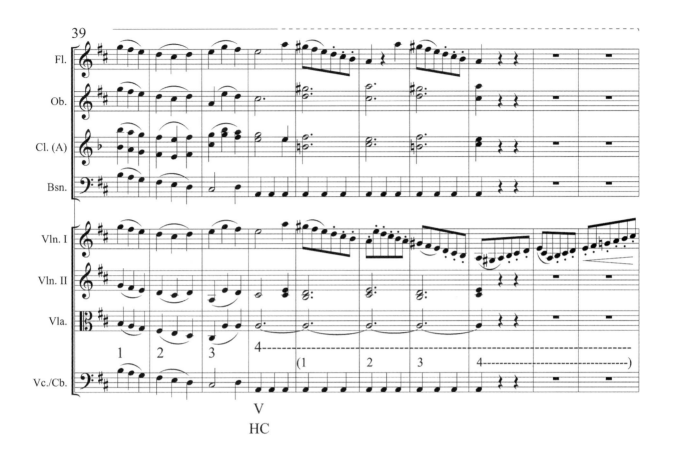

EXAMPLE 5.2 *continued*

EXAMPLE 5.2 *continued*

EXAMPLE 5.2 *continued*

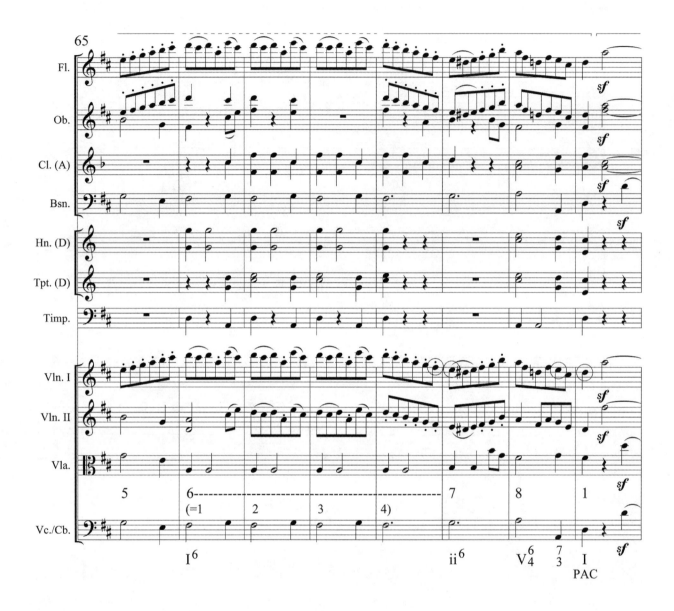

EXAMPLE 5.2 *continued*

The second part consists of its usual two segments: a portion leading to the home dominant (mm. 29–48) and the thematic return (mm. 49–80). The former includes an extension of the home dominant for several measures preceding the thematic return; thus, mm. 29–42 alone provide the underlying content of the B section. These fourteen measures can be viewed as a contraction of sixteen. To understand this, we need to examine the sequence that launches the second part of the minuet. The rapid descending fifth sequence beginning in m. 35 is introduced by four-measure sequential units beginning in m. 29. Example 5.3 recomposes this passage with an exact sequence of mm. 29–32 in the following four measures. Comparing this recomposition against Haydn's version, we observe that in the third measure of the second unit the sequence breaks off, avoiding the expected arrival on G major harmony. Instead a new "pseudo-sequence" begins; the harmonic basis of mm. 35–38 is descending fifths (B, E, A, D), but the melodic content is not exactly repeated between mm. 35–36 and 37–38. There is enough of a sequence, though, to convey that mm. 35–38 constitutes a four-measure unit; combined with its internal repetition and the subsequent hastening of surface chord changes in mm. 39–40, mm. 35–42 give the impression of a sentence design. This breaking off of the initial sequence in m. 35 in favor of this eight-measure sentence motivates our hypermetric reading of m. 35 as 3 = 1. Haydn could have written the eight-measure recomposition provided in Example 5.3 and followed this with his eight-measure sentence; this is why we mentioned earlier that mm. 29–42 can be viewed as a contraction of sixteen measures into fourteen. This interpretation rests on understanding pitch structure, but Haydn's sudden *forte* in m. 35 vividly and directly projects the unexpected change in direction that occurs here. As is often the case with performance indications, this change of dynamics does not merely provide an increase in volume but is intimately connected to the thematic content.

EXAMPLE 5.3 Recomposition of mm. 29–34 as eight-measure unit

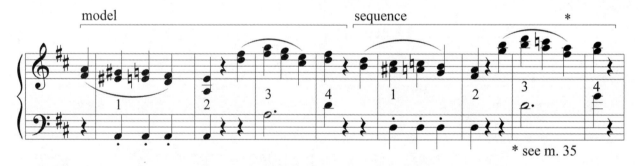

Before leaving the B section, we will point out three details. First, notice the deployment of the chromatic descending figure from the end of the initial antecedent phrase at the beginning of B. In the Haydn string quartet movement studied above, we also noted the re-use of a cadential figure as an initiatory melodic gesture in the analogous location. Second, there is an imitative relationship between the outer parts in the pseudo-sequence of mm. 35–38. Even though the imitation is inexact, it is unmistakable since this passage consists of only two lines, each doubled at the octave. This might be viewed as related to the hidden imitative relationship mentioned in mm. 1–4. Third, this B section is one that does not tonicize a new key; instead, it heads directly back to the home key and transforms V from a key area into the dominant of the home key. Note that the controlling harmony for a sizable expanse of the B section—mm. 32–40—is D major in root position. However, this D major harmony is circumscribed by A major chords at the boundaries of B. Thus, there is a prolongation of the dominant from the end of the first part of the minuet until the thematic return, but internal to that prolongation is, in fact, a strong presence of root-position D major. Once we are aware of the multiple levels on which harmony operates, these D major sonorities do not diminish the tension of the extended dominant and the desire for tonal return coordinated with the thematic return.

In A′, the antecedent phrase is the same as before, and the closing phrases are simply transposed into the tonic key. The only element that is substantively modified is the consequent phrase, which is further expanded from twelve to sixteen measures (mm. 57–72). The additional four measures result from a repetition of the presentation (mm. 61–64 = mm. 57–60). The upper instruments have a four-measure presentation, and then the lower instruments have their own. Thus, the imitative relationship between upper and lower instruments that was submerged in mm. 1–4 is explicit here. The expansion within the continuation—the stasis on the I^6 harmony—is the same harmonically as before, but the melodic content is altered. The expansion in mm. 66–69 unfolds the descending sixth D6–F♯5 in response to the quickly ascending sixth E5–C♯6 in the measure preceding the expansion. The F♯5 at the end of the expansion promptly leads to E5 over ii^6 and the ensuing dominant and to melodic closure at m. 72.

Two other aspects of the consequent phrase in A′ bear noting. First, the bass line at the start of the consequent does not solidly articulate tonic harmony. Instead, the lower strings (and two measures later the lower winds) emphasize the dominant. It is only when the melody goes into the bass for the presentation by the lower instruments that D occurs in the bass register. Note that the timpani is silent during the first four measures of the phrase, and re-enters only to reinforce the return of D. The second aspect is perhaps less evident but is a wonderful detail. In m. 64, the descending chromatic figure from m. 7 is incorporated, though altered. Harmonically, the progression $I^6 - [V^7]\ V^7 - I - ii^6$ replaces a chain of parallel thirds leading between I^6 and V. Hypermetrically, the figure no longer has a strong–weak placement, as it falls on hyperbeats 4 and 5 rather than 7 and 8. This conflict between the memory of the original hypermetric placement of this melodic figure and the hypermeter established by the immediate context has the effect of diluting the strength of hyperbeats in the latter, thereby increasing the phrase's desire for both tonal closure and a strongly projected hypermetric downbeat. In writing this thematic return, Haydn makes sure to "outdo" the expanded consequent from the minuet's first part!

We offer only a few brief comments on the trio; the score, with hypermetric annotations, is provided as Example 5.4. Trios are usually "simpler" in one or more ways compared to their framing minuets (or scherzos). In orchestral works, there is almost always a reduction in instrumentation, as is the case here. Often, the dynamics are softer, the harmonic rhythm slower, and the lengths of sections shorter. All of these occur in this trio. Note that the trio's first part is only sixteen measures in length; mm. 97–112 are a written-out repeat of mm. 81–96 to allow for a very slight harmonic alteration (in mm. 102–103 the upper strings briefly depart from their repeated D major chord).[4] Due to the lack of tonal motion in the initial twelve measures, the first part constitutes only a single phrase, leading from the tonic to a PAC in the key of the dominant.

EXAMPLE 5.4 Haydn, Symphony No. 101 in D Major ("Clock"), III, mm. 81–160

Example 5.4 *continued*

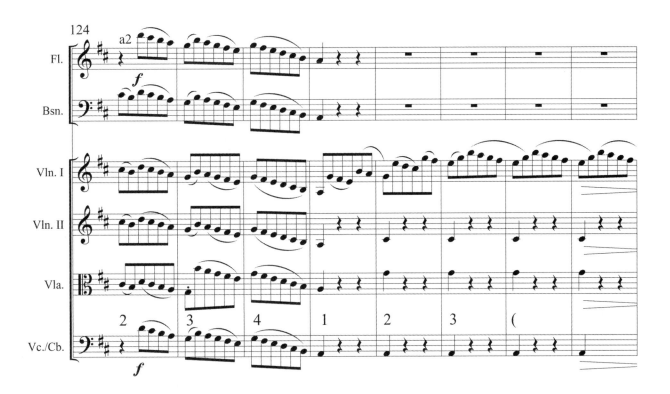

EXAMPLE 5.4 *continued*

Example 5.4 *continued*

EXAMPLE 5.4 *continued*

As in the minuet, the B section returns quickly to the tonic key and does not tonicize any other keys. The chord at the start of B—F♯ major in first inversion—is a shock, reharmonizing the F♯4 from the start of A with this chromatic chord. We can understand this chord as part of a motion from the dominant at the end of A to the D major chord reached early in the B section. Example 5.5 provides a literal chord reduction of this passage at (a) and shows how it can be understood as a contraction of an ascending 5–6 sequence at (b). Example 5.5 also points out that the goal of B is the home dominant, which is reasserted at m. 127 and extended until m. 136. Thus, as we saw in the minuet, there is a salient root-position D major chord subsumed within the larger prolongation of the dominant from the end of A to the end of B. We have suggested one hypermetric interpretation of B; we view the repetition in mm. 121–122 and in mm. 130–135 as outside of the underlying hypermeter.[5]

EXAMPLE 5.5 Sequential basis of B

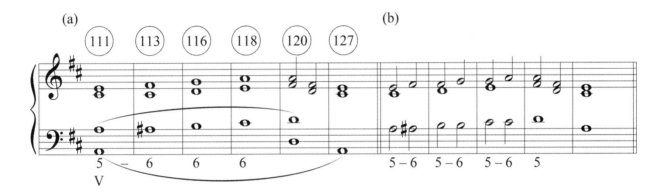

The most fascinating component of the trio is its extensively rewritten thematic return (mm. 137–160). As at the start of B, the introductory vamp lasts only two measures (and here it is also placed in a higher register), but it is now much more vigorously cut off by the full ensemble—not a solo flute. (Thus, we have shown the third measure of A′ as a hypermetric downbeat.) When the opening melody re-enters, it does so in the bass, and this motivates a recomposition that includes strong harmonic changes. In place of the placid twelve-measure tonic pedal, there is an overall progression of $I - vi - IV - ii^6 - V^{6-5}_{4-3}$ spanning mm. 137–148. This phrase seems destined for closure; in addition to the harmonic progression, there is a clear arrival on scale degree 2 in the melody over the ii^6 harmony (m. 145). Instead, the phrase breaks off, and after some silence the *pianissimo* D major chords return. The cellos and basses provide an independent bass line that introduces C♮ to create $[V^4_2]$ IV, a conventional signal of post-cadential function. Thus, although we have not yet had a PAC in D major during the trio, there is a feeling that the trio is already past the point of such a cadence. There are further melodic closes at m. 156 and m. 160—and the former is reinforced by an A–D leap in the cellos and basses—but look at the horns. Already at m. 154 they have begun to sustain a tonic pedal in a low register (D2/D3). The trio ends on its tonic harmony, but there is never a true PAC. This qualification of closure is possible because the trio is only the middle section in the larger minuet–trio–minuet design.

Finally, the hypermeter in mm. 150–160 requires comment. Throughout the trio, we have understood the onset of the main flute melody to correspond with a hypermetric downbeat. We do so as well here, but there are two complications. First, the flute enters after *three* measures of vamp (rather than four or two). Second, and more significantly, the added bass line suggests a hypermeter non-aligned with the flute's melody. Since the bass line remains on C♮ during the first measure of the flute melody, the bass line suggests that this measure is hyperbeat 4 in a quadruple hypermeter. This reading is further reinforced by the onset of the long tonic pedal in the horns in the next measure. There is a conflict here between the hypermetric cues of the accompaniment and those of the melody; when this is the case, the larger melodic design generally predominates. Here, the eighth-note melody is presented twice—mm. 153–156 and 157–160—and its implied quadruple hypermeter gradually subsumes the accompaniment's competing hypermeter.

This movement has a very straightforward harmonic language—none of the chords introduced in Chapter 4, for example, are found. Primarily we have focused on the movement's more distinctive treatment of phrase design and hypermeter. While minuets and scherzos often play with our expectations concerning phrase lengths and manipulate hypermeter in interesting ways, many also have remarkable tonal features. Although tonal features may be highlighted somewhat less here than in other chapters, as we proceed to movements by Beethoven and Brahms there will be increasing discussion of tonal elements.

Beethoven, Piano Sonata in A♭ Major, op. 26, II

In the second movement of Beethoven's Piano Sonata in A♭ Major, op. 26, we find a very lively scherzo, marked *Allegro molto*, which encloses a serene trio. Both scherzo and trio sections have remarkable formal and tonal features. We will discuss the scherzo first, then the trio, and finally the connection between scherzo and trio.

Example 5.6 provides an annotated score of the scherzo, and a cursory glance reveals it to be a rounded binary form. The repeat of the first part is written out (mm. 9–16 = mm. 1–8) to permit the addition of some passing tones (compare, for example, m. 1 with m. 9, m. 2 with m. 10). Wanting to ensure that the first part is not played *four* times (!), Beethoven writes "*La prima parte senza repetizione*" in the score. The second part (mm. 17–67) receives its customary exact repeat, and the thematic return occurs at the pickup to m. 45 with the melody placed into the left hand. It is subsequently played by the right hand eight measures later. We turn now to a closer look at tonal organization.

The scherzo, as is expected in a multi-movement work of Beethoven's time, is in the key of the overall work, here A♭ major. But this is not the key established in the scherzo's opening measures. Instead, we hear a cadential progression in E♭ major in mm. 1–4. The motion to A♭ major in mm. 5–8 results simply from transposing mm. 1–4 up a fourth. In addition to the off-key beginning, the scherzo's initial harmony is not a tonic or a dominant of E♭ major but its supertonic; in terms of the eventual A♭ major, the initial chord is submediant. This non-tonic beginning, and specifically its F minor chord, has implications for the design of the second part. Finally, note the continuous ascent of the upper line in the first part from C5 to A♭5: (A♭–B♭)–C5–D♮–E♭–[F]–E♭, (D♭–E♭)–F–G–A♭–[B♭]–A♭5. This, too, influences the subsequent course of the music.

EXAMPLE 5.6 Beethoven, Piano Sonata in A♭ Major, op. 26, II, mm. 1–67

EXAMPLE 5.6 *continued*

The second part opens with an ascending sequence that connects the A♭ harmony from the end of the first part to a C harmony that is vastly extended (mm. 24–44). As shown in Example 5.7, the sequence is a 5–°7 variant of the ascending 5–6 sequence. Although the melodic material is directly based on the opening music, the placement of the melody with respect to the harmony has changed. In the initial F minor chord, the melody moves from third to fifth; at the start of part 2, the melody moves from chordal fifth to seventh. As a result, the melodic line needs to descend, at least temporarily, and after a two-measure delay the G♭ moves to F (m. 20). The larger melodic framework is still an ascent, but a much slower one, progressing from E♭ (m. 17) to F (m. 20) to G (m. 24), where each of the latter two tones is approached by a local descent. Supporting the G is the extended C major harmony, which is destabilized through addition of its seventh and later its ninth, clarifying its function as dominant of F minor. Thus, we see the logic of Beethoven's pause on the C major harmony: he is preparing the thematic return in a perfectly appropriate way—with the dominant of its initial harmony. An expansion of the home dominant would be less effective here, as it would not lead as strongly to the initial harmony and it would undercut the emphasis on the key of the dominant in the first few measures of the thematic return. In the upper part, there is a clear connection as well: the motion from E♭ to F to G ultimately leads to A♭ at the thematic return. Just as with the earlier motions to F and G, the approach to A♭ comes from above, the seventh—B♭—having been introduced already at m. 26.[6]

EXAMPLE 5.7 Voice-leading representation of mm. 16–45

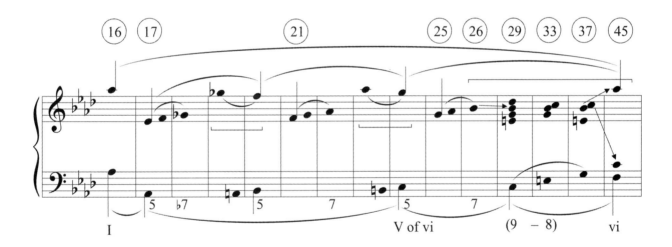

We have remarked already that the principal melody occurs in the left hand at the thematic return. Initially, it is not the lowest voice; the bass motion is the same as at the beginning, simply transposed down an octave. In the third and fourth measures of the return, the left-hand melody does function as the bass voice (with the addition of a syncopated chromatic passing tone—E♮—that recalls, albeit briefly, the extended dominant of F minor from earlier). What is less immediately apparent in the thematic return is that the eighth notes in the upper register are an embellished version of the middle voice from the opening. The pitches corresponding to the middle voice in mm. 1–8 have been circled on the score in mm. 45–52.

The repetition of the melody by the right hand has a few significant effects. By emerging after the left-hand statement, it powerfully conveys the ascending sweep characteristic of this material. Although the left-hand statement momentarily breaks this sweep in mm. 49–52 by shifting down a fifth rather than up a fourth, one can nonetheless trace a motion from the C4 at the start of the left-hand statement all the way to the A♭5 at the end of the right-hand statement (m. 60). Yet the phrase is not over at m. 60 since the running eighths of the left hand have arrived only on scale degree 3. The I^6 internally expands the phrase, and the PAC arrives four measures later (m. 64). Both during the phrase expansion and the four-measure codetta that begins at m. 64, the upper part lands on C6—first supported by [V] ii, then I^6, and finally I. This focus on C6 is a beautiful outcome of the ascending melody, taking the focal pitch of m. 1 and giving it a climactic registral treatment and supporting it eventually with root-position tonic harmony.

While the expansions at the end of the scherzo's final phrase attract the most attention, there is a subtle recomposition at the very beginning of this phrase. Consider the eighth notes in the left hand in m. 53. The note F does not arrive until the fourth eighth note; on the downbeat, only A♭ and C sound. As we pointed out in Chapter 1, two pitches that form the interval of a third usually suggest the root and third of a chord, and this is clearly the case here since the preceding measure contains root-position A♭ major. Thus, this final statement of the principal melody begins from tonic harmony with only a vague suggestion of its characteristic F minor chord at the last instant before the next change of chord. We might not even hear this brief suggestion of F minor at all, but it is worth noting that Beethoven alters the eighth notes in m. 53 from the ones in the right hand eight measures earlier in a way that is consistent with a nod towards the F minor chord. In m. 45, the fourth eighth note was C (not F), as the lowest part in the left hand provided the F for the F minor chord.

The trio certainly fulfils our expectation for simplification: the surface rhythm and harmonic rhythm are slow and consistent, the texture is exclusively chordal, and the outer voices proceed almost entirely in parallel tenths. The score appears in Example 5.8 and a voice-leading representation in Example 5.9. The form is binary (not rounded binary), and the dominant at the end of the first part is handled as V of the principal key (not as a key area of its own). The dominant harmony extends from the end of the first part all the way to the cadential dominant at the end of the second part; note the bass motion through the octave A♭2–A♭3 across mm. 75–89.

There is one striking parallelism between the first and second parts of the trio. As shown by the brackets in Example 5.9, the bass line's initial approach to the dominant and its approach to the subsequent return of the dominant are the same: scale degree 4 (G♭) prolonged first by a lower neighbor (F) and then a chromatic passing tone (G♮). This might not seem a particularly unique or salient melodic motion, but the sonorities that accompany the bass F are striking, albeit different. In the first part, the upper voices move to the notes of ii$^6_5$; usually with a bass embellishment the upper voices either shift to be somewhat more consonant with the bass, or they simply stay on their original notes. Moving to a different sonority that is not consonant with the simultaneous bass embellishment stands out. In the second part, the F initially supports [V$^6_5$] IV but in the ensuing measure the fifth of the chord is raised, temporarily producing an augmented triad [V$^6_♮$] IV. In addition, the motions of the melody are related in these two locations. As shown by the dotted brackets

EXAMPLE 5.8 Beethoven, Piano Sonata in A♭ Major, op. 26, II, mm. 68–95

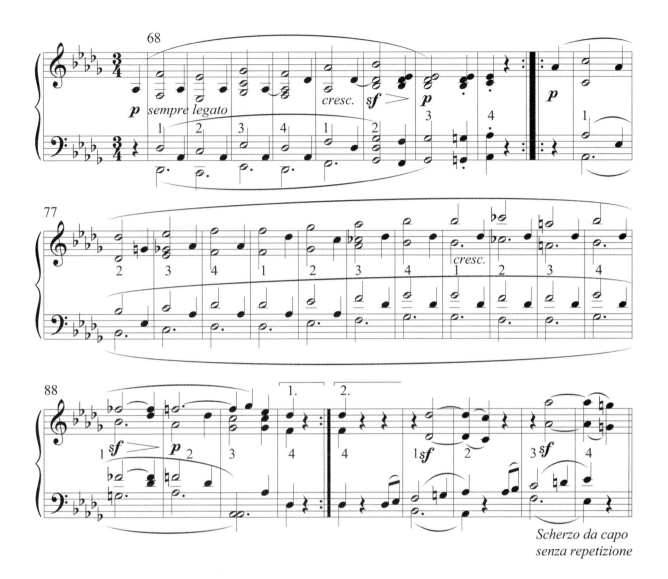

Scherzo da capo
senza repetizione

Example 5.9 Voice-leading representation of the trio

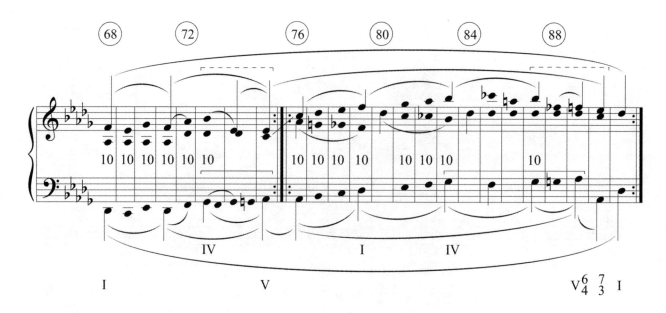

in Example 5.9, in both instances there is a leap downward from B♭, although it does not occur in the same alignment with the bass line. Further, the leap is not to the same pitch—E♭ the first time, F♭ the second. However, the F♭ serves to delay E♭ and does resolve there once the dominant harmony arrives. The strongest argument for this melodic relationship, though, is the minimal melodic motion in this trio; the leaps B♭4–E♭4 and B♭5–F♭5 are the only leaps that span an interval larger than a third.

A remarkable formal feature of this movement is the presence of a retransition between the trio and the *da capo* return of the scherzo. This type of retransition was rare in the eighteenth century but became quite common during the nineteenth century. Here, the thematic material derives entirely from the scherzo, reversing the tonal motion of mm. 1–8 as a way of modulating smoothly back from the trio's D♭ major. We will encounter a similar retransition in the scherzo movement by Brahms to which we now turn.

Brahms, Piano Sonata in F Minor, op. 5, III

The scherzo movement from Brahms's Piano Sonata in F Minor, op. 5, shares many similarities with the Beethoven movement just studied. In addition to a retransition between the trio and *da capo* return of the scherzo, Brahms's scherzo also begins with a non-tonic harmony, which again has implications for the tonal structure of the scherzo's second part. But Brahms's scherzo is much more experimental. There are no exact repeats, and the written-out repeat of the first part is considerably more varied than in the Beethoven. The tonal goal of the first part is an unexpected one—the subdominant—and the beginning of the second part is thematically independent from the rest of the scherzo. We will examine these and other features of the scherzo first, and subsequently turn to the lengthy trio.

An annotated score of the scherzo is provided as Example 5.10. With its left-hand pattern of a low bass octave followed by two higher chords, the scherzo's opening resembles a waltz,

EXAMPLE 5.10 Brahms, Piano Sonata in F Minor, op. 5, III, mm. 1–100

EXAMPLE **5.10** *continued*

EXAMPLE **5.10** *continued*

EXAMPLE 5.10 *continued*

and it possesses the strongly projected four-measure hypermeter characteristic of a waltz. Decidedly less waltz-like are the tonal elements. The first part of the scherzo consists of sixteen measures, leading to the subdominant and not to the usual relative major. Moreover, the way Brahms approaches this arrival is unusual: a stepwise, and almost fully chromatic, bass line traces the diminished twelfth from E♮ up to B♭. There is a sense of two parallel phrases—mm. 1–8 and 9–16—due to the similarity in the melodic material at corresponding locations in these two passages. However, the chord in m. 8 is iv^6, which is not suitable as a goal harmony. Thus, the feeling of two phrases is illusory, as a single tonal motion connects the beginning with eventual arrival at the key of B♭ minor. But, tonally speaking, what exactly constitutes the beginning of this scherzo? The initial chord—°7—is not only non-tonic but, in fact, dissonant. At first, we think it will resolve to tonic harmony in m. 2, but note that the fifth above the bass note F is displaced by the sixth (D♭); in harmonic terms, a VI⁶ sonority replaces the expected i. In m. 3, we encounter $^{o6}_{5}$, an inversion of the opening chord, and only at m. 4 does an F minor chord arrive, but it is in first inversion. And, in m. 5, it is transformed into an applied chord to the subdominant! Combined with the stepwise motion of the bass throughout mm. 1–16, the de-emphasis of tonic harmony contributes to the unsettled, turbulent quality of this opening.

In the preceding Beethoven scherzo, the repeat of the first reprise was written out to allow for the addition of a few passing tones. In the Brahms, the recomposition of mm. 1–16 in mm. 17–36 is much more extensive. Overall, the pianist's hands exchange material. This occurs most literally in mm. 17–20 (= mm. 1–4) and mm. 25–28 (= mm. 9–12), where the left hand states the former right-hand melody in melodic inversion. Notice that, although the harmonies are quite similar, there is a slight stabilization of F minor in the initial four measures of the varied repetition: the second measure now presents i⁶ (rather than VI⁶) and the fourth measure lands on i rather than i⁶. The segments corresponding to mm. 5–8 and 13–16 are more freely varied; Example 5.11 provides simplifications of mm. 5–8 and its varied repetition in mm. 21–24. The simplification reveals the transfer of F–G♭–A♭–B♭ from right hand into the left, and the partial transfer of the A♭–B♭–C–D♭ from left hand into the right. The transfer of the latter is, in fact, somewhat more complete as in m. 22 the B♭ is delayed by an embellishing A♮. Harmonically, the most significant change is in the first measure (m. 21), where an applied chord of the Neapolitan replaces [V⁶₅] iv.[7] The final segment of the first part is expanded by four measures in its varied repetition. Due to the repetitions, we can easily discern that mm. 29–36 represent an expanded and varied repetition of mm. 13–16. Notably, it is the two measures that depart furthest from their model (mm. 13–14) that are stated multiple times—an expansion Brahms highlights through his *sostenuto* indication.[8] The varied repeat ends with a clear restatement of its final measure (m. 36 = m. 16); notice the recomposition of the penultimate measure that enables a root-position dominant chord and thus a perfect authentic cadence in mm. 35–36, in contrast to the stepwise bass motion in mm. 15–16.

EXAMPLE 5.11 Voice-leading simplifications of mm. 5–8 and 21–24

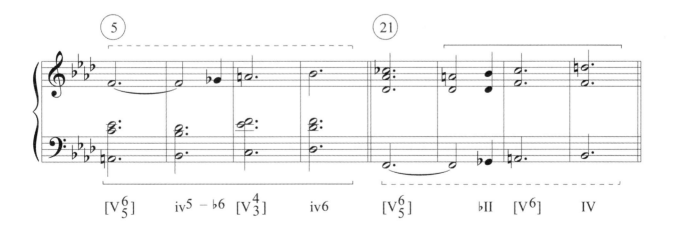

We noted above the stepwise motion through the diminished twelfth from E♮ up to B♭ during the scherzo's first part. The second part continues the ascent from B♭ (m. 37) up to G (mm. 50–69), dividing the span at D♭ (m. 42) and E♮ (m. 46) and thereby projecting the opening diminished seventh harmony linearly. The unusual bass design of B leads smoothly to the return of the diminished seventh at the onset of A' (m. 70), the non-dominant preparation responding to an idiosyncrasy of the thematic material. As in the first part, the bass ascent during B is stepwise, although here the stepwise motion happens more slowly; the bass tones participating in the ascent occur every other measure: B♭ (m. 36), C♭ (m. 38), C (m. 40), D♭ (m. 42), E♭ (m. 44), E♮ (m. 46), F♯ (m. 48), G (mm. 50–69). After the arrival on D♭ (m. 42), the upper line moves in parallel tenths with the bass; in mm. 36–42, the upper line descends from B♭6 to F6. These observations are summarized graphically in Example 5.12. Note that within mm. 42–50 the chords in odd-numbered measures are subsidiary to those that participate in the pattern of parallel tenths.[9] This entire passage is principally organized around the large linear motion in the bass rather than standard harmonic progressions; this is why we have not provided a detailed harmonic analysis on the score.

EXAMPLE 5.12 Voice-leading representation of mm. 36–70

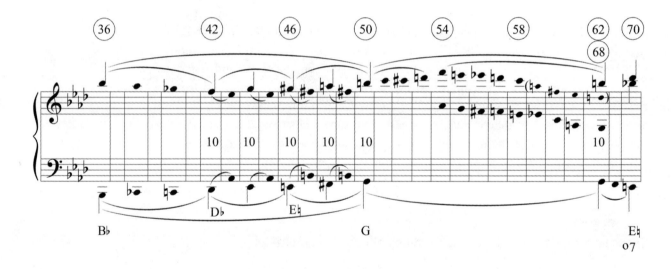

We have addressed the tonal design of the B material, but we have not commented on two unusual aspects of its formal design. First, due to the discontinuous gestures in mm. 38–41, the B section does not seem to begin until the arrival on D♭ major and the continuous right-hand material at m. 42. For this reason, on the score we have labeled mm. 38–41 as a transition to the B section. There is, in fact, some blurring of the boundary between the end of A and the start of this transition. The descending arpeggio that marks the cadence on B♭ minor at the end of A (m. 36) is answered by the bass in the next measure; the latter seems simply like a one-measure post-cadential extension. However, these two measures provide the thematic material for both of the two-measure units within the transition in mm. 38–41. From a tonal perspective, mm. 36–37 (beat 2) provide a close to the A section, but thematically they prepare the transition to the B section. Blurring of boundaries between sections is typical of Brahms's style, and we will encounter more elaborate overlaps in the Brahms works studied in Chapters 7 and 8. The second unusual aspect of the B section is its thematic independence from the A section. As we have seen in the Haydn and Beethoven examples, B is normally a development of material from A. In the Brahms, however, the rhythmic pattern from the transition (mm. 38–41) serves as the basis for every measure in mm. 42–62; the rhythm from the scherzo's first measure disappears completely until m. 63. There is thus a stark contrast in thematic material that begins at m. 42—a contrast more typically found between a scherzo and a trio than between the A and B sections of a scherzo (or of a trio). In A′ only the rhythmic pattern from the scherzo's opening returns, which means that the scherzo's contrasting rhythmic motives are not brought into direct conflict or reconciliation. It is notable, though, that in the approach to the final cadence (mm. 87–95), the rhythmic content becomes dramatically simpler: each measure consists of a half-note octave followed by a quarter-note chord. This may be viewed as a liquidation of the rhythmic content to its underlying basis; this long-short succession is suggested by the tonal content of the two rhythmic figures. In m. 1, the brief C is a passing tone between D♭ and B♭; similarly, in m. 42, the F is prolonged through arpeggiation and then moves to D♭ on beat 3. (Of course, the half-note to quarter-note motive is present throughout mm. 42–54 in the left hand.)

In A′ we encounter yet another variation on the opening material. Both right and left hands give the opening melody (mm. 70–73), combining the modes of presentations seen in the first part and its written-out varied repeat. The first eight measures of A′ closely resemble the corresponding portion of A, but the presence of F minor is further stabilized. Both in the second and fourth measures of A′ is there a root-position F minor chord. It is only at the eleventh measure of A′ (m. 80) where significant divergence from A occurs in order to avoid modulation. After an expansion of the phrase through the sequential repetition of the diminished seventh arpeggio figure, a cadential segment (mm. 87–94) leads to closure at m. 95. A short codetta further extends this already massive phrase of twenty-six measures (mm. 70–95).

Particularly beautiful is the trio's placement in D♭ major, since it thereby seems to germinate from the trio-like D♭ major passage that began the scherzo's second part.[10] With its soft, slow-moving, homorhythmic texture, the trio provides necessary and obvious expressive contrast. The trio's phrase design and hypermetric structure also contribute to this effect. Throughout most of the scherzo, the bass line announces a forceful change of harmony at each downbeat. At the trio's third measure, this fails to occur; instead there is a syncopation at the level of the measure, and this becomes the trio's most distinctive rhythmic feature. We provide a score with hypermetric annotations as Example 5.13.

As the annotations on Example 5.13 suggest, the syncopated figure maintains a consistent placement on the second hyperbeat. This hypermetric identity is strongly established by the beginnings of the trio's first two phrases. When the gesture returns at the end of the third phrase (mm. 129–132), it is easily heard with the same hypermetric placement due to the end of the two-measure melodic parallelisms in mm. 123–128. After the symmetrical eight-measure phrases in mm. 101–116, the asymmetry within mm. 117–132 is striking; the sixteen-measure phrase does balance the previous two phrases, but is subdivided as 6 + 6 + 4. Brahms returns to this thematic material at the end of the second reprise and fashions a version that preserves four-measure hypermeter (mm. 192–203).

EXAMPLE 5.13 Brahms, Piano Sonata in F Minor, op. 5, III, mm. 101–212

EXAMPLE 5.13 *continued*

Dal segno sino al Fine.

The second part of this trio is noteworthy for two bold phrase expansions. The first occurs in mm. 139–153 where an eight-measure unit is expanded to fifteen measures. This phrase is especially similar to the trio's second phrase (mm. 109–116), which makes the expansion of the [°7] V particularly obvious. Recognizing the expansion explains a seeming anomaly: the phrase consists of an odd number of measures and the concluding dominant chord (m. 153) seems a measure too short. When the expansion is taken into account, however, it is clear that the final chord would only last one measure in the underlying prototype. Many phrase expansions maintain relatively periodic surface hypermeter, but this one decidedly does not. In fact, without awareness of the deeper level of hypermeter, the conclusion of this phrase—which provides the dominant arrival that sets up the thematic return—feels awkward. Within the expansion, a nice touch is the inclusion of the syncopated gesture in the second measure (m. 146). Somewhat puzzling is the chromatic slide to Gb in the bass that momentarily produces a dominant seventh of Cb major. Brahms appropriately revisits this harmony in A′.

The remaining phrase expansion is much longer than the previous one, and it is used to prepare the trio's climax. In A′, the second phrase begins as a minor-mode variant on the trio's second phrase. At the end of its fourth measure, the phrase goes off track tonally, rhythmically, and registrally. The phrase at first seems headed for Fb major (mm. 166–168) but ultimately goes to Cb major (mm. 169–172), a destination that seems related to the tonal content of the expansion just before A′. Rhythmically, the characteristic half-note to quarter-note succession is augmented from three beats into three measures (mm. 169–171); the six-measure unit in mm. 166–171 expands a four-measure model through this written-out deceleration. As the goal Cb major triad (bVII) unfolds into the home dominant, the rhythmic content further hints at the passage's digressiveness through the bass line's reintroduction of the *scherzo*'s primary rhythmic idea. The entire passage from mm. 166–179 occurs in a very high register. The impression that these measures constitute a large parenthetical insertion is confirmed by the arrival of I^6 at m. 180; I^6 is the chord that should have occurred at the phrase's fifth measure. Brahms does not allow the phrase to end in a half cadence at this point, but keeps reiterating these long-expected measures (with the glorious melodic arpeggiation Db, F, Ab, Db connecting consecutive hyperdownbeats). These repetitions culminate with a restatement of the latter portion of the final phrase from the first part, in invertible counterpoint (mm. 192ff.). Previously this phrase was not consonant with four-measure hypermeter, but this recomposed version is. Especially significant is the arrival of the trio's structural dominant on a hyperdownbeat (m. 200) and its interaction with the right-hand melody. The right-hand chord is tied over from the previous measure and thus is not a syncopation—as everywhere else in the trio—but a suspension. It is normative for a suspension to enter in a metrically weak position and sustain through a stronger beat. Thus, the stylistically marked syncopation is transformed into a stylistically unmarked suspension. This final phrase, then, not only brings hypermetric resolution to the material originally presented at the end of the trio's first reprise but also provides a climactic working out of the trio's characteristic rhythmic motive. After this powerful buildup—there is essentially a single tonal motion from tonic to dominant spanning mm. 162–200—Brahms provides a tonic harmony only at the start of an eight-measure retransition that leads to the *da capo* repeat of the scherzo.

SUGGESTED ASSIGNMENTS

The ultimate goal of analysis is to identify what is special or unique about a particular work. To that end, we suggest you proceed through the following steps:

1.   Identify the main formal divisions and subdivisions (A, B, A′, retransition, codetta, etc.).

2.   Identify important motives that are repeated/developed in the course of the movement.

3.   Examine features of the phrase rhythm, that is, the interaction of phrase design and hypermeter.

4.   Identify important features of the overall tonal organization and details of the harmony, particularly in more complex passages. You may want to prepare a simplification of the voice leading of certain passages, identifying harmony, hypermeter, important motives, etc.

For each of the five pieces below, we have provided a few questions to point towards some of the movement's unique aspects. We encourage you to study the music on your own and to complete the analytic steps listed above before considering our questions.

Haydn, String Quartet in B♭ Major, op. 76, no. 4, III

1.   Identify several techniques by which Haydn develops the opening eighth-note motive.

2.   Compare the harmonic progressions and outer-voice motions of mm. 1–8 and 29–36.

3.   What are the chords in mm. 17–18?

4.   How does Haydn's deployment of the cello in mm. 9–29 clarify the formal-tonal organization?

5.   What is the formal function of mm. 37–50?

6.   In what way(s) is the thematic material of the trio similar to that of the minuet?

Haydn, String Quartet in C Major, op. 74, no. 1, III

1.   We studied the end of the minuet in Chapter 3 (see Example 3.17) as an example of a three-measure parenthetical insertion (mm. 56–58). This thematic material originates in mm. 11–12. What is the formal function of mm. 11–12 within mm. 1–14?

2.   Upon what model is the tonal structure of mm. 15–23 based? (In what other work studied in this chapter was a similar progression used at the same formal location?)

3.   What is the formal function of mm. 27–31?

4.   This is a minuet in which one might say that the thematic rounding occurs twice. Explain and speculate on why Haydn might have included the additional statement of the opening material.

5. Comment on the Db in m. 40. What pitch did we expect here? What does the Db "trigger"?

6. Compare the first violin line in the first five measures of the minuet to that in the first five measures of the trio.

7. In addition to the melodic similarity noted in the preceding question, what other similarities are there between the thematic materials of the minuet and those of the trio?

8. What is the formal-tonal role of mm. 97–112? How is the modulation from m. 112 back to the *da capo* restatement of the minuet achieved?

Haydn, String Quartet in F Major, op. 74, no. 2, III

1. Why do mm. 1–4 not constitute a complete phrase? How could one rewrite m. 4 so that mm. 1–4 would be a complete phrase? If one undertook such a rewriting, to what phrase design would mm. 1–8 correspond?

2. Describe the phrase design of mm. 18–37. Comment on the relationship of this passage to mm. 1–8 (and the hypothetical recomposition of mm. 1–8 mentioned in the preceding question).

3. What is the formal function of mm. 38–41?

4. What melodic relationship exists between the end of the minuet and the start of the trio?

5. What is the formal-tonal role of mm. 68–78? On what earlier measures are mm. 68–69 based, and what is the effect of this on the listener?

Beethoven, Violin Sonata in C Minor, op. 30, no. 2, III

1. Why is there no repeat sign in m. 18?

2. Comment on the significance of the piano left hand in m. 16 (beats 1 and 2).

3. With what harmony does Beethoven prepare the scherzo's thematic return? Does this provide a smooth harmonic return, or is another type of connection present?

4. Comment on the relationship between the piano and violin parts in the trio.

5. With what harmony does Beethoven prepare the trio's thematic return? How many measures in total are occupied by this harmony?

Brahms, Cello Sonata in E Minor, op. 38, II

1. This "quasi Menuetto" is unusual in the length of its upbeat: the piano part has more than a complete measure before the principal melody begins. What implications does the lengthy upbeat have for hypermeter throughout the minuet?

2. The initial pair of notes F–E and the motive of a descending semitone (especially $\hat{6}$–$\hat{5}$ in minor) permeates both minuet and trio. Explain.

3. Compare the phrase design of mm. 2–14 and 60–76.

4. Is the trio an example of binary or rounded binary form? Justify your answer.

6 Classical Sonata Form

Sonata form in the Classical period—as expressed in the music of Haydn, Mozart, and early Beethoven—is an expansion of rounded binary form, where the initial part is the exposition and the second part contains both the development and the recapitulation. Both parts are repeated, as specified in the score through repeat signs, though the repeat of the second part is rarely taken in modern performances. As the dimension of sonata-form movements grew in the nineteenth century, repeats disappeared, leaving a three-part design: exposition–development–recapitulation. Although sonata form does appear in various types of movements, it is almost always found in the first movement of instrumental works such as sonatas, trios, quartets, and symphonies. All of our examples are first movements of such works.

There is always a danger in defining a model of Classical sonata form, since there are many exceptions to the "rule." Still it is helpful to have in mind the norm for sonata form in both the major and minor modes.[1] Thematically, the **exposition** typically contains an initial theme, a transitional passage leading to a second theme, and a closing section that may involve a full-fledged theme and/or shorter phrases. The content of the **development** is harder to define; it may include new material, but typically involves development of motives and themes from the exposition leading to a retransition. The **recapitulation** normally follows the exposition's ordering of material. In many sonata forms, additional closing material—referred to as a **coda**—follows the recapitulation. Unlike thematic content, tonal structure differs in major- and minor-mode sonata forms. In the major mode, the initial theme is in the tonic key, and the following transition will typically lead to V of V.[2] The second theme and closing section will then appear in the key of the dominant. The development digresses from the dominant but eventually returns to it for a retransition leading to the opening theme in the tonic. In the recapitulation, it is normally the transition to the second theme that is rewritten to remain in the tonic, ending on the dominant of the home key. The remainder of the recapitulation presents a transposed version of the corresponding exposition material. In a movement in the minor mode, the transition to the second theme in the exposition typically leads to V of III, and the second theme and following material are written in the key of the relative major (III).[3] The development section leads eventually to V and the retransition, and the transition in the recapitulation is usually rewritten to remain in the tonic key, ending on its dominant. The remainder of the recapitulation presents a transposed version of the corresponding exposition material, though often some—or even all—occurs in the parallel major. This preserves the modal quality of this material, which thereby retains more of its original expressive import. Again, bear in mind that this is a general description of the norm, subject to a wide variety of modifications.

	Exposition			Development	Recapitulation	
	‖: th.1 – trans. – th.2 – cl. mat.:‖:			( )	th.1 – trans. – th. 2 – cl. mat.:‖	
Major:	I	[V] V ----V ------		-V^7, I	I	
Minor:	i	[V] III --- III -----		-V^7, i	i/I	

FIGURE 6.1 Basic Models of Classical Sonata Form

A chart of the basic thematic/tonal models outlined above is provided in Figure 6.1. As indicated by the repeat signs, the formal design is binary, though once the repeat signs are removed, the form is ternary. From a tonal perspective, sonata form falls into two large parts, as indicated by the brackets at the bottom of Figure 6.1. Thus we must be careful to define exactly what it is we are describing about sonata form. The formal design is binary as long as the repeats remain intact, but its tonal design is also binary—but a different binary: the first part contains the exposition and development and the second part the recapitulation. It is useful to distinguish the two by terminology: **formal design** vs. **tonal structure**.

In this chapter we will examine two opening movements in some detail: Mozart's Piano Sonata in F Major, K. 332, and Beethoven's Piano Trio in C Minor, op. 1, no. 3. The Mozart is straightforward in its formal-tonal organization, while the Beethoven is more complex in its formal design.

Mozart, Piano Sonata in F Major, K. 332, I

In almost all respects, the initial movement from Mozart's Piano Sonata in F Major, K. 332, reflects the standard practice of the Classical period for a sonata movement in the major mode. The score of this movement with analytic additions—to be discussed below—is provided in Example 6.1, and Figure 6.2 provides a chart of the movement's formal-tonal organization. The left column of Figure 6.2 lists the three major sections (Exposition, Development, and Recapitulation) and their subdivisions. The center column provides corresponding measure numbers, and the right column indicates key areas and important harmonic motions within these keys. As a first step in our analysis, we will talk through the formal divisions, then go back and discuss some important features of the melody, the harmony, and the metric organization.

The opening theme of this sonata movement is in two parts, both ending with perfect authentic cadences in the tonic. It is this strong tonal closure as well as the introduction of new melodic material that creates a two-part initial theme. This theme is followed by a transition (T1) that leads to V of V (mm. 37–40), preparing the statement of the second

EXAMPLE 6.1 Mozart, Piano Sonata in F Major, K. 332, I

EXAMPLE **6.1** *continued*

EXAMPLE 6.1 *continued*

EXAMPLE 6.1 *continued*

EXAMPLE 6.1 *continued*

EXAMPLE 6.1 *continued*

EXAMPLE **6.1** *continued*

EXPOSITION

Theme 1

part 1	1–12		I
part 2	13–22		I
Transition (T1)	23–40	leads to	V of V

Theme 2

antecedent	41–48		C(V): I – V
consequent	49–56		I
Transition (T2)	56–70	leads to	V

Closing section

closing theme	71–76		IV – I
expanded repetition	77–86		
closing phrase	86–93		I

DEVELOPMENT

initial phrase	94–101		I
repetition (octave lower)	102–109		I
extension (based on T2)	109–123, 123–132	leads to F(I):	III♯

RECAPITULATION

Theme 1

part 1	133–144		I
part 2	145–154		I
Transition (T1)	155–176	leads to	V

Theme 2

antecedent	177–184		I – V
consequent	185–192		I
Transition (T2)	192–206	leads to	V

Closing section

closing theme	207–212		IV – I
expanded repetition	213–222		I
closing phrase	222–229		I

FIGURE 6.2 Outline of Mozart, Piano Sonata, K. 332, I

theme in the key of the dominant, C major. Theme 2 consists of a sixteen-measure antecedent-consequent construction, ending with a perfect authentic cadence (mm. 55–56) in C major. Rather than proceeding directly to closing material, theme 2 is followed by a second transition passage (T2), which contains a descending fifth sequence in the parallel minor mode and leads once again to V of V. Now the closing theme enters, although it does not open as we might expect with the local tonic (C major), but with the subdominant harmony. This six-measure phrase is then repeated in varied form an octave higher and expanded, leading to a perfect authentic cadence (m. 86) and a final closing phrase.

The development opens with an eight-measure phrase in the key of the dominant, which is subsequently repeated an octave lower. Although by no means the only possibility, continuing the key from the end of the exposition into the start of the development—however briefly—is the most common tonal strategy at this formal juncture. This tonally closed unit (mm. 94–109) is followed by a transitional passage based on the earlier transition leading from the end of theme 2 to the closing theme, that is, T2, only here the sequence leads us from the lower register to the one an octave higher. The goal of this motion is the A major chord, reached in m. 123. This A major chord has the potential to be V of vi, but it never functions in that capacity. It has been marked III♯ on the score, and eventually we must consider why Mozart would make an A major chord the goal of harmonic motion in the development section. For now we note that the C♯ is subsequently replaced by C♮ preparing the entry of V^4_3 and then V^7 to reintroduce the opening theme in the tonic key.

The recapitulation follows standard procedure. The only change from the exposition comes in the transition to theme 2 (T1), which is rewritten to lead to V rather than V of V. Thus the entire recapitulation remains in the tonic key.

Having taken this brief descriptive walk though the movement, we will now go back to the beginning to examine various parts in greater detail. Our discussion will increasingly focus on the musical elements that make this movement unique and memorable, although we will continue to make some general comments on Classical sonata form. A solid understanding of standard sonata-form procedures, in fact, helps to reveal the truly distinguishing features of a particular movement.

Exposition

The first theme, part 1, consists of three four-measure hypermeasures, as indicated by the Arabic numbers between the staves in Example 6.1. Initially, these hypermeasures seem unusually distinct due to the clear changes in rhythm and texture. A close look at mm. 1–12 reveals elements that bind the twelve measures together and that also have significance for the movement as a whole. The melodic line contains two important motivic components: the arpeggiation of the tonic triad (marked with brackets in mm. 1–2, 6–7, and 10), and the upper neighbor of scale degree 5, that is, D5 (mm. 5 and 9). The melody's lower range between the two iterations of D5 highlights this pitch, as does its function in m. 9 of introducing the decorated return of the arpeggiation of the tonic triad. The varied return of the opening arpeggiation coincides with the melody's most active rhythm and provides momentum towards the ensuing cadence. A third, less obvious, component of mm. 1–12 is the gradual descent of a fifth from C5 to F4: C5 (m.2)–B♭4 (m.3)–A4 (m.5)–A4 (m.9)–G4 (m.11)–F4 (m.12). These notes are circled on the score. Note that although the A4 in

m. 5 continues on down to F4 in m. 7, the latter motion has been interpreted as extending A4 until it reappears at m. 9.[4] This delay on A4 thus articulates a clear division of the fifth into two thirds: C5–B♭4–A4 (mm. 1–5) and A4–G4–F4 (mm. 9–12). Before moving on to the second part of theme 1, there is one final feature of the first part worthy of note, namely the weak hemiola pattern implied by the interaction between melodic contour (duple) and meter (triple) in mm. 5–6 (right hand) and 7–8 (left hand), marked by dotted brackets on the score. Mozart's *legato* slurs provide further clarification that the hemiola is not strongly projected. Like the other features we have noted in the opening twelve measures, however, this implicit hemiola pattern is developed later.

The second part of theme 1, stated in the upper octave, is clearly based on the primary motivic component of the movement, the descending arpeggiation of the tonic triad (bracketed on the score). Despite this motivic connection, the higher register, new dotted rhythms, and simpler texture make the second part of theme 1 rather contrasting from its first part. Particularly satisfying, then, is the exact return of the melody at the final cadence (compare mm. 19–20 with 11–12). In the cadential melody, note that B♭ is consistently picked up and resolved an octave lower in an inner voice rather than proceeding by step to A in its own register. At the juncture between the two parts of theme 1, B♭ quickly returns in the upper voice—on the last beat of m. 12—and moves by step down to A. At the end of the second part of theme 1, B♭ does not return immediately in the upper voice, but there is a longer-range connection to the A5 in m. 24, a connection that is sealed with the reiteration of B♭5–A5 across mm. 25–28. This extends a connective thread across the otherwise sharp juncture between theme 1 and the transition.

Theme 1 ends with a two-measure extension that reiterates the cadential harmonies and the melody's central C–F fifth in the two registers explored during the theme. These repetitions give theme 1 an unusually strong close, as does its separation from the ensuing transition by a beat of rest. These features set the stage for quite a shock when the transition begins: the gentle floating down from C6 to C5 proceeds not to C4 but to C♯4. The dynamics shift to *forte*, and the simple harmonies from the end of theme 1 give way to an onslaught of diminished seventh sonorities (mm. 25–26 and 29–30). We have already observed the presence of one connection across this musical chasm—the resolution of the B♭5 "hanging" in the upper line to the A5 in m. 24. Note that this A5 is preceded by a rising D minor arpeggio (bracketed on the score). Thus, the first two measures of the transition are a variant on the first two measures of the initial theme! Many transitions begin with a relatively literal reuse of the start of the initial theme; Mozart's disguised variant in this movement is more exceptional. Example 6.2 provides a simplification of the transition's tonal content, along with some analytic notations. If one removes the sixteenth-note elaborations from the first two measures of the transition, it becomes apparent that the arpeggiation of the D minor chord in mm. 23–24 builds upon another element of theme 1: the conflict of three half notes against two measures of triple meter (i.e., hemiola).[5] This pattern is repeated in mm. 27–28 and then three successive times beginning in mm. 31–32. As shown between the staves, the two-measure pattern is initially grouped into two metric units of four measures each, then into three units of two measures each. This fragmentation of four-measure into two-measure units increases the transition's drive towards its tonal goal—the V of V at m. 37. As is typical for the end of a transition in a sonata form, the goal harmony is reiterated across several measures (mm. 37–40). Also common is the brief rest after the transition.

EXAMPLE 6.2 Voice-leading simplification of mm. 22–40

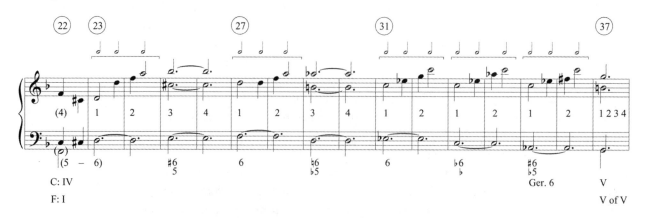

The shift into the minor mode during the extension of V of V is not uncommon either; this modal shift permits a brightening in color when the second theme begins.

The exposition's overall tonal motion thus far is I – V of V, preparing the second theme in the key of V. Note the use of a German augmented sixth chord (mm. 35–36) immediately before the arrival on V of V. Augmented sixth chords frequently occur at the ends of modulatory passages, where they clarify the new key by pointing out its dominant. In the case of a modulation to the key of the dominant, the augmented sixth chord is closely related to the initial tonic harmony. In this piece, the initial tonic triad is F–A–C, and the German augmented sixth in the key of the dominant is F♯–A♭–C–E♭ . To put it differently, the initial tonic triad can be construed as a subdominant harmony in the key of the dominant, and the German augmented sixth represents a chromatic intensification of that subdominant.[6] Like the "hanging" B♭5, this tonal connection spans the sharply articulated boundary between first theme and transition.

The second theme consists of two eight-measure phrases, grouped into 4 + 4, an antecedent leading to V in the local key and a consequent leading to a perfect authentic cadence. The theme begins from the inner-voice tone E5, but in the next measure G5, so carefully prepared by the preceding transition, is stated above it, and from there descends by step to D5 supported by V. The notes in this descent are indicated by upward-directed stems added to the music. The consequent phrase traverses the same path, this time completing the descending fifth G5–C5. The last three notes of the descent, E5–D5–C5 (mm. 55–56), have been circled to highlight the linkage to the following transition, which elides with the final measure of the second theme. The linkage is subtle: E5–D5–C5 (right hand, mm. 55–56) answered by E4–D4–C3 (left hand, mm. 56–58).[7]

The following transition (in its tonic-key version from the recapitulation) was discussed in Chapter 1 in the section on Diatonic Sequences; see Examples 1.13a and 1.13b and the accompanying discussion. It is by no means common to have a transition between the second theme and the closing material; we have designated mm. 56–70 as a transition because of its reduced melodic content and the presence of sequence. The one feature of this sequence important to note here is that the hemiola pattern, while implicit earlier, now becomes explicit in mm. 64–65 through the harmonic rhythm, use of bass register, and the dynamic changes. As noted above, this transition leads us once again to V of V in preparation for the closing material, which opens with subdominant harmony. Note that because of the formal boundary between the end of the transition (m. 70) and the start of the closing material (m. 71) V does not proceed to IV; the subdominant harmony represents the beginning of a new phrase. Launching the closing material from subdominant harmony fits well with its slower rhythms and chordal texture, bringing a calmer mood after the minor mode and hemiola conflicts of the preceding transition.

In Figure 6.2 we have shown a "closing theme," which is repeated in expanded form, and a "closing phrase." The amount of material within the closing section of an exposition can vary considerably, as the perfect authentic cadence at the end of the second theme has already performed the exposition's necessary tonal "work." As a result of this variability, we will use a variety of terms in discussing closing sections: closing theme, closing phrase, and codetta. It is not always obvious which term best suits a given portion of the closing section, and some analysts simply demarcate the subdivisions—marked by authentic cadences—within the closing section without giving them further labels. We feel, however, that even if there is ambiguity about the distinction between, say, a closing theme and a closing phrase, it is preferable to reflect carefully on the construction of the closing section and attempt to reveal something about how its organization is similar to, or different from, the closing sections of other expositions. Thus, "closing theme" signifies a phrase or group of phrases that possesses a length and melodic interest relatively commensurate with theme 1 or theme 2. A "closing phrase" is a single phrase that does not approach the scale of a theme. Finally, codetta refers to a short passage of repeated cadential gestures. Bear in mind, though, that the most important formal boundary is the one between the second theme and the closing section; this moment is always articulated by a perfect authentic cadence in the secondary key. This is usually the first such cadence, except in cases where the melodic material of theme 2 is revisited immediately afterwards. In that much less common situation, the next perfect authentic cadence in the secondary key would mark the move from second theme to closing section.

Returning to the Mozart, we see that the closing theme consists of two phrases (mm. 71–76 and 77–86). The initial phrase, which is the first six-measure phrase in the exposition, ends with an imperfect authentic cadence. The phrase is repeated an octave higher and is heading towards a perfect authentic cadence at m. 82, but it is evaded through the substitution of first-inversion C major harmony and the melodic leap up to G5. Only after an additional four measures does the perfect authentic cadence occur. These intervening measures (mm. 82–85) therefore represent an internal phrase expansion that arises through parenthetical insertion (due to the sharply contrasting musical content).

Development

The development opens with an eight-measure phrase that might first appear to be a new idea. Compared to Haydn and Beethoven, Mozart was fond of including a new theme in his developments. In some respects this material is new, but careful examination reveals similarities with earlier material, particularly the opening of the second theme. The fleeting sixth G4–E5 of this earlier theme is now expressed as the broader arpeggiation G4–C5–E5, and the top voice G5, which was introduced in the second measure of theme 2, is here delayed until the third measure. If we consider longer-range melodic continuities within the development's first phrase, we observe a neighbor motion G5–A5–G5 that soars above the third E5–D5–C5, which moves towards closure in the phrase's second and fourth measures but only attains C5 in its final measure. The prolongation of scale degree 5 by its upper neighbor while a lower line moves from scale degree 3 to scale degree 1 is exactly analogous to the last four measures of the first part of theme 1 (mm. 9–12). So this new idea incorporates important features of earlier ideas. This phrase is then repeated an octave lower (mm. 102–109), the final measure eliding with the following sequential passage. Since this sequence leads back to the upper octave, there is a registral connection between the G5 prolonged throughout the development's initial phrase and the G♯5 as part of the Italian augmented sixth chord leading to the A major chord (III♯) at the end of the sequential passage (mm. 122–123).

This A major chord is clearly articulated as a tonal goal, and we should ask ourselves why Mozart has made III♯ rather than V the harmonic goal of the development section. There is no definite answer, but we can note that this intermediate goal divides the space between V (end of exposition) and I (beginning of the recapitulation), thus dividing the large-scale bass motion of a fifth into two thirds. Recall that the opening theme, part 1, descends a fifth, clearly divided into the thirds C5–B♭4–A4 and A4–G4–F4. We should not overstate this connection as there are a few other instances where Mozart ends a development on III♯, but imagining this very long-range connection stimulates a tantalizingly rich hearing of the tonal motion across this development. The A major chord is sustained over four measures, then changed into an A minor chord in preparation for the connecting V^4_3 chord that leads back to the tonic and the opening theme. Mozart does not do the expected here, but rather states V^7 in the upper register and *piano* before beginning the restatement of the opening idea in the lower octave, which was carefully prepared by the V^4_3.[8] The result is that B♭5, the dissonant seventh, is not resolved in that register until the second part of theme 1. This delayed resolution of B♭5 to A5 recalls the connection we heard earlier between the end of theme 1, part 2, and the following transition.

Recapitulation

There is no need to discuss the recapitulation at great length, since the primary difference is that the tonic key prevails throughout. As is usually the case, the necessary modification occurs during the transition between the first and second themes, and it is achieved in the most common manner. The transition begins exactly as in the exposition (mm. 155–163 = 23–31), several measures are recomposed (mm. 164–172 only roughly correspond to mm. 32–36), and the final measures of the transition exactly transpose the corresponding ones from the exposition (mm. 173–176 transpose mm. 37–40). Although the second theme and closing material are unmodified except for transposition, their placement into the tonic key reveals a connection to the first theme that was previously obscure. The striking subdominant harmony at the beginning of the closing theme (m. 207) now harmonizes D5, the upper neighbor of C5 and a central element in the first part of theme 1. Further, in the approach to its perfect authentic cadence, the closing theme now outlines the fifth C5–F4, the same fifth outlined across the first part of theme 1 (and also, given the tonic transposition, across theme 2 in the recapitulation).

At first glance, this movement seems to be a study in contrast. There are a wide variety of melodic and rhythmic figures, sharp dynamic changes, and oppositions between different registers. Many formal boundaries feel abrupt due to these contrasts and the frequent use of rests at major junctures. One of the contributions of analysis is to reveal connections among seemingly disparate materials and to bridge formal divisions. Analysis can provide a balance between local detail and overall organization, enriching our experience of this movement whether as a listener or as a performer.

Beethoven, Piano Trio in C Minor, op. 1, no. 3, I

In comparison to the Mozart, the initial movement of Beethoven's Third Piano Trio is larger in dimension and bolder in its dramatic expression. In most, but not all respects, it conforms to the norm for a Classical sonata form in the minor mode. The exposition consists of two distinct thematic groups, the first in the tonic and the second in the relative major (III). This is followed by a closing section that confirms the new key. The development begins from III and progresses to V with a lengthy expanse of iv in between. Thus the exposition and development chart an overall tonal course found in many Classical sonata-form movements in the minor mode: i – III – iv – V. With one notable exception, the recapitulation follows the same order of events as in the exposition, except that the transition to theme 2 is rewritten to stay in the tonic key. So far, very normal. However, as we shall see, the divisions of these larger formal sections and their tonal contents are not so predictable.

An outline of the movement's formal-tonal organization is provided in Figure 6.3. Like Figure 6.2, the left column lists the major formal sections and their subdivisions, the middle column lists the corresponding measure numbers, and the right column lists the basic harmonic motion of each formal unit. A copy of the score with analytic additions—identification of formal units, important motives, hypermeter, and, where appropriate, harmony—is provided in Example 6.3. We will refer to both Figure 6.3 and Example 6.3 throughout the following discussion.

Exposition

The first theme consists of two phrases with distinct melodic content (labeled *a* and *b*); both phrases end on the dominant.[9] As a whole, these two phrases create the impression of a very large antecedent, thereby giving rise to the expectation that a consequent will follow. Indeed, the opening idea does return (m. 31), but at a different pitch level (A♭), which leads to the dominant of the secondary key (III) at m. 39. The expected consequent is instead the transition to the secondary key! It is common in Classical sonata form for the transition to begin with the same melodic content as the start of the first theme (though usually at its original pitch level). Since the expected consequent does not materialize, this means that theme 1 ends with a half cadence. Unlike second themes and closing themes, which invariably end with perfect authentic cadences, a first theme may end with either type of authentic cadence or with a half cadence. Compared to Haydn and Mozart, Beethoven was fond of ending first themes with a half cadence, a choice that often contributes to a feeling of agitation or breathlessness, as it does here.

EXPOSITION

Theme 1

phrase 1 (a)		1–10		i – V
phrase 2 (b)	presentation	11–18		i – V
	continuation	19–30		V

Transition

phrase 1 (a')	31–39	E♭ (III):	IV – V
cadential expansion			
(based on b)	39–58		V

Theme 2

presentation by piano	59–67	I
presentation by strings	67–75	IV
continuation	76–98	IV – V – I

Closing section

closing theme (initially		
based on a)	98–(110)–124	I – I^6 – ♭II^6 – V– I
codetta (based on b)	124–137	I

DEVELOPMENT

development of a	138–176		I – ♭VI – ii/iv
development of b	176–198	c(i):	iv – V
retransition	198–213		V

RECAPITULATION

Theme 1 – Transition

phrase 1 (a)	214–223	i – V
phrase 2 (a″)/transition	224–242	I – ♭II^6 – V
cadential expansion		
(based on b)	242–261	V

Theme 2

presentation by piano	262–270	i
presentation by strings/piano	270–278	i – VI – iv
continuation	279–301	iv – V – i

Closing section

closing theme (initially based	301–(313)–327	i – i^6 – ♭II^6 – V – i
on a)		

CODA (based on b)   327–360   i

FIGURE 6.3 Outline of Beethoven, Piano Trio, op. 1, no. 3, I

EXAMPLE 6.3 Beethoven, Piano Trio in C Minor, op. 1, no. 3, I

EXAMPLE 6.3 *continued*

EXAMPLE 6.3 *continued*

EXAMPLE 6.3 *continued*

EXAMPLE 6.3 *continued*

EXAMPLE 6.3 *continued*

EXAMPLE 6.3 *continued*

EXAMPLE 6.3 *continued*

EXAMPLE 6.3 *continued*

EXAMPLE **6.3** *continued*

EXAMPLE 6.3 *continued*

EXAMPLE 6.3 *continued*

EXAMPLE 6.3 *continued*

We will point out two features of the initial phrase (mm. 1–10). On first hearing it sounds like an introduction, given its slow rhythms and ending on an embellished dominant with fermata. In other words, the second phrase (mm. 11ff.) sounds like the start of theme 1. However, motive *a* returns at the beginning of both the development and recapitulation (as well as to initiate the transition and the closing section), and thus mm. 1–10 really are an integral part of theme 1. Second, note that the opening phrase's length results from the varied repetition of mm. 3–4 a step higher, thus expanding an eight-measure phrase to ten. An underlying quadruple hypermeter, then, is present, and it will persist as a surface hypermeter throughout much of the movement.

The second phrase (mm. 11–30) is a sixteen-measure sentence whose continuation is expanded by four measures through the extensive repetitions of the goal dominant harmony. The phrase opens with a five-note descending figure (motive *b*), which is employed extensively at various points throughout the movement. Here its statements articulate the prolongation of E♭5 by its upper neighbor note, shown by the large slur in Example 6.3. In mm. 17–18, the melody progresses to the covering third above, G5, thus preparing the continuation, which prolongs the dominant. The continuation's lack of harmonic motion and its progressive rhythmic intensification resemble the end of a transition more than the end of a first theme. This impression is furthered by the rests at the end of the phrase. The keen listener knows that the prolonged G major harmony cannot prepare a second theme in E♭ major, but it seems that Beethoven is trying to unsettle the listener's evolving sense of the exposition's formal design.

As noted above, the transition to theme 2 opens with a statement of motive *a*, beginning with an A♭ chord, which is the pivot in the modulation to E♭ (III): VI/IV. This prominent placement of A♭ recalls the expansion in mm. 5–6 of theme 1. Since the transition begins on A♭, its fifth and sixth measures introduce the Neapolitan sixth chord of E♭ major, a striking sound that is exploited later. After a passing secondary diminished seventh chord, the dominant of the new key arrives and is expanded across mm. 39–58. Beethoven thus "outdoes" the dominant expansion from the end of theme 1 when he has arrived at the proper dominant to prepare theme 2. This post-cadential expansion divides into two parts, the first (mm. 39–46) based on multiple statements of motive *b*. As in the transition from the Mozart movement, modal mixture temporarily darkens the color until theme 2 arrives. Unlike the Mozart, the transition ends softly and is not followed by any rests. Note that Beethoven easily could have introduced rests immediately before theme 2 by using a gesture like the last two measures of theme 1. (Imagine transposing mm. 29–30 to B♭ and substituting that in place of Beethoven's mm. 57–58.) Instead, he fills in this juncture with two measures that prepare the mode and mood of theme 2, possibly because he had deployed such a decisive break after theme 1 and wanted to ensure that the exposition did not become too sectionalized. The hypermeter further contributes to the recessive quality at the end of the transition. Ever since the second phrase of theme 1, quadruple hypermeter has been strongly projected, but this is not the case in the second part of the transition's post-cadential expansion. Measures 47–50 and 51–54 are hypermeasures, but the beginning gesture of mm. 47 and 51 does not recur at m. 55. Instead, there is a drawing out of the hypermeasure (to eight measures), coordinated with the reduction in dynamics and rhythmic activity.

The second theme (mm. 59–98) is a massively expanded sixteen-measure musical sentence, clearly divisible into various components. It opens with a four-measure basic idea in the piano that is then repeated. This is followed by a further presentation of the same idea by the violin a fifth lower, concluding with the subdominant harmony in m. 75. Sentences usually begin with two statements of the basic idea, but this one has four, although the dialogue between piano and violin gives the overall impression of binary grouping. In works such as duo sonatas and trios, melodic ideas (and even complete themes) are frequently repeated more than one would find in a solo sonata (or in a symphonic work) in order to give more members of the chamber ensemble the opportunity to shine. The sentence's continuation spans twenty-three measures (mm. 76–98), a length even greater than the sixteen measures of the expanded presentation. The vast size of this phrase builds up tension for the perfect authentic cadence that will close theme 2 and confirm the secondary key. Beethoven's *calando* marking in the middle of the continuation adds to the suspenseful effect. The continuation prolongs the subdominant, first IV, then its modal equivalent, iv, until the dominant is reached in m. 92. Overall the harmonic motion of this sentence is $I^{(6)} - IV^{(6)} - V - I$.

The hypermetric organization of Beethoven's second theme is interesting. Due to the arrival of E♭ major in the first measure of the second theme (m. 59) and the hypermeter of the preceding transition, m. 59 seems to be hypermetrically strong. Yet the melody enters after the downbeat with an upbeat figure that leads to the next downbeat, whose strength is further projected by the trill. This suggests that m. 60 initiates the theme's hypermeasures, and this is why we have designated both mm. 59 and 60 as hypermetric downbeats. The most common scenario for consecutive hypermetric downbeats is, in fact, exactly this one— an accompaniment pattern launches a hypermeasure and the melody enters later and reorients the hypermeter. This one-measure hypermetric shift in mm. 59–60 is confirmed by the start of the continuation at m. 76 (not at m. 75).

A representation of theme 2 is provided in Example 6.4. It is most significant, then, that the piano enters *fortissimo* on a weak measure (m. 91) as if to shift back to the original hypermeter, but without success. As far as tonal contents are concerned, the initial four-measure idea elaborates a descending third B♭5–A♭4–G4 progressing in parallel tenths with the bass. This idea is subsequently repeated a fifth lower (violin), E♭5–D♭4–C4, supported by subdominant harmony. As shown in Example 6.4, there is a voice exchange between the outer parts leading to m. 76, the beginning of the continuation. Not shown here, but clearly marked on the score, are the subsequent voice exchanges prolonging the subdominant harmony. In the final approach to the dominant, the E♭5 is picked up once again, which then leads to D5 supported by V in the local key at m. 92. Measures 92–97 provide an interesting study in levels of harmonic activity. It is possible to label every chord in this succession, but at the largest level they all fall within the dominant scale-step. Looking at the overall picture, there is no descent of a fifth from the initial B♭5, as one might expect, given that themes ending with a perfect authentic cadence often feature an embellished stepwise descent to that melodic goal. This fifth will occur later in conjunction with the closing theme.

A simplification of the closing theme (mm. 98–124) is provided in Example 6.5. The theme's initial portion is a variant of the 5–6 sequence. After the fifth measure, this line, which enters on the third beat of the measure, disappears, leaving the inner voice, which proceeds in an 8–10 pattern with the bass. The end of the sequence and the change in rhythmic texture articulate the vi chord in m. 106 as a tonal goal, but it initiates a linking

EXAMPLE 6.4 Voice-leading representation of mm. 59–98

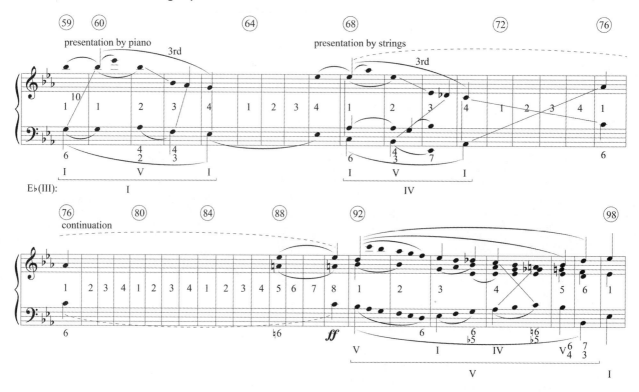

EXAMPLE 6.5 Voice-leading simplification of mm. 98–124

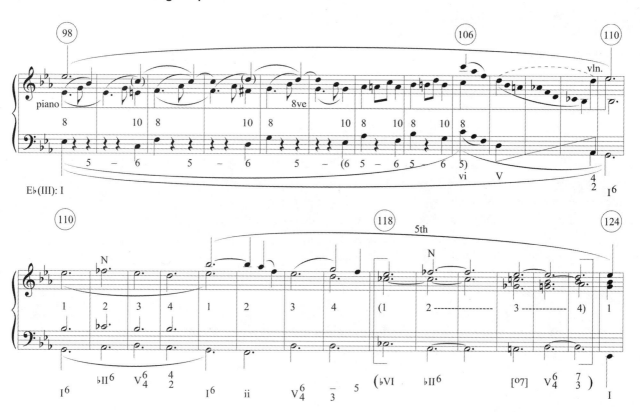

passage to I^6, the real goal, in m. 110. As shown in Example 6.5, this passage prolongs E♭5 while the inner line traverses an entire octave from E♭4 to E♭5. The final portion of this theme then opens with a four-measure idea (mm. 110–113) that decorates E♭5 by its chromatic upper neighbor F♭5, harmonized by the Neapolitan sixth chord, recalling its use near the start of the transition to prepare V of the secondary key. In the varied repetition of this idea (mm. 114–117), the violin line reaches up to B♭5 and from there descends by step to local closure, finally articulating the descending fifth that had not occurred earlier within theme 2. At the last minute, closure is thwarted by the deceptive harmonization of E♭5 by ♭VI, which initiates a six-measure parenthetical insertion utilizing once again the characteristic sound of the Neapolitan sixth chord. As indicated in Example 6.5, this parenthetical insertion is itself an expanded four-measure unit (based directly on mm. 110–113), resulting from the extension of the melody's second and third pitches. Like the second theme, then, the closing theme ultimately consists of a single tonal motion—in our terminology, a single musical phrase.

The codetta is based on varied statements of motive *b* by all three instruments (indicated on the score by brackets). The return of both motive *a* and motive *b* during the closing section provides an immediate feeling of unity for the exposition as a whole and also highlights the change in expressive character experienced during theme 2.

Development

The development opens with an abbreviated statement of the opening phrase from theme 1 that leads from the parallel minor of III (E♭) to initiate a second statement of this idea in B major, enharmonically C♭ major or ♭VI in relation to E♭. It soon becomes apparent that this is only an intermediate goal between E♭ and the C^7 chord—V^7 of ii—which is reached in m. 152 (***ff***). This harmony is then extended over the next twenty-four measures until it resolves to the F minor chord in m. 176. This is the pivot in the return to C minor: ii in E♭ = iv in C minor. The next section of the development deploys motive *b* in all three instruments. The first presentation is in F minor (iv), the second in A♭ (VI), to which the lowered seventh is added in m. 191. This harmony has the potential to become V^7 of ♭II, but instead Beethoven rewrites the G♭ as F♯, transforming the chord built on A♭ into the German augmented sixth chord, which resolves to V in m. 198. Overall mm. 176–197 extend the subdominant harmony, changing it from stable triad to a chromatically altered harmony, the augmented sixth chord, requiring resolution. The extended A♭ – A♭^{7} section beginning in m. 184 functions within this larger prolongation of the subdominant as a composing-out of the triad's third. In characteristically Beethovenian fashion, the goal dominant from m. 198 launches a sizable retransition (mm. 198–213). Recognizing the development's main harmonic arrivals reveals its contribution to the movement's tonal motion thus far: i – III – iv – V.[10]

Recapitulation

Our investigation of the recapitulation will be relatively brief, focusing on areas where it differs from the exposition. The first change comes immediately after the first phrase, where, instead of motive *b*, we get a lengthy phrase based on *a*. This phrase opens with a statement of the first two measures of *a* by the cello in C major. The bass line descends almost chromatically to A♭, which supports varied statements of this motive by the violin in D♭ (♭II), another manifestation of this movement's fascination with the Neapolitan. We might expect the A♭ to continue its descent to G; the A♭7 harmony at m. 236 could have been enharmonically reinterpreted as a German augmented sixth, as it was immediately before the retransition. Instead the bass ascends chromatically to C followed by F–F♯–G. A representation of the voice leading of this passage is provided in Example 6.6. At the deepest level it shows the extension of tonic harmony and scale degree 3, first E♮4, then E♭5, by its upper neighbor F5. At the cadence in mm. 240–242, E♭5 descends to D5 and on to the third below. Scale degree 2 is then transferred to the upper octave (D6) for the initial statement of motive *b* by the piano at the outset of the post-cadential expansion.

EXAMPLE 6.6 Voice-leading representation of mm. 224–242

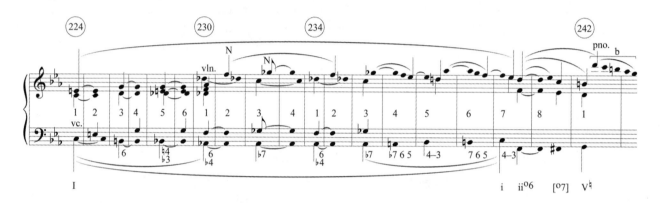

There are two important consequences of Beethoven's extensive recomposition of the early stages of the recapitulation. First, the quick departure from literal recapitulation and the tonal remoteness of the Neapolitan provide a developmental quality. It is as if the impulse for exploration has carried over from the development proper into the recapitulation. There are many instances in Classical sonata-form movements where something "developmental" occurs early on in the recapitulation. The second result of Beethoven's recomposition is a fusion of theme 1 with the transition. We are waiting for the second phrase of theme 1, but it never comes. Instead, the new developmental phrase leads to the dominant, which receives the same post-cadential expansion as did the dominant of the secondary key at the end of the exposition's transition. Fusion of first theme and transition into a single section in the recapitulation occurs quite often in the repertoire. This tactic avoids repeating some of the material that had already occurred in the tonic key in the exposition. Moreover, in movements that close the first theme with a perfect authentic cadence, it eliminates that cadence, which would usually mean that the close of the second theme provides the recapitulation's first perfect authentic cadence in the tonic key.

The second theme and closing theme are much the same as in the exposition, except, of course, they are in the tonic key rather than III. Only in the final measures of the closing theme—after the thwarting of closure by the deceptive progression—is there substantive change. Compare mm. 118–124 of the exposition with mm. 321–327 in the recapitulation. In the exposition, recall that the melody's second and third pitches were extended by a measure each. In the recapitulation, the third pitch is further elongated and when it does move it incorporates a seemingly innocuous embellishment in the violin part (mm. 326–327). The new embellishment E♭5–D5–C5 provides a link to the ensuing statement of motive *b* at the outset of the coda. The coda's prominent use of motive *b* over tonic harmony is particularly satisfying since this was precisely the thematic element largely absent from the recapitulation. As noted above, the recapitulation omits the second phrase of theme 1, and the codetta is discarded as well. Motive *b* is only present in the post-cadential expansion before theme 2, and there it expresses dominant rather than tonic harmony. Notably, the coda ends with the same material that closed the exposition's codetta. As a result, the coda is tightly integrated with the recapitulation, seeming almost like a wonderfully inventive expansion of the codetta rather than a thoroughly new section.

Many commentators have written about Beethoven's "C minor style," especially in regards to his "Pathétique" Piano Sonata, Third Piano Concerto, and fate-knocking Fifth Symphony. These and other of Beethoven's C minor works have a particularly urgent dramatic quality, and writers throughout the eighteenth and early nineteenth centuries opined extensively about the expressive qualities of the different keys (although, by no means, did they agree!). Our piano trio movement is Beethoven's first published work in C minor, and it certainly does not contradict the notion of a dramatic C minor style. Many features discussed in our analysis—such as the sometimes obsessive reiterations of motive *b*, the premature transition rhetoric at the end of theme 1 in the exposition, the vast single-phrase designs of the second and closing themes, and the recomposition of theme 1 in the recapitulation— play important roles in creating the movement's bold expression.

SUGGESTED ASSIGNMENTS

The ultimate goal of analysis is to identify what is special or unique about a particular work. To that end, we suggest you proceed through the following steps:

1. Identify the main formal divisions and subdivisions (themes, transitions, closing sections, etc.).

2. Identify important motives that are repeated/developed in the course of the movement.

3. Examine features of the phrase rhythm, that is, the interaction of phrase design and hypermeter.

4. Identify important features of the overall tonal organization and details of the harmony, particularly in more complex passages. You may want to prepare a simplification of the voice leading of certain passages, identifying harmony, hypermeter, important motives, etc.

For each of the four pieces below, we have provided a few questions to point towards some of the movement's unique aspects. We encourage you to study the music on your own and to complete the analytic steps listed above before considering our questions.

I. Examine one or both of the following movements in the minor mode.

Mozart, Piano Sonata in A minor, K. 310, I

1. The first theme is divided into an antecedent phrase and a modulating consequent/transition.

    (a) What is Mozart bringing out in the *calando* measures (mm. 14–15)?

    (b) How is the consequent/transition expanded?

2. Note that theme 2 begins with a four-measure idea that is subsequently repeated in varied form and expanded. Examine this phrase carefully.

3. What is the relationship between mm. 35–40 and 40–45?

4. Development section: Identify the various subdivisions, noting harmonic progressions and larger goals. Specific questions:

    (a) Why does Mozart change the spelling of the C^7 chord of m. 56 in the next measure?

    (b) Speculate as to why Mozart might have changed the spelling of the embellishing diminished seventh chord in m. 55, replacing the D♭ with C♯, especially considering that the change makes no sense in the local context. The answer might have to do with the harmonic goal of the phrase.

5. Consider changes made in the recapitulation compared to the exposition.

    (a) How are the phrases beginning in m. 88 (the transition) and later in m. 121 expanded?

    (b) What is/are the structural and/or expressive effect(s) of the latter phrase expansion?

Beethoven, Piano Sonata in C Minor, op. 10, no. 1, I

1. On what phrase design is theme 1 based? How has it been expanded?

2. Take a careful look at the transition to theme 2. How is the modulation to III accomplished?

3. Theme 2, although lengthy, consists of a single phrase. Explain how Beethoven manages to do this.

4. What is unusual about the development section? How do you explain B♭ minor/D♭ major within the context of C minor? Stated differently, what is the controlling key of the development section, and how does that relate to the overall tonal progression of the movement up to the recapitulation?

5. What is unusual about the tonal progression of the recapitulation?

6. In our discussion of Beethoven's Piano Trio, op. 1, no. 3, we mentioned that his C minor sonata forms tend to be highly dramatic. Do you feel this is the case in this piano sonata? By referring to specific elements in the music and your analysis of it, defend your choice.

II. Examine one or both of the following movements in the major mode.

Beethoven, Piano Sonata in G Major, op. 14, no. 2, I

1. Comment on the treatment of the $\frac{2}{4}$ meter in the opening measures.

2. Comment on the relationship of the outer lines in mm. 47–58. What implications might this have for the hypermeter?

3. Trace the thematic origins of the development and identify its main arrivals (about four). Then consider the following:

    (a) Launching the development in the parallel mode of the tonic key is not uncommon. Explain why it is so effective here. (What element of theme 1 might hint at G minor?)

    (b) What trick is Beethoven playing on the listener in mm. 99–103?

    (c) The retransition occurs in two segments. Identify these segments and explain how the second one prepares for the recapitulation (in ways other than providing dominant harmony).

4. The coda includes a restatement of theme 1 in the tonic key. Explain how this restatement is more "stable" than the original version of theme 1.

Beethoven, Violin Sonata in F Major, op. 24 ("Spring"), I

1. What is the formal organization of the first theme and transition? (It may be interesting to compare your analysis to our discussion of the corresponding portion of Beethoven's Piano Trio, op. 1, no. 3.)

2. Upon what pattern is the harmonic progression of mm. 26–33 based? How does it compare to the corresponding portion of the recapitulation?

3. On what phrase design is the second theme based? What melodic interval unfolds over the span of this theme?

4. What is the function of the A major chord that frames the development section? Can you explain the role of the harmony between these poles?

5. The coda, mm. 210–247, opens like the development section, except a fifth lower. What is the function of the D major chord in mm. 210–213?

6. Explain the harmonic basis of mm. 222–227. What interesting relationship do you notice between mm. 222–223 and 224–225?

7. In the second part of the coda (mm. 232–247), there is a shocking moment. Where is this? Why is it so shocking, and how does Beethoven handle its harmonic resolution? (And how is that harmonic resolution different than elsewhere in the movement?)

7 Sonata Form in the Nineteenth Century

The Classical model of sonata form—as described in the previous chapter—persists well into the nineteenth century, but at the same time certain changes also start to appear, beginning with the middle-period works of Beethoven. Here we find all of the repeat signs disappearing, leaving a clear ternary design, and an expanded harmonic language. We will encounter both in the first work examined in this chapter, the first movement of Beethoven's Piano Sonata in F Minor, op. 57. Schubert's music brings two significant innovations. The first, the three-key exposition, expands the path from tonic to dominant in the exposition to include an intervening key with its own theme. For example, the exposition from the first movement of the String Quintet in C Major, D. 956, consists of three distinct tonal areas (C–E♭–G), each with its own theme. This type of expansion of the dimension and tonal language of first-movement sonata form influenced subsequent generations of composers.[1]

A more radical change, one that is peculiar to Schubert, is the replication of the key scheme of the exposition in the recapitulation but transposed to end on the tonic. For example, in the first movement of the Piano Quintet in A Major ("Trout"), D. 667, the recapitulation begins in the subdominant; that is, I – V of the exposition is answered in the recapitulation by IV – I. In the fifth movement of the same work, I – IV (exposition) is answered by V – I (recapitulation). Most radical in this regard is the key succession in the work's second movement. An initial statement of three themes follows the key scheme F major – F♯ minor – D major, which, following a transition to G, is answered by A♭ major – A minor – F major! Schubert has been criticized for this procedure, which potentially avoids rewriting the transition in the recapitulation to remain in the tonic key, though, in fact, he rarely transposes the exposition without some rewriting. In his late works, Schubert reverts to the standard practice of the tonic return at the outset of the recapitulation, yet often this tonic becomes V of IV; the tonal structure remains innovative but basically within the framework of the Classical model. This hybrid procedure occurs in the first movements of works such as the Piano Trio in E♭ Major, D. 929, and in the C major string quintet mentioned above.

This brief survey is not intended to provide a comprehensive overview of innovations in nineteenth-century sonata form—a huge topic—but rather to point toward two important areas of change: the expansion of content to compensate for elimination of repeats and the expansion of the tonal language. Above it was noted that we will begin our investigation with the first movement of Beethoven's Piano Sonata in F Minor, op. 57. We will then examine the opening movement of another work in F minor, Brahms's Clarinet (or Viola) Sonata, op. 120, no.1.

Beethoven, Piano Sonata in F Minor, op. 57, I

Beethoven's Piano Sonata in F Minor, op. 57, is one of his compositions that has acquired a nickname: "Appassionata." It is a stormy work where—unlike in his Symphony No. 5 in C Minor—the minor mode persists even throughout the last movement. Like the first movement of the Fifth Symphony, the opening movement of the "Appassionata" is dominated by the rhythmic motive of three eighth notes leading to a longer note, and its obsessive use contributes greatly to the music's power. In its initial utterance, this rhythm accompanies the pitches C–D♭–C. Our analysis will reveal that the neighbor-note motive C–D♭–C (and its major-mode counterpart C–D♮–C) appears in multiple other guises as well, pervading the tonal landscape. We will focus on this germinal idea in our commentary.[2] In terms of overall formal design, the repeat of the exposition has been eliminated, and there is a substantial coda that significantly extends the movement. Before examining this movement in detail, we will talk though its formal-tonal organization, a chart of which is provided in Figure 7.1. The score with a few added notations is provided in Example 7.1.

In its overall plan, the exposition follows a traditional path with theme 1 in the tonic key and theme 2 in the relative major. The first theme is divided into two phrases, an antecedent that leads to the dominant and a modulating consequent that takes us to the new key (III). The second theme consists of a four-measure idea followed by its varied and extended restatement that changes to the parallel minor of III. The closing theme extends this modal change.[3] The development is divided into two parts, the first based on theme 1 and the second on theme 2. Part 1 opens with a statement of theme 1 in E major, enharmonically F♭ major or ♭VI in A♭ (III), which is followed by a sequence that begins in E minor and leads through C minor back to A♭, now A♭^{7} or V^7 of D♭ (VI in the tonic key). This passage looks complicated, but once we examine what Beethoven has written, we realize he has prolonged the key of the relative major by a chain of descending major thirds, A♭ – E/e – c – A♭, and the return to A♭ becomes V of D♭. This leads to part 2 of the development, which opens with a sequence based on theme 2 that continues the pattern of descending thirds leading from VI through iv to ♭II in the tonic key. This leads us to the dominant and preparation for the return.

The recapitulation follows the order of events as they occurred in the exposition with the transition to theme 2 rewritten to remain in the tonic key. Theme 2 begins in the parallel major, but then reverts in the varied restatement to the minor mode. The closing theme now emphasizes ♭II (rather than ♭II in A♭), an important feature of this movement from the very beginning. This leads to a weak close in the tonic in m. 203. More is needed to bring the movement to a satisfactory conclusion. What follows is not just a closing phrase or codetta, but an extended coda, really a second development section. It opens with a phrase based on theme 2 that leads us to ♭II^6 in m. 218. This coincides with a change of surface pattern (arpeggios) which progresses from ♭II^6 to iv^6, which is extended, and leads eventually to the cadential $^{6-7}_{4-3}$ and a perfect authentic cadence (m. 240). This is followed by a closing phrase, initially based on theme 2, which not only confirms closure, but in the end also allows the built-up energy to dissipate.

EXPOSITION
Theme 1
    antecedent   1–16   f: i – V^6
    modulating consequent/   17–34   i – [V^7] III
      transition
Theme 2
    statement   35–39   A♭ (III): I
    varied statement   40–51   I/i
Closing section
    closing theme   51–65 $i^{5–♭6}$ – ♭II – V^7 – i
    bridge to development   65–66

DEVELOPMENT
part 1 (based on theme 1)
    theme 1   67–78   ♭VI (E)
    sequence   79–93   ♭vi – iii – I
    extension   94–108 $I^{♭7}$ (=V^7 of D♭)
part 2 (based on theme 2)
    sequence   109–123   f: VI – iv – ♭II
    retransition   123–135 $°7$ – V^7

RECAPITULATION
Theme 1
    antecedent   136–151   f: i – V^6
    consequent/transition   152–173   I – V^7
Theme 2
    statement   174–178   I
    varied statement   179–190   I/i
Closing section
    closing theme   190–203 $i^{5–6}$ – ♭II – V^7 – i

CODA [=second development]
    phrase 1 (based on theme 1)   203–210   f: I – VI
    phrase 2 (based on theme 2)   210–217   VI – i^6
    cadential buildup   218–239   ♭II^6 iv^6 [$°^6_5$] – V – i
    closing phrase   239–262   i

FIGURE 7.1 Outline of Beethoven, Piano Sonata, op. 57, I

EXAMPLE 7.1 Beethoven, Piano Sonata in F Minor, op. 57, I

Example 7.1 *continued*

EXAMPLE 7.1 *continued*

EXAMPLE **7.1** *continued*

Example 7.1 *continued*

c minor

Ab major (completes cycle of descending major thirds)

extension
(prepares part 2 of development)

$A^{b7} = V^7$ of VI (Db major)

EXAMPLE **7.1** *continued*

Example 7.1 *continued*

EXAMPLE 7.1 *continued*

EXAMPLE **7.1** *continued*

EXAMPLE 7.1 *continued*

EXAMPLE 7.1 *continued*

Closing theme

EXAMPLE 7.1 *continued*

CODA – phrase 1 (based on theme 1)

phrase 2 (based on theme 2)

E<small>XAMPLE</small> 7.1 *continued*

EXAMPLE 7.1 *continued*

EXAMPLE 7.1 *continued*

Exposition

A graphic representation of theme 1 and the opening statement of theme 2 is provided in Example 7.2. The antecedent phrase, a sixteen-measure sentence, opens with a four-measure idea that progresses from i to V^6, which supports the neighbor-note figure C5–D♮5–C5. The repetition of this idea occurs a half-step higher, establishing from the very beginning an emphasis on ♭II and on D♭, the upper neighbor of scale degree 5. This is followed by an eight-measure continuation that begins with a restatement of the C5–D♮5–C5 figure, thus articulating a larger pattern of C–D♭–C over mm. 1–10, shown in Example 7.2 by the larger slur. Motion from D♭–C is thereby established as a primary motivic component of the movement, as is the interchange between D♭ and D♮. Immediately after restating C5–D♮5–C5 in mm. 9–10, we hear three statements of D♭2–C2 in the bass in the pervasive rhythmic motive mentioned above. Finally, at the end of the phrase D♭4–C4 is harmonized by VI^6 – V^6, a non-cadential progression. This is one of the rare instances where the overall organization of melodic material—and the long chord and fermata in m. 16—clearly indicate the end of a phrase despite the absence of a normative cadential progression. The pause on this tense first-inversion, rather than root-position, dominant harmony adds to the suspenseful atmosphere.

The consequent opens with a varied restatement of the initial four-measure idea now extended to six measures. The C5–D♮5–(C5) figure of mm. 21–22 is answered in m. 23 by

EXAMPLE 7.2 Voice-leading representation of mm. 1–39

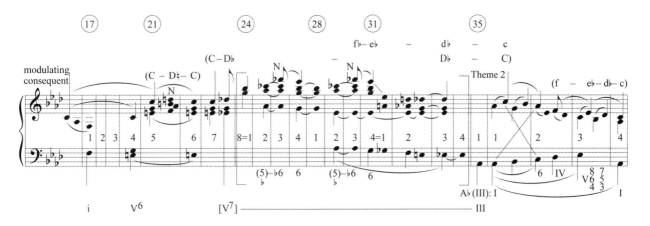

C5–D♭5, the latter now harmonized as the seventh of the dominant in the key of the relative major. The resolution of this dissonant seventh and completion of the neighbor-note motive will not occur until the start of theme 2 (m. 36). Meanwhile we have an eleven-measure extension of the new dominant harmony, which is shown in Example 7.2 as a parenthetical insertion. This passage emphasizes the minor mode, thus anticipating the closing theme in A♭ minor.[4] As indicated by the upper-most line of letters above the staff in Example 7.2, the top part of this insertion articulates the neighbor-note figure F♭6–E♭6 in mm. 26–27, which is then repeated in mm. 30–31 and, following transfer to the lower octave, continues its descent to C5 as part of theme 2 in m. 36. Not only is the resolution of the dissonant D♭ withheld until theme 2, but there is also linkage between the insertion and theme 2, as this idea reappears as F4–E♭4–D♭4–C4 in mm. 37–39. Once again we have the interchange between ♭$\hat{6}$ and $\hat{6}$, now F♭ and F♮ in the key of A♭. And, in the restatement of the first four measures of theme 2, the mode shifts back to minor precisely at the melody's arrival on scale degree 6 (m. 42)![5]

A graphic representation of the closing theme is provided in Example 7.3. The initial melodic gesture is the descending third C♭–B♭–A♭, which is then restated a sixth higher (A♭–G♭–F♭ in m. 52). This leads to D♭5, the upper neighbor note of C♭, first supported by ♭II in the local key, then, following transfer to the lower octave, as seventh of the dominant resolving to C♭ and tonic harmony in m. 55. As shown in Example 7.3, mm. 51–55 articulate a modally altered statement of the neighbor-note motive from theme 1, as C♭–D♭–C♭ in the context of the new key. The expanded repetition of this four-measure idea is an octave higher (mm. 55–61). The expansion comes at the end, where the upper neighbor, now D♭6, is first extended (m. 59), and then led through C♭6 (m. 60) supported by [°7] V, to B♭5 supported by V, and finally to A♭5 for local closure in m. 61. This melodic descent is shown in Example 7.1 by the addition of stems to the notes D♭6 (m. 59), C♭6 and B♭5 (m. 60), and A♭5 (m. 61). The registrally expanded descending third occurring over the span of the closing theme, shown in Example 7.3 by the large slur, is an expansion of the motivic gesture that

EXAMPLE 7.3 Voice-leading representation of mm. 51–61

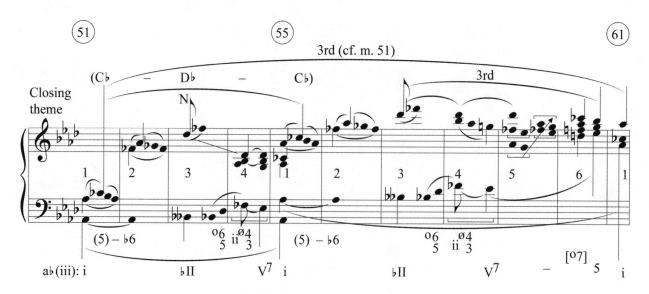

opens the phrase. The remainder of the exposition (mm. 61–65) extends the local A♭ minor tonic harmony, leading to an open octave on A♭.

Development

The development opens with a statement of theme 1 in E major, which we hear as VI (F♭) in relation to A♭ minor, the exposition's closing key. Following the modal change to E minor (m. 79), a sequence leads through C minor back to A♭ (mm. 87–108), which, with the addition of its seventh, G♭, leads to D♭ major in m. 109 for the second part of the development. Example 7.4 offers a graphic representation of the *underlying* structure of the entire development. The purpose of this type of graph—as opposed to ones like Examples 7.2 and 7.3—is to show *underlying* connections; this necessitates registral simplification and omission of detail. From a melodic perspective, C♭ within the exposition's closing A♭ minor becomes B♮4, scale degree 5, in E major, which is prolonged throughout the development's initial phrase and retained as top note at the modal change to E minor (m. 79). As we progress from m. 79, the beginning of the sequence, the main melodic line is no longer emphasized, but rather is buried within the arpeggios. In fact, by the time Beethoven has reached the A♭[7] chord, the emphasis has clearly shifted to the seventh, G♭ (see esp. mm. 91–93), which is represented in Example 7.4 as coming from an inner voice. The entire passage from mm. 94–108, represented in our abstract sketch by parentheses, extends this dissonant harmony until its resolution in m. 109. This parenthetical passage is directly based on the extension of V of III that prepared theme 2 in the exposition, except transposed down by fifth since the imminent recall of theme 2 will be in the key of D♭ (VI).[6]

EXAMPLE 7.4 Voice-leading representation of development

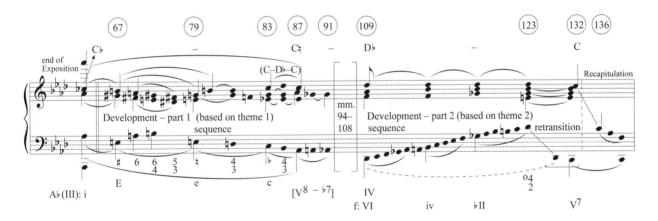

The second part of the development opens with sequential statements of the opening of theme 2 that progress from VI (m. 110) through iv (m. 114) to ♭II (m. 118), the latter two arrivals approached through deceptive progressions (i.e., as vi of the preceding key). Up to this point, the hypermeasures are all quadruple, but the connection between ♭II (which is subsequently respelled enharmonically in m. 119) and the diminished seventh chord with

D♭4 as the lowest note (m. 123) requires an additional measure, as the motion is achieved through an ascending 5–6 sequence. Note that this dramatic arrival on the diminished seventh, which launches the retransition, completes a two-octave ascent in the bass from D♭2 (m. 109) to D♭4 (m. 123). The following arpeggios leading to m. 130 are based entirely on this one diminished seventh chord. Beginning in m. 130 the right-hand part holds its position, while the left hand crosses over, first stating D♭ in the same octave position as in m. 109 (D♭2), then D♭5, then D♭2–C2 and D♭5–C5 in the primary rhythmic motive. In Example 7.4, we suggest large-scale connections involving these D♭2–C2 motions in both of the structural outer voices.

Recapitulation

Beethoven follows Classical procedure by rewriting the transition to theme 2 to remain in the tonic key. One result is that the neighbor-note motive of this passage, which in the exposition was F♭–E♭, is now at the original pitch level: D♭–C. Statements of this idea in mm. 165–166 and 169–170 are marked in the score by brackets. This passage is followed by theme 2, the initial statement in F major and the extended restatement returning to the minor mode in preparation for the closing theme.

   A graphic representation of the closing theme is provided in Figure 7.5. In the initial statement, scale degree 3 (here A♭) is prolonged by its upper neighbor (B♭), first harmonized by ♭II, then as seventh of the dominant. As in the transition, the transposition maps some former F♭–E♭ motions onto D♭–C; note especially the bass line in m. 193 (bracketed in Example 7.5). Like at the end of the exposition, the repetition of this four-measure idea is an octave higher and extended as the melodic descent to closure unfolds. The details are slightly varied, as the continuation of B♭5 through A♭5 to G5 occurs in the left-hand part, temporarily covered by the figuration above. The recapitulation, though, ends as did the exposition with a few measures of tonic harmony (mm. 200–204 = mm. 61–65)—except instead of the open octave sustained throughout m. 65, the momentary F octave at the start of m. 204 immediately launches the coda.

EXAMPLE 7.5 Voice-leading representation of mm. 190–200

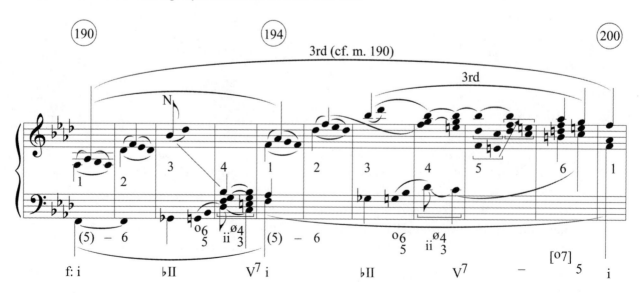

Coda

A graphic representation of the voice leading of the coda is provided in Example 7.6. The coda opens with an eight-measure phrase based on the ascending arpeggiation portion of theme 1. The phrase leads from i to VI, above which the top part articulates the neighbor-note motive F6–G♭6–F6. This is followed by an extended statement of theme 2 that leads us to ♭II^6 in m. 218, whose arrival is marked by a change in surface pattern (sixteenth-note broken chords). From this point the harmony progresses through a passing $^6_3$ chord in m. 220 to the iv^6 chord in m. 222, whereupon parallel $^6_3$ chords traverse two octaves to the iv^6 in m. 227, an arrival also marked by a change in surface pattern. The top voice soars from B♭4 to B♭6 over this extended subdominant harmony with D♭, the pervasive upper neighbor of C, as the lowest note. As in the development, the bass specifically traces the stepwise ascent from D♭2 to D♭4. This D♭4 (m. 227) progresses to D♮4 (m. 229) on its way to C (m. 231), a reference to the interchange between D♭ and D♮ as neighbors to C from the very beginning of the movement.[7] The harmonic progression supporting this motion is iv^6 – [$^{o6}_{5}$] – V. Meanwhile the top voice descends by step B♭6–A♭6–G6, but this can be interpreted as a motion to an inner voice. B♭, now the dissonant seventh of the dominant harmony and an octave lower (B♭5), is still very much in evidence. It is extended over the next four measures, while the bass re-articulates the D♭–C motive four more times (mm. 235–238). This dissonant seventh then resolves to A♭5 in m. 239 covered by F6.[8]

EXAMPLE 7.6 Voice-leading representation of mm. 203–249

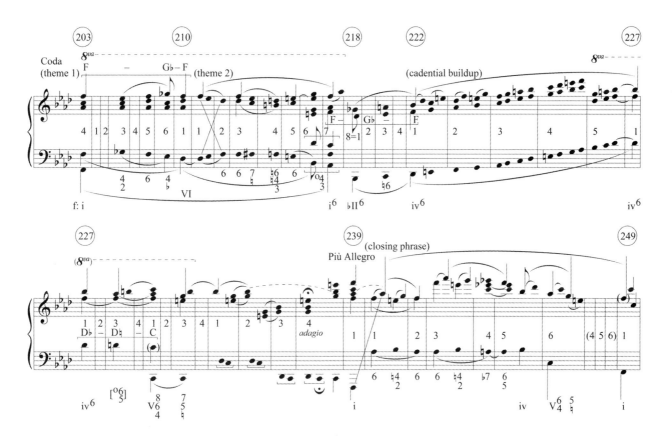

Though the cadence at the *più allegro* ends conclusively with F6 in the top-sounding part, we must be aware of the importance of A♭5 as the resolution of the preceding dissonant seventh. Indeed A♭5 emerges as primary in the following altered statement of theme 2, which leads to B♭5 supported by subdominant harmony in m. 244 (= m. 247), and from there the top voice descends by step through A♭5 to G5, supported by V^{6-5}_{4-3}, and then to an implied F5 over tonic harmony in m. 249. This implied F5, which completes the descent to closure, is immediately covered by scale degree 5. In the following measures (not shown in Example 7.6) there are several references to the D♭–C motive, and, as the movement comes to an end, C4, then C5, persists until it fades away entirely.

Despite its length, this movement displays a characteristically Beethovenian economy of material. We have especially focused on the deployment of neighbor-note motives, particularly the use of scale degree 6 (usually ♭$\hat{6}$) as an upper neighbor to scale degree 5, either in relation to the tonic F or to local tonics. In the development, we also noted the prevalence of modulation by falling third. These two ideas are not unrelated: in F minor, a 5–6 motion exchanges F–A♭–C with F–A♭–D♭, or in harmonic terms an F chord (or key) with the chord (or key) a third lower. Sometimes this interrelationship of linear and harmonic entities is explicit, as in the closing theme. In the exposition, a 5–♭6 motion in the first two measures of the closing theme generates the pitches of F♭ major, which (notated as E major) becomes the first key area of the development. In the recapitulation, the same 5–♭6 move— but now in relation to F—brings forth the pitches of D♭ major, which turns out to be the first key area of the coda. Elsewhere the linear 5–6 motion is less explicit on the musical surface, but with falling-third modulations an element of 5–6 motion remains embedded in the underlying voice-leading structure.[9]

Brahms, Clarinet (or Viola) Sonata in F Minor, op. 120, no. 1, I

With this Brahms movement we are entering a new sound world. In contrast to the expansive dramatic works of Beethoven, Schubert, and even earlier Brahms, this late work is compact, devoid of extensive repetitions. There is also a clear difference in Brahms's harmonic language, which is manifest at times in chord-to-chord syntax as well as the means by which changes of tonal center are achieved. Brahms's harmony is sometimes difficult to understand, particularly when viewed in light of the clarity of the Classical style. It is at times Classical, at times decidedly non-Classical, but always logical. Once we unravel what is taking place in this movement, we will discover that it is a musical essay on the linear motion 5–6, which pervades many levels of the structure.

An annotated score is provided in Example 7.7 and an outline of formal-tonal organization in Figure 7.2. Following a precedent established by Schubert, the exposition consists of three themes in three different keys. Here, however, the second key is very dependent on the first key and is not confirmed with a cadence. To varying degrees, downplaying of the second key is Brahms's standard practice in his three-key expositions. Why then do analysts refer to such structures as three-key expositions? The answer lies in a subtle shift in the conception of sonata form during the nineteenth century. In the eighteenth century, sonata form was defined by tonal structure, namely the polarity between the two keys presented in the exposition. Haydn occasionally reused his first theme as the

EXPOSITION

"introduction" (pno.)	1–4		
Theme 1 (cl.)	5–12	f:	i – V
continuation	12–24		V (VI^6 – iv^6 – $\flat$II^6)
Theme 1 restatement (pno.)			
→ Transition	25–37		i – V – [V^7]
Theme 2	38–52	D$\flat$ (VI):	I^6 = c: $\flat$II^6
Theme 3			
statement 1 (pno.)	53–56	c (v):	V – i – [V] V
statement 2 (cl.)	57–60		V – i – ii$^{ø6}_5$
augmentation (pno.)	61–68		V – i – [V] V – V
continuation	68–76		V
Closing section			
closing phrase	77–81		i – ii$^{ø6}_5$ – V^7 – i
expanded repetition	81–89		i – ii$^{ø6}_5$ – V^7 – i

DEVELOPMENT

phrase 1 (based on theme 2)	90–100	A$\flat$ (VI of c):	I^6 – ii$^6_5$ – V – i
phrase 2 (based on theme 2)	100–115	E ($\flat$VI of A$\flat$):	I^6 – [ii^{ø7} – V^7] vi
phrase 3 (based on theme 3)	116–130	c$\sharp$ (vi of E):	i – to f$\sharp$ ($\flat$ii of f)
retransition (based on theme 1)	130–137	f$\sharp$ ($\flat$ii):	i – V^6 = f: i$^{6–5}$

RECAPITULATION

Theme 1	138–145	f:	i – V
dominant extension	145–152		V
Theme 2	153–167		I^6 – i^6
Theme 3			
statement 1 (pno.)	168–171		V – i – [V] V
statement 2 (cl.)	172–175		V – i – ii$^{ø6}_5$
augmentation (pno.)	176–183		V – i – [V] V – V
continuation	183–191		V
Closing section			
closing phrase	192–196		i – ii$^{ø6}_5$ – V^7 – i
expanded repetition	196–205		i – ii$^{ø6}_5$ – V^7 – i
closing phrase (based on theme 1)	206–213		i – ii$^{ø6}_5$

CODA

CODA	214–236	V – i

FIGURE 7.2 Outline of Brahms, Clarinet Sonata, op. 120, no. 1, I

EXAMPLE 7.7 Brahms, Clarinet Sonata in F Minor, op. 120, no. 1, I

EXAMPLE 7.7 *continued*

EXAMPLE 7.7 *continued*

EXAMPLE 7.7 *continued*

EXAMPLE 7.7 *continued*

EXAMPLE 7.7 *continued*

EXAMPLE 7.7 *continued*

EXAMPLE 7.7 *continued*

EXAMPLE 7.7 *continued*

second theme, simply transposing it (the so-called monothematic exposition). During the nineteenth century, thematic contrast came to be as important as tonal structure in defining the thematic sections of an exposition. Thus, strong thematic contrast allied with a relatively weak key change can suggest a three-key, three-theme model. In the clarinet sonata, Brahms's third key (C minor) is cadentially confirmed, providing the local tonal closure necessary at the end of an exposition. Like the Classical model, there is a two-key polarity underlying Brahms's exposition, but there is also a new melodic idea in a different key wedged between these tonal poles. Brahms's handling of the three-key exposition can be viewed as a consolidation of Schubert's three-key innovation with the Classical two-key tradition. In reading our analysis of this sonata, bear in mind that "theme 2" signifies something different than what "theme 2" denotes in an eighteenth-century sonata exposition.

Brahms's development section consists of four phrases, the first two based on theme 2. The first phrase is in the key of Ab major, VI in relation to the dominant from the end of the exposition. The second phrase begins in the key of E major, enharmonically bVI of the preceding Ab major, and it leads to C# minor for the third phrase, which is an elaborate combination of all three themes. This third phrase leads to F# minor for the final phrase, which is based on theme 1. These last two keys, C# and F# minor, enharmonically Db and Gb minor, bvi and bii in relation to F minor, play important roles in this movement. This last phrase is marked as a retransition, but this is not a retransition in the Classical sense of leading back to the tonic through the dominant. There is no dominant, but rather, as we shall see, a 6–5 linear motion, the reverse, in a sense, of the 5–6 motion that introduces the development.

The recapitulation follows the sequence of events of the exposition, the main change occurring in theme 2, which is now in the parallel major (F major). The next significant change comes with the addition of a reminiscence of theme 1 after the closing phrase, which leads to a beautiful coda, where the main melodic note of the movement, C5, persists, growing ever fainter, but never relinquishing its position.

Exposition

A detailed representation of the voice leading of mm. 1–38, that is, up to theme 2, is provided in Example 7.8. The sonata opens with a four-measure "introduction" stated by the piano in open octaves, the main features of which are the decoration of C5 by its upper neighbor, Db5, and the subsequent descent by step to F4 via Gb4—not G♮4—immediately creating a dark modal quality that characterizes much of the movement. The Gb and the extended neighbor, Db, become important features of this movement. We have placed "introduction" in quotation marks because, although the piano's hollow octaves of mm. 1–4 seem like a preparation for the clarinet's ensuing melody, they present thematic material that is integral to theme 1.[10] In fact, towards the end of theme 1 (mm. 19–24) the clarinet restates mm. 1–4 in their entirety, with only slight rhythmic variation. This tension over the formal connectedness of mm. 1–4 with the subsequent music highlights the chromatic Gb4 of m. 4. Although we understand this pitch to resolve to F4 in the piano accompaniment in m. 5 (and have therefore drawn a large slur in Example 7.8 between C5 in m. 1 and F4 in m. 5), there is a certain hesitancy to this resolution. This tentativeness is enhanced by Brahms's *decrescendo* in m. 4 and the delay of the piano chord in m. 5 until the second beat.

EXAMPLE 7.8 Voice-leading representation of mm. 1–38

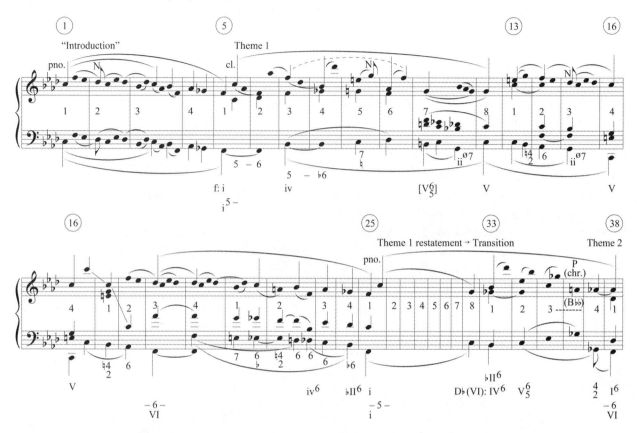

Not only do these musical details draw attention to the chromatic G♭4, signaling its importance to the movement, but they also sow the seed for a recomposition of this passage near the end of the coda.

The main feature of theme 1 is the descent of a fourth from C5, supported by tonic harmony, to G4, supported by the dominant. It has already been noted that 5–6 linear motion operates throughout the movement at multiple levels, almost as an *Ur*-motive. Looking now to the details of the harmony and voice leading in theme 1, we see that its initial tonic harmony is extended by a 5–6 linear motion, as is the following subdominant (5–♭6). As a result, Brahms has immediately reintroduced the two important decorative pitches of the introduction, D♭ and G♭. Note that the following two chords—the C^7 chord of m. 9 and D♭ chord of m. 10—have not been labeled. The problem with simply labeling them as V^7 – VI is that this would suggest they function at the same level as the preceding subdominant and following cadential pattern. Instead, they extend the subdominant until its chromatic manifestation, V$^6_5$ of V, is introduced on the downbeat of m. 11. This is an excellent example of the distinction made in earlier chapters between chord and harmonic scale-step, which may encompass many chords. The harmonic underpinning of this phrase is i – iv – V (mm. 5, 7, 12), which is expanded by 5–6 motions and passing chords.

The following four measures (mm. 13–16) extend the dominant, the clarinet melody making clear reference to the neighbor-note pattern from the piano "introduction." A varied repetition of these four measures begins, but in the third measure (m. 19) Brahms introduces a D♭ chord above F, which becomes the point of departure for the clarinet's complete restatement of the piano "introduction," which now functions to close theme 1. What are we to make of this D♭^{6} sonority? This is not D♭ introduced by its dominant, but F with D♭ above, displacing C5. As indicated by the lowest level of Roman numerals in Example 7.8, this sonority participates in a 5–6 motion that connects mm. 5 and 19. Looking ahead in Example 7.8, we see that this motion is reversed between mm. 19 and 25, where we are firmly back on tonic harmony for the seeming repetition of theme 1 that turns out to be a transition. Note that in these final measures of theme 1 the harmonic progression outlines descending thirds, "VI^6" – iv^6 – ♭II^6; thus, a direct progression from ♭II^6 to i—without an intervening V—accompanies the tonal and thematic return at m. 25.[11]

The first eight measures of the transition basically follow the same path as mm. 5–12 of theme 1, and thus their interpretation has not been written out in Example 7.8. This is followed by a brief passage leading us back once again to a D♭ chord over F, now with A♭ rather than D♭ as the top note (m. 38). The initial melodic descent of the fourth C5–G4 (mm. 25–32) is shown to be embedded within the third C5–B♭4–A♭4 (mm. 25–38), where B♭4 is supported by ♭II^6, by now a familiar sound, which is the pivot for the local modulation to D♭ (VI). As shown in the bass (stems up), there is an ascending line leading from this bass B♭ of this pivot through C, supporting V$^6_5$ of VI, to D♭, but as an inner voice above the bass F. Though the motion to D♭ is stronger than before, Brahms leads us back to the same bass note as before, F, and once again via G♭. For the first time in this movement, the quadruple hypermeter is expanded by one measure (m. 36) to accommodate the chromatic passing tone A♮4. This brief delay during the extension of V^7 of D♭ lends some gentle support to the arrival on the D♭^{6} sonority of m. 38.

Example 7.9 is an abstract representation of the structure of this movement up to theme 3. We have already discussed mm. 1–25, which overall present the voice-leading motion 5–6–5 over F. This motion is embedded within a larger version of the same progression leading to theme 2. This is what was meant earlier by the statement that this 5–6 idea pervades deeper and deeper levels of musical organization. Though we can speak of a modulation to D♭ in a local sense, D♭ is never stable or cadentially confirmed. As shown below Example 7.9, this D♭^{6} chord ultimately becomes the pivot in the modulation to the dominant, the key of theme 3.

EXAMPLE 7.9 Tonal summary of exposition

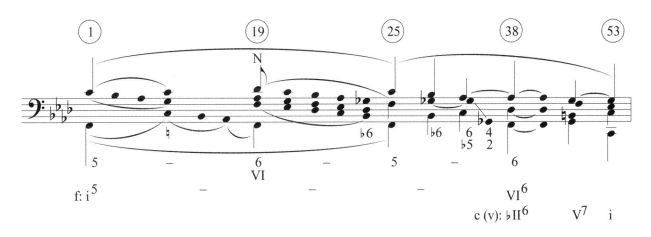

We have not provided a representation of themes 2 and 3; instead refer to the annotated score (Example 7.7). The rhythmic drive of theme 3, with its repeated rhythmic pattern ♩ ♪ ♪ ♪ 𝄽 ♪ ♩, provides a contrast to the legato-like and registrally expansive first theme. The initial statement of theme 3 is shared by clarinet and piano, but then the clarinet predominates. This is followed by an augmentation of the rhythmic pattern in the piano[12] above which the clarinet begins an elaborated descent from the sustained G5 in m. 61 directed toward closure in the local key. Though this line concludes on C5 in m. 67, the harmony is directed beyond this point to the dominant in the next measure, preceded by the descent in octaves from Ab5 to D5. The following elaboration of the dominant begins with an augmentation of this descent in the piano part, imitated two beats later by the clarinet (mm. 68–69). This gesture is then stated a step lower beginning from G5 (mm. 70–71), and the imitating clarinet line once again reaches C5 on the downbeat of m. 72. Here, too, closure is avoided by transforming the tonic into V^7 of iv, where we now hear an elaborated descent from this Ab5, the clarinet leading and the piano following (mm. 72–73). The descent once again outlines the diminished fifth Ab5–D5, at which point the line skips to the lower octave for the answering descent from G4 (mm. 74–76). After the first two steps in the piano descent, Brahms separates the notes by rests, creating a written-out *ritardando*. If we expect finally to hear melodic closure to C4 on the downbeat of m. 77, the beginning of the closing phrase, we are once again disappointed.

The closing phrase occurs twice: in mm. 77–81 which elides with an expanded repetition in mm. 81–89. A representation of the expanded version (mm. 81–89) and the first measure of the development is provided in Example 7.10. Here we can see the melodic emphasis placed on scale degree 2 in the local key, D5, first harmonized as V of V, then later by its diatonic counterpart, $\text{ii}^{\emptyset 6}_5$. The long-awaited resolution to local scale degree 1 occurs in the clarinet part, as C4, at the end of the phrase. Note the connection to the beginning of the development section via a 5–6 motion above the bass note C.

EXAMPLE 7.10 Voice-leading representation of mm. 81–90

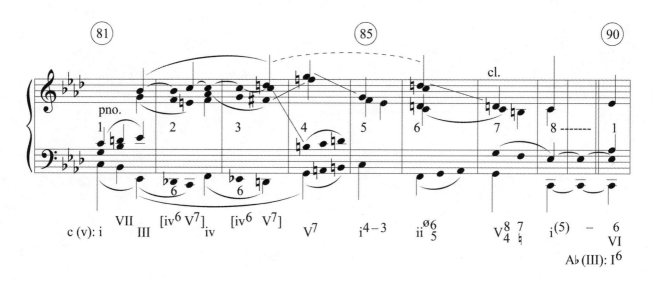

Development

A representation of the voice leading of the entire development is provided in Example 7.11. Before examining each of the four phrases in some detail, take note of the voice-leading connection at both ends. We have just observed that the connection between exposition and development is a 5–6 motion above the bass note C. The connection between development and recapitulation reverses this motion, that is, 6–5, now over the bass note F (mm. 136–138). In this instance the 6–5 motion is elaborated by an intervening embellishing German sixth chord. The D♭⁶ chord (m. 136) is heard initially as V⁶ in the key of F♯ (G♭) minor.

The first phrase of the development is based on theme 2, and our representation of the voice leading once again eliminates rhythmic displacements. The main feature of this phrase is the descent of a fifth within the local key of A♭ from the opening E♭4 via transfer to the

EXAMPLE 7.11 Voice-leading representation of development

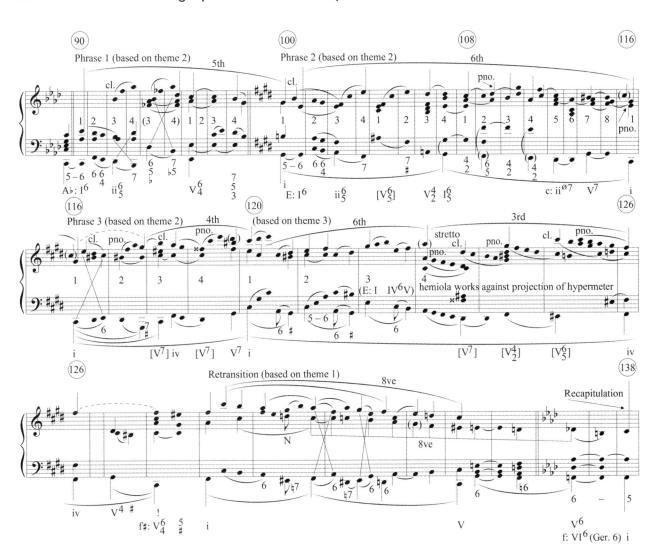

upper octave to G♯4 [A♭4] on the downbeat of m. 100. The transfer to the upper octave is accomplished by repetition of the voice exchange of the third and fourth measures (the piano part is an octave higher in mm. 94–95 compared to mm. 92–93). The repetition of these measures is modally altered, incorporating F♭ and thereby anticipating of the change of mode at the end of the phrase (m. 100). This two-measure phrase expansion has been indicated by the (3 4) between the staves on Example 7.11.

The second phrase presents a further expansion of the same idea (theme 2) a third lower.[13] Once again Brahms has used the bass note as pivot to change the key. That is, the tonic note of the previous key, A♭/G♯, is retained as the third of the new key, E major. This phrase can be divided into two parts, the first leading from m. 100 (I^6) back to the point of origin (m. 107), although with a seventh added in the clarinet (D♯5). Note that this seventh chord resolves to another seventh chord, part of a descending fifth sequence alternating between $\frac{4}{2}$ and $\frac{6}{5}$ chords that breaks in m. 111. There is a registral connection between the bass G♯2 at the outset of the sequence (m. 107) and the D♯2 (m. 112), which supports $ii^{\varnothing7}$ in the key that is the goal of this phrase, C♯ minor. Between these two landmarks, the bass had been displaced upwards during the sequence, but in Example 7.11 we provide bass notes in the lower octave parenthetically to show the implied stepwise connection in the bass as the modulation from E major to C♯ minor unfolds. Arrival at the C♯ minor goal in m. 116 coincides with the completion of the melodic descent of a sixth E5–G♯4. Note that G♯4 (A♭4) was also the melodic goal of the development's first phrase (m. 100).

The fact that this new key for phrase three (C♯ minor) is stable—i.e., begins with a root-position local tonic harmony—places it in association with the stable point of origin of this motion, namely the C minor at the end of the exposition. The intervening keys of A♭ major and E major result from successive 5–6 motions; they are subsidiary tonalities between C minor and C♯ minor (=D♭ minor), whose relationship may be considered a manifestation of 5–6 at a very deep level of structure. The third phrase opens with a bold four-measure idea (mm. 116–119), marked *forte* and *marcato*, that is a thoroughly transformed version of theme 2—the *dolce* theme that has dominated the development thus far. As before, the melody is split between the two instruments, but now the clarinet leads (E5–D♯5–C♯5) and the piano provides the ascending chord (B♯4–F♯5–A5–G♯5). The passage sounds entirely different not only due to the dynamics but also the plunge into minor mode and the altered scale-degree placement of these melodic motives. The left hand of the piano maintains its earlier role, but instead of moving in half notes it proceeds in quarter notes, thereby revealing a hidden connection between themes 1 and 2. The bass motion in the first two measures of theme 2 was nothing other than an augmentation of mm. 1–2! Starting in m. 120, theme 3 provides the thematic content for this C♯ minor phrase, strengthening the connection between C minor and C♯ minor suggested above. The latter portion of the phrase focuses on the descending fifth motive from the end of theme 3, and—as in the exposition—convincing local melodic closure is hard to achieve. A stretto-like series of imitations of this motive along a succession of secondary dominants leads to a momentary F♯ minor chord at m. 126 with full stability arriving only at m. 130. We leave further details of the voice leading of this phrase for you to explore with the aid of Example 7.11.

The development's last phrase, beginning in m. 130, anticipates the thematic return. The top part descends a fifth, C♯6–F♯5, then continues its descent, completing the octave. This overlaps with an inner part that continues one step beyond the octave to resolve the

D♭ to C (6–5) over the bass note F. Despite the thick piano texture, these two lines emerge due to the quasi-canonic relationship between them in mm. 130–131, an intricacy made plain by Brahms's careful upward stemming of the inner part. It was noted previously that the D♭⁶ chord in m. 136 is, enharmonically, V⁶ in the key of F♯ minor. We would also point out that the bass motion leading into this chord—G♯–F♯–F♮ in mm. 134–136—is enharmonically equivalent to A♭–G♭–F, the pitch motion that led to the exposition's statements of theme 1 (i.e., mm. 4–5 and 23–25).

Example 7.12 is an abstract representation of key relationships in the movement so far, eliminating transient tonal centers, such as D♭ in the exposition and both A♭ and E in the development. The main keys of the exposition are F and C minor, and those of the development are a half-step higher, D♭ [C♯] and G♭ [F♯] minor. These are the pitches that were prominent in mm. 1–4!

EXAMPLE 7.12 Tonal summary of movement

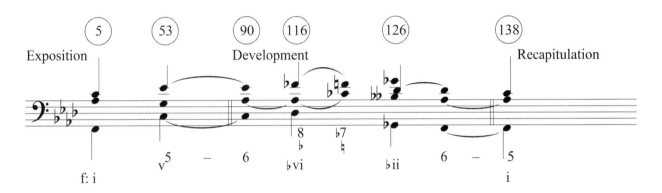

Recapitulation and Coda

The changes in the recapitulation, beyond the use of more elaborate figuration in both the clarinet and piano parts, are the following:

1. The extension of the first phrase of theme 1 is rewritten to lead directly to theme 2, which is now in the parallel major. (There is no second statement of theme 1 by the piano to launch a transition between themes 1 and 2.)

2. Themes 2 and 3 are in the tonic (F major, F minor).

3. There is a new closing phrase, based on theme 1, that begins in m. 206 and leads to the coda.

A representation of this new closing phrase plus the opening measures of the coda is provided in Example 7.13. The first four measures, which unfold over a tonic pedal, are perfectly straightforward, presenting no analytic challenges, but the voice leading and particularly the harmonic syntax of the next four measures are unusual. The succession of chords in mm. 210–213 is e♭⁶ – C°⁷ – b♭⁶ – (G♭^{maj7}) – G°⁷, which then occurs in first inversion and resolves as ii°⁶₅. This seems to make more sense if we understand this motion as occurring in relation to an implied bass B♭, as shown in Example 7.13, which is finally stated at the end of the fourth measure (ii°⁶₅). In other words, this appears to be a variant of the opening statement of theme 1 (compare mm. 8–11 and especially the triplet-embellished restatement in mm. 28–31). The recapitulation's new closing phrase leads to the extended dominant harmony at the beginning of the coda, above which the clarinet line descends a fifth once again to closure, though immediately covered by the ever-present C5.

EXAMPLE 7.13 Voice-leading representation of mm. 205–219

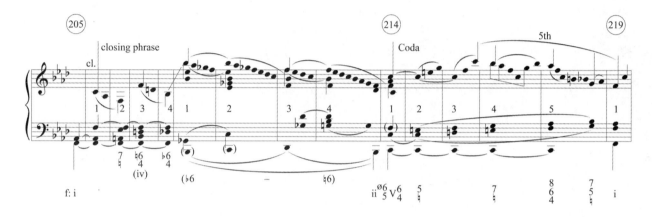

The coda concludes with two *sotto voce* reminiscences of the piano "introduction." We observe something is absent—the chromatic G♭. In fact, neither G♭ nor F♯ makes a single appearance, even as an embellishing tone, during the entire coda. This contributes to the greater stability of mm. 227–236 compared to mm. 1–4, as do the presence of harmony (rather than open octaves) and the conclusion with Picardy third. Although the end of the coda strongly references mm. 1–4, thereby framing the movement thematically, it also alludes to the final phrase of the development (esp. mm. 130–132). At the start of the F♯ minor phrase of the development, there was a quasi-canonic effect within the piano part, as the F♯5–C♯6 fifth was answered by the C♯5–F♯5 fourth. This same answering of a fifth with a fourth occurs at the end of the coda (m. 227, m. 231), suggesting again the central importance of the F♯ minor phrase to the development.

SUGGESTED ASSIGNMENTS

Schubert, Piano Trio in B♭ Major, D. 898, I

1. In Classical sonata form, the recapitulation is marked by a double return, that is, a coordinated return of the opening theme and the tonic key. In this movement the thematic return and tonal return do not coincide. What, then, are the possible explanations for the thematic return in ♭VI?

2. Consider these aspects of the exposition:

    (a) How does the D major chord, mm. 18ff., function within the context of theme 1? Likewise, what is the function of the A major chord, mm. 44ff., in the transition to theme 2?

    (b) In theme 1, note the use of A♭ in m. 9. How does it function in this context? How is this detail developed later in the movement? Hint: check out the coda.

    (c) In theme 2, how does Schubert modulate to the dominant? What is the structure of theme 2?

    (d) What is the tonal organization of the closing theme?

3. The development section is divided into two parts followed by a retransition (prolongation of V), then the thematic return in G♭ (♭VI). Part 1, mm. 112ff., is based on theme 1; part 2, mm. 139ff., is based on theme 2. Consider the following:

    (a) What is the tonal organization of each part of the development?

    (b) What is the combined tonal organization of these parts? Relate it to the coda.

    (c) What is the function of the thematic return in ♭VI in this larger scheme?

Brahms, Clarinet Sonata in E♭ Major, op. 120, no. 2, I

This movement is as complex as the one we already examined in this chapter. Understanding of its organization comes in many stages.

1. Step 1 is always to understand the formal organization at many levels. Where does the development section begin? Is there a coda? If so, where (and how) does it begin? Then determine the divisions of the major sections—themes, transitions, etc.—noting major tonal connections.

2. Step 2 is to examine various sections in some detail, paying attention to phrase rhythm, harmony, and important features. Here you may want to be selective, choosing specific passages for careful scrutiny. Here are several suggestions:

    (a) Consider mm. 1–10.

        (i) Explain the harmony in mm. 5–8.

        (ii) What is the function of mm. 9–10?

        (iii) Note the use of G♭ in m. 8 and again in m. 9. How is this detail developed later in the movement?

(b) The phrase in mm. 10–21 stops abruptly. What is Brahms doing here? How does he accomplish the modulation to V? What happens at the corresponding spot in the recapitulation?

(c) What is the relationship between the clarinet and piano left hand in mm. 22ff.? Does this type of relationship occur elsewhere?

(d) What seems to be the function of mm. 26–27? In the next phrase as well, what is going on with the phrase design?

(e) Explain the harmony and voice leading of mm. 44–52. This might require a simple reduction.

3. More difficult to explain are the following and how they function within a broader context:

(a) mm. 113–126

(b) mm. 150–166

(c) mm. 73–102

8 Ternary Form

Ternary form—normally designated A B A or A B A′—is based on the principles of contrast and repetition. The portion designated B provides a contrast to A, and the second A is either an exact repetition (written out or *da capo*) or a varied repetition (A′) of the first part. In the Baroque period, ternary structures were frequently formed by pairing two movements, e.g., Menuet I and Menuet II, where the individual movements were invariably in binary form, each complete in itself. The larger ternary design resulted from repetition of the first movement: Menuet I (A) − Menuet II (B) − Menuet I (A).[1] The equivalent in vocal music of the period was the *da capo* aria. This type of composite ternary form was expressed in the Classical period as the Minuet − Trio − Minuet and later as the Scherzo − Trio − Scherzo. As we saw in Chapter 5, the individual components were most always in rounded binary form.

Though one can find examples of single movements in ternary form in the Classical period (especially in slow movements), this is a form most often associated with character pieces, particularly piano pieces, of the nineteenth century, no doubt because it is well suited to the expression of strongly contrasting, often lyrical, ideas. There are many examples in the piano music of Schubert, Schumann, Chopin, Mendelssohn and Brahms, to name a few. Here we frequently find the ternary form expanded internally by a retransition leading back to a varied repetition (A′) and externally by a coda, often combining elements from both the A and B sections. In this chapter we will examine three representative works: the second movement of Beethoven's Piano Sonata in D Major, op. 10, no. 3, Schubert's *Impromptu* in G♭ Major, op. 90, no. 3, and Brahms's *Intermezzo* in B♭ Minor, op. 117, no. 2.

Beethoven, Piano Sonata in D Major, op. 10, no. 3, II

We begin our investigation with one of Beethoven's most tragic slow movements. This is a highly dramatic work that expresses a wide range of emotional states from dark and foreboding to lyrical but somber, from intense to tranquil. Overall it has a very serious quality, only briefly providing a glimpse of a brighter world. A copy of the score with analytic additions—indications of larger and smaller formal divisions, harmony, hypermetric organization, and motivic repetitions—is provided as Example 8.1, and an outline of formal-tonal organization is provided in Figure 8.1. We will begin by talking through the movement in a general way, focusing on aspects of formal design and rhetoric. We will then examine the movement from a more technical perspective, focusing on voice leading and longer-range connections.

A				
phrase 1 (motive *x*)	1–9	d: i		
phrase 2	9–17	i	→	VII (C)
phrase 3				
initial statement	17–21		→	v (a)
varied repetition	21–26			v
closing phrase	26–29			v
B				
phrase	30–38	III (F) →		V♯
retransition	38–43			V♯
A′				
phrases 1 and 2 combined	44–56	i	→	VI (B♭)
phrase 3				
initial statement	56–60	Ger. 6 – V – i		
varied repetition	60–65			
Coda				
phrase (motive x)	65–76	i		
closing phrase	76–87	i		

FIGURE 8.1 Outline of Beethoven, Piano Sonata in D Major, op. 10, no. 3, II

The A section, mm. 1–29, is divided into three phrases and a fourth closing phrase. The first phrase, which has a dark, foreboding, quality is closed in the tonic key of D minor. The melodic content of the first measure is an important motive that is developed over the course of the movement; it is bracketed and labeled *x* on the score. This is followed by what comes closest to a real melody in this movement. This second phrase begins as a lyrical, rather somber, idea that leads eventually to a perfect authentic cadence in the unexpected key of C major (VII). As we approach the cadence, the music expands registrally and dynamically, offering a brief glimpse of sunlight in an otherwise dark environment. This is followed by a four-measure phrase leading to a cadence in A minor (v), internal to which the initial gesture, the German augmented sixth resolving to the dominant, is repeated in embellished form, followed by the dramatic gesture extending the diminished seventh chord (*forte*) leading to the cadential pattern in mm. 20–21. The melodic gesture at the cadence is a descending fifth (E5–A4), though not a complete descent by step. This four-measure idea is then repeated in varied form with increased intensity, once again leading to a cadence on A4.[2] The closing phrase supplies the fully stepwise descent of a fifth missing in the previous two cadences. The notes of the descent are circled on the score (Example 8.1).

EXAMPLE 8.1 Beethoven, Piano Sonata in D Major, op. 10, no. 3, II

EXAMPLE **8.1** *continued*

EXAMPLE 8.1 *continued*

Example 8.1 *continued*

EXAMPLE 8.1 *continued*

The B section initially offers a strong contrast to the preceding material. The opening measures, in F major (III), present a calm exterior, but this relative tranquility is short-lived, giving way to the intensity of the repeated gesture of m. 35, which takes us to the G minor harmony of m. 36, the pivot in the modulation back to the tonic. Here the intensity of m. 35, which is repeated a step higher in m. 37, is interrupted by the fleeting repeated three-note gestures in the right-hand part over the G minor harmony. This pattern is then repeated and extended for six measures over the dominant harmony beginning in m. 38. This leads us back to the varied repetition of A.

The A′ section begins as expected, but instead of a complete statement of the opening phrase, Beethoven presents us with a thirteen-measure phrase that combines features of the first two phrases. He begins with the opening five measures of the first phrase (the passage leading to the subdominant), though with more activity in the accompaniment than before, but this then leads to a new connective passage taking us to a higher octave and the latter part of the second phrase leading to a cadence in B♭ major (VI). This connective passage—featuring three successive statements of motive *x*—proceeds from the subdominant harmony in m. 48. As shown on the score, the following 5–♭6 motion creates a ♭II^6 chord, which is subsequently heard as IV^6 in the key of B♭ (VI). This E♭ harmony is then altered to its minor form before leading to the dominant seventh chord of the new key in m. 51. This last chord is loaded with potential meaning. Enharmonically it is the German augmented sixth chord that originally led us to A minor, but here it will eventually lead us to an arrival on B♭. But Beethoven isn't quite ready to get us there yet, and instead he pulls back once again to the G minor harmony via a chromatic change in the bass that emphasizes this deceptive resolution of the F^7 chord. The reason for Beethoven's choice of B♭ as the eventual goal of this extended phrase becomes immediately clear in the following phrase. B♭ becomes the bass note of the following German augmented sixth chord leading us to the dominant and eventually to the tonic in the original key of D minor. As before, this four-measure idea is repeated with greater intensity, but here leading to a coda rather than to a brief closing phrase.

Though the coda opens softly with statements of the *x* motive in the bass on i, then VI, it is clear from the very beginning, especially with the repeated figure in the right-hand part, that this is going to build in intensity. And, indeed, it does build to the V$^{6-7}_{4-3}$ in mm. 72–73, repeated an octave lower in the next two measures. This leads to a closing phrase beginning in m. 76, the first part of which is based on statements of the second half of motive *x*. This is followed by the gesture G♯5–A5 stated three times like the tolling of a bell as the melodic line descends the final third to closure. The music settles ominously in the dark lower register before two fleeting statements of C♯–D and the final two beats of the bass drum. A most effective ending to this dark, but beautifully expressive, work!

We now return to the beginning of this movement to examine certain passages in greater detail. An interpretation of the initial phrase is provided in Example 8.2. The metric organization of this nine-measure phrase is interesting. Something is unusual, at least for an opening phrase, but just *how* it is unusual may not be immediately apparent. The hypermeter is clearly duple (or quadruple) with m. 5 falling on a hypermetric downbeat, and if we continue in this pattern m. 9 does as well. Measure 10, the start of the second phrase, is also a hypermetric downbeat. Successive downbeat measures are not uncommon, but there is one problem with this interpretation, namely that m. 6, where we hear the repetition of the opening motive a step higher, is also heard as a downbeat, that is, as a beginning.

EXAMPLE 8.2 Voice-leading representation of mm. 1–9

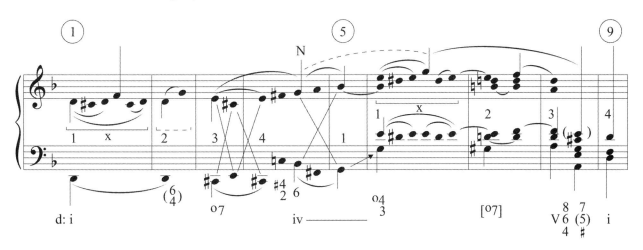

In fact, this motivic association is crucial to our interpretation of long-range pitch connections. So a better interpretation of the hypermetric organization is that the successive downbeat measures occur within the phrase, in mm. 5 and 6.

The *x* motive of m. 1 articulates the third D4–F4, and in the next measure F4 moves temporarily to its upper neighbor, G4. This is followed by a diminished seventh chord prolonged by a double voice exchange between the outer parts, after which $[V_2^4]$ iv leads the top line back to the upper neighbor G4 via its leading tone. However, this time the motion continues beyond the G4 to B♭4 as part of another voice exchange. This concludes the first half of the phrase. The second part of the phrase opens with a statement of motive *x* a step higher than in m. 1, resulting in the transfer of the upper neighbor, here the upper third of the motive, to G5. This note moves down by step to F5, first harmonized by [°7] V and then as part of the cadential $^6_4$. The continuation does not occur in this register, but rather an octave lower, where E4, the resolution of F5/F4, is implied by the context (over the sounding leading tone). This brief excursion into the upper octave will be immediately exploited by Beethoven, as will the distribution of notes of a descending line in different registers.

If we direct our attention back to the score, we see that the next phrase begins in the upper octave with a decorated descending third leading to F5 supported by tonic harmony in m. 10. A stem has been added to this note in Example 8.1 to show its importance. A graphic representation of the material immediately following would show this F5 progressing down to D5 through the passing E5, which is decorated by its own third. The D5 then moves down to C♯5 over dominant harmony, and this is followed by D5–F5 supported by a voice exchange with the bass. This is followed by a repetition of the upbeat figure that leads once again to F5 and tonic harmony in m. 12, then F♯5 leading to the upper neighbor G5, recalling the equivalent motion in the first phrase. The gesture here leading to m. 13 is a replica of the opening of this second phrase, but a step lower; it leads to E5 supported by VII (C major). In the continuation of the phrase we expect the line to continue its descent to C5, but Beethoven retains E5 on the downbeat of m. 15. In the repetition of the cadential pattern that follows we do get the expected descent to local closure, but only after transfer to yet another octave higher and resolution two octaves below that. The notes of the descent (E5–D4–C4) are indicated in Example 8.1 by added stems.

As it turns out, the descent to local closure in C major prolongs the tone that initiated the descent, E5, which is reinstated on the downbeat of m. 20 via its upper neighbor. We are now in the key of the dominant, and the following cadential pattern outlines a descending fifth (E5–A4), though not a fully stepwise one. The expanded repetition of this phrase also articulates this fifth similarly, and it is left to the closing phrase to complete the descent by step to local closure. Though the preceding phrases are articulated from one another by cadences, they are united by a single long-range pitch connection, the descending fifth.

A representation of the voice leading of the B section is provided in Example 8.3. The purpose of this example is to show the connections to the opening material, despite the very different character of the music. Here we are once again in the lower octave with F4 as the main melodic note, which is subsequently prolonged by its upper neighbor G4, introduced here by the unharmonized chromatic passing tone F♯4. This is followed by a descent through E♭4 to D4, first supported by the secondary dominant leading to the G minor chord in m. 36, the pivot in the modulation back to D minor. Not shown in this reduction are the three-note figures that elaborate this harmony, which on the one hand interrupt the flow of the music from m. 35 (*ff*) to m. 37 (*ff*), but on the other hand prepare the figuration that extends the dominant in mm. 38–43. The longer-range connection across these measures leading to the A′ section is F4/III – E4/V♯ – D4/i.

The final portion of this movement to be examined is the coda leading to the final phrase; a representation of the voice leading of this passage is provided in Example 8.4. The first six measures extend the tonic, the top voice traversing the entire octave from D4 to D5 chromatically with the harmony at the terminal points being i and i^6. This is followed by the standard cadential pattern $ii^{ø6}_{5}$ leading to the cadential $^6_4$ supporting the continued ascent through E5 to F5. The V^{6-5}_{4-3} chords are elaborated by the three-note embellishing pattern introduced in the B section, functioning primarily here, as there, to extend the dominant. The voice leading shown in Example 8.4 represents the norm, that is, the regular

EXAMPLE 8.3 Voice-leading representation of mm. 30–44

EXAMPLE 8.4 Voice-leading representation of mm. 65–76

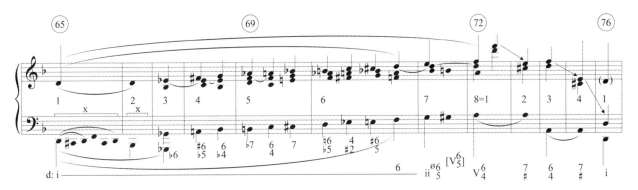

resolution of $\frac{6}{4}$ to $\frac{5}{3}$ in two octaves, without trying to represent all aspects of the elaboration. Again we find a descending third distributed over several octaves. We must wait to hear this descending third in the same octave in mm. 82–84 as the bell tolls, and even here the final note of resolution, D4, is delayed.

Schubert, Impromptu in G♭ Major, op. 90, no. 3

One could hardly find a greater contrast to the Beethoven movement than this impromptu by Schubert. Both are highly expressive works, but, whereas the Beethoven is a somber, intense work, the Schubert is mostly tranquil, almost like a lullaby. The annotated score is provided in Example 8.5, and an outline of formal-tonal organization is provided in Figure 8.2.

The A section consists of an a b b′ design, each eight measures in length. The first eight measures are further divided into an antecedent leading to the dominant and a consequent ending with a perfect authentic cadence. The b phrase, which emphasizes ii, then IV, also concludes with a perfect authentic cadence, as does the following varied repetition of the phrase. This frequent coming to closure contributes to the music's sense of peace and well-being. The B section provides contrast. Its controlling mode is minor, E♭ minor (vi), with an internal excursion to C♭ major (VI in E♭ minor). More important, perhaps, is that the phrase lengths are no longer predictable. The B section consists of two phrases, both expanded. Though the phrases are not parallel, that is, they do not consist of the same material, they are related by the characteristic rhythm of the left-hand part in their opening measures, which helps in identifying where phrases begin and end. The basis for the phrase expansion is indicated on the score. The first phrase is expanded internally by a slightly varied repetition of the first three measures, which gives the initial impression that the hypermeter has now shifted from quadruple to triple, and externally by extension of the goal harmony, C♭, by an additional four measures (mm. 36–39). The second phrase is also expanded internally, in this case by varied repetition of its first four measures. A particularly beautiful moment occurs in m. 49, where Schubert leaps up to G♮5, momentarily breaking away from the restricted range of the melody. This phrase is followed by a brief retransition leading back to the opening material.

A

a antecedent	1–4	G♭: I – V
consequent	5–8	I – V – I
b	9–16	[V] ii – [V] IV – V – I
b′	17–24	

B

phrase 1	25–39	e♭ (vi): i → VI
phrase 2	40–51	°7 – i – ii⁶ – V – I
retransition	51–54	I – iv/G♭: ii – V$^6_5$

A′

a antecedent	55–58	G♭: I – V
consequent	59–62	I – V – I
b′ expanded	63–74	[V] ii – [V] IV – V – I

Coda | 74–86 | I

FIGURE 8.2 Outline of Schubert, Impromptu, op. 90, no. 3

The A′ section consists of an exact repetition of the a period and an expanded version of the b′ phrase. This four-measure internal expansion (mm. 70–73) begins with the substitution of IV⁶ for the expected tonic (the expected fourth hyperbeat), which is followed by a varied repetition of mm. 67–69. The final measure of this phrase, m. 74, overlaps with the harmonically interesting coda. It will be discussed further below, but here we note another one of the special expressive moments in this piece. In the coda the repeated underlying melodic progression is G♭4–F4–G♭4. Three times Schubert has approached the leading tone by the descending arpeggiation C♭5–A♭4–F4 (mm. 77, 81, and 82), but the fourth time the music leaps up to E♭5, the ninth of the dominant, an extremely effective moment in this very beautiful work.

A representation of the voice leading of the a and b phrases of the A section is provided in Example 8.6. The antecedent of the a period proceeds to what Schenkerian analysts refer to as an interruption. In an interruption, the melodic line descends as far as scale degree 2 supported by V, but instead of completing the descent to closure, this motion is interrupted and returned to its point of departure, in this case scale degree 3. The consequent, then, completes the motion. This is a very common paradigm in tonal music. The b phrase counters this strong pull toward closure with an ascending fifth A♭4–E♭5 divided into two overlapping thirds, the first progressing to ii and the second to IV at the climax of the phrase (m. 12). This ascending fifth is subsequently answered by a descending fifth a step lower (D♭5–G♭4),

EXAMPLE 8.5 Schubert, Impromptu in G♭ Major, op. 90, no. 3

Example 8.5 *continued*

EXAMPLE 8.5 *continued*

EXAMPLE 8.5 *continued*

EXAMPLE 8.5 *continued*

EXAMPLE 8.5 *continued*

EXAMPLE 8.5 *continued*

EXAMPLE 8.6 Voice-leading representation of mm. 1–16

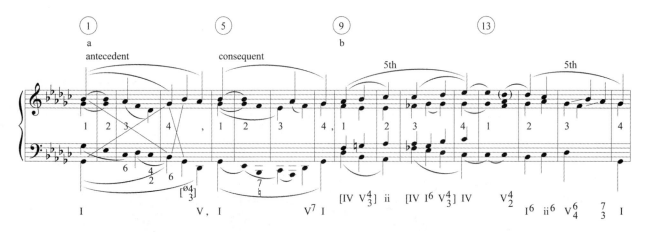

concluding with a perfect authentic cadence. As shown in Example 8.6, the descent through Bb4 and Ab4 to Gb4 is delayed until the final moment.

A representation of the voice leading of both phrases of the B section is provided in Example 8.7. The initial part of the first phrase, including the varied repetition of its first three measures, prolongs the local tonic, Eb minor. As shown in Example 8.7, the melodic motion in these measures occurs at two levels, a descending fifth from Bb4 to Eb4, a motion to an inner voice represented by downward-directed stems, and the slower-moving upper line that descends a third from Bb4 to Gb4. This takes us to m. 31, which becomes the point of departure for the modulation to Cb major (VI). There is an immediate descent of a fifth to the downbeat of m. 32, above which Gb4 is retained, and from that point there is a clear descent of a fifth to the perfect authentic cadence on Cb in m. 35. Overall, then, there is a descent of a third Bb4 to Gb4 followed by a descent of a fifth from Gb4 to Cb4. Together these form a descending seventh, replacing an ascending step from Bb4 to its upper neighbor, Cb5. Looking ahead, we see that the music indeed does arpeggiate up to this Cb5 in m. 39. So, if we were to represent only the deepest level of connection across this span of fifteen measures (mm. 25–39), it would show Bb4, supported by an Eb minor chord (i) progressing to its upper neighbor Cb5, supported by a Cb major chord (VI).

Measures 35–39, the extension of the goal harmony, is worthy of some scrutiny. The local tonic is initially prolonged by a neighboring motion involving the minor subdominant chord, followed by a progression involving the German augmented sixth chord. When dealing with so many flats, it takes a moment to determine the notes of this chord. Begin with the lowered sixth degree of the scale, which is Abb, then above it add major third (Cb), perfect fifth (Ebb) and augmented sixth (F♮): Abb–Cb–Ebb–F♮. The repetition of these two measures of extension involves two subtle changes. First, the neighboring motion involves the regular subdominant (IV[6]) and the German sixth chord is replaced by $^{o6}_{5}$ of V, Ab having replaced the earlier Abb. These very subtle changes in color are typical of Schubert's repetitions.

The first four measures of the second phrase, which are repeated, return us to Eb minor. Cb5, the upper neighbor, is now harmonized as seventh of $^{o}7$ leading to Bb4, harmonized

EXAMPLE 8.7 Voice-leading representation of mm. 25–54

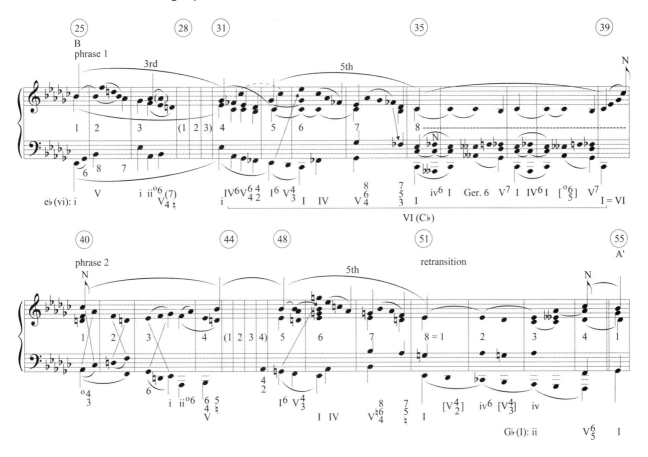

by the dominant (end of m. 43). The varied repetition ends with V_2^4, which leads now to G♮ in the bass (I^6) passing on down to E♭. We have already noted the melodic leap up to G♮5 at this point, a simple motion that seems to open up an entirely new sound world. This motion covers a descent from B♭4 to E♭4 at the cadence in m. 51. This is followed by a brief connection back to the opening material. Here B♭4 is reintroduced by its upper neighbor, C♭5, this time harmonized as seventh of the dominant.

The final section we will examine in some detail is the coda, which contains a wonderful example of enharmonic use of the augmented sixth chord. A representation of mm. 74–82 is provided in Example 8.8. In the first four measures the harmony progresses to the minor subdominant, which prepares for its chromatic alteration as the German augmented sixth chord. The second time Schubert respells the augmented sixth chord enharmonically as a dominant seventh chord (D–F♯–A–C as opposed to E♭–G♭–B♭♭–C♭), which leads to the minor Neapolitan (written as G–B♭–D rather than A♭♭–C♭♭–E♭♭). But he then pulls us back once again to G♭ major by re-employing this dual-function chord as an augmented sixth chord resolving to V_{4-3}^{6-7} – I.

Though this work seems to float by almost effortlessly, it is actually very complex. As always with Schubert, there are some interesting harmonic twists, and, as the work progresses, we encounter some sophisticated manipulation of the lengths of musical phrases.

EXAMPLE 8.8 Voice-leading representation of mm. 74–82

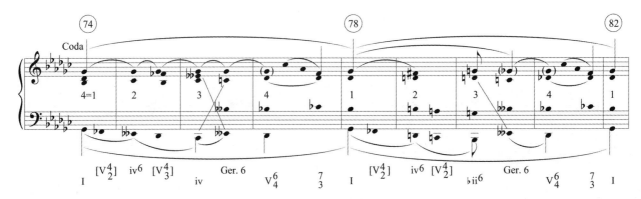

Brahms, Intermezzo in B♭ Minor, op. 117, no. 2

Brahms indicates to the performer to play this intermezzo very expressively (*con molto espressione*). It is, in fact, a deeply expressive work, much of it gentle and flowing, yet at other points somewhat agitated. And though the dynamic level remains predominantly soft, there are places where the music builds to *forte*, most notably at the climax in mm. 67ff. Technically, this is an extremely sophisticated work, in which phrases are often expanded and overlapped, the end of one almost indistinguishable from the beginning of the next. The harmony is at times crystal clear, at other times momentarily obscured by surface embellishment. A copy of the score is provided in Example 8.9, and an outline of its formal-tonal organization is provided in Figure 8.3.

This intermezzo is in a ternary form that is expanded internally by a retransition leading back to A′ and externally by a coda. Both the A and B sections consist of parallel phrases in antecedent-consequent relationship, and, as we shall see, the two ideas are motivically related. The goal harmony of the intermezzo's first phrase, the dominant, is extended, melting seamlessly into the beginning of the second phrase, which is expanded internally by a digression to the key of the dominant. But the real goal is the relative major, D♭, the key of the B section. The antecedent phrase of the B section ends on an F major chord (III♮), a fleeting reference to the dominant of the main key, and, for the first time in this piece, the consequent phrase ends with a strong cadence, an imperfect authentic cadence in the local key. The approach to this cadence is the first time the dynamic level reaches *forte*. The B section is followed by a retransition that leads us back, again almost seamlessly, to the opening material, this time with D♮ rather than D♭ in the bass. Otherwise the antecedent is largely the same as in the beginning. However, the consequent phrase is substantially rewritten, leading to the climax of the piece, the tritone-related progression ♭II^7 – V$^4_3$ harmonizing scale degree 4, first E♭6, then dropping down to E♭4 in preparation for the coda. The coda further prolongs the dominant until the first perfect authentic cadence of the piece and the first tonic triad in root position three measures before the end of the intermezzo! Even here, the arrival at scale degree 1 is delayed by a suspension.

A representation of the voice-leading structure of both phrases of the A section is provided in Example 8.10, and an account of the chord-to-chord harmonic syntax is indicated

A			
antecedent	1–9	b♭:	i⁶ – V⁷
modulating consequent	9–22		i⁶ – vi/D♭: iv
B			
antecedent	22–30	D♭ (III):	V⁷ – I → III♯
consequent	30–38		V⁷ – I – IV – V – I
retransition	38–51	b♭:	[Ger. 6 – V⁷] V⁷
A′			
antecedent	51–60		i⁶ – V⁷
consequent	60–72		i⁶ – ♭II⁷ – V⁷
Coda	72–85		V♮6 – ♭6 – 5 – i

FIGURE 8.3 Outline of Brahms, Intermezzo in B♭ Minor, op. 117, no. 2

on the score. The meaning of the opening progression is not immediately clear; it leads to a B♭ minor chord in first inversion, first with B♭4 as the top note, then F5. What follows is a diatonic sequence of root-position seventh chords progressing by descending fifths from i⁷ (third beat of m. 2) to ii°⁷ (m. 5). Melodically the top voice reaches up to A♭5, the seventh of the tonic chord, and then the top voice descends in parallel tenths with the bass (alternating with sevenths in a 10–7 pattern) until m. 5, where there is a voice exchange with the bass prolonging ii and E♭5. The descending third from this E♭5 is then repeated in the next measure supported by dominant harmony. At this point we expect that this E♭5, now the dissonant seventh of the dominant, will resolve to D♭5 supported by tonic harmony, but this expectation is never realized. Instead Brahms extends V⁷, melodically approaching the seventh once again from a third above. This leads us to the expected D♭5 (m. 8), harmonized not by the tonic but presented as an accented passing tone over an extended dominant harmony. Following the cascading arpeggio down to the low E♭, this dominant harmony is transformed into °⁴/₃.³ Once the dissonant D♭ resolves to C5 over E♭ on the third beat of m. 9 and this leads to B♭4 over D♭ in the bass (i⁶) on the downbeat of m. 10, we have already begun the consequent phrase. This is what was meant earlier by our comment that the two phrases overlap almost seamlessly. The antecedent phrase has been expanded by the extension of the dominant harmony and the composing-out of the third E♭5–D♭5–C5 over a span of four measures (mm. 6–9). This third is part of a larger motion of a descending fifth F5–B♭4 crossing the phrase boundaries.⁴

The consequent phrase begins as before, but this time the top voice reaches up from F5 to B♭5 initiating a series of secondary dominant seventh chords leading back to F5 over D♭. This is not a seventh chord, but an augmented sixth chord initiating a four-measure parenthetical excursion to F minor that is abruptly cut short by the reintroduction of this

EXAMPLE 8.9 Brahms, Intermezzo in B♭ Minor, op. 117, no. 2

EXAMPLE 8.9 *continued*

EXAMPLE 8.9 *continued*

EXAMPLE 8.9 *continued*

EXAMPLE 8.9 *continued*

EXAMPLE 8.10 Voice-leading representation of mm. 1–23

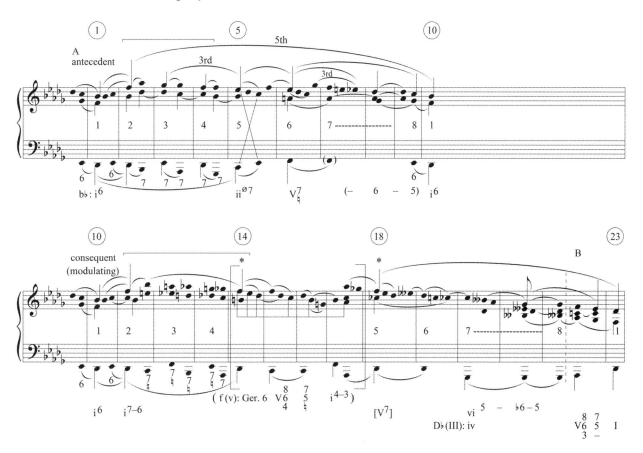

same chord on the downbeat of m. 18, now spelled with a C♭ rather than a B♮ in the inner part. These two chords are marked with asterisks in Example 8.10.[5] This chord then leads to the G♭ minor chord in m. 20, the pivot in the modulation to D♭ major (III): vi/iv. This harmony is extended over three measures (mm. 20–22), further expanding the phrase. This is a tricky passage to decipher, but in essence this G♭ harmony is colored by a 5–♭6 motion (D♭–E♭♭), momentarily transforming the minor subdominant into a Neapolitan chord. The voice leading once again continues across the phrase boundary, which is indicated by the vertical dotted line in Example 8.10. The gesture initiating the new phrase is F4–E♭4–D♭4, a motion to an inner voice. In the immediate context this F4 is a passing tone, and thus its notation in Example 8.10 without stem. But, as we shall see, this note retains its important function in the B section as third of the local tonic.

Before proceeding to the B section, we want to point to an important feature of the opening phrase, since this feature is extensively exploited later in the intermezzo. This feature is the reaching up from the F5 in m. 2 to A♭5 and the return by step to F5 two measures later. Though the motion continues beyond this second F5 to E♭5 (m. 5), Schenker's unpublished analysis of this intermezzo identifies F5–A♭5–G♭5–F5 as an important motivic idea exploited later on.[6] This idea is marked on the score with a bracket and on our representation of the voice leading of the two phrases of the B section, which is provided as Example 8.11.

EXAMPLE 8.11 Voice-leading representation of mm. 23–38

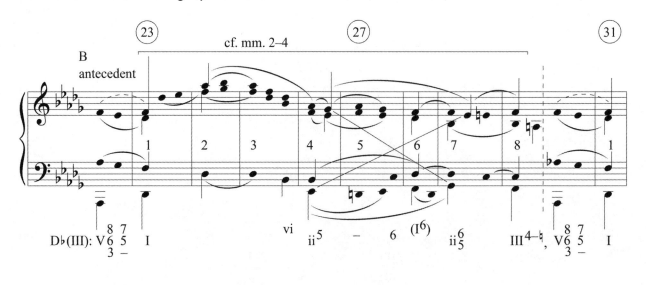

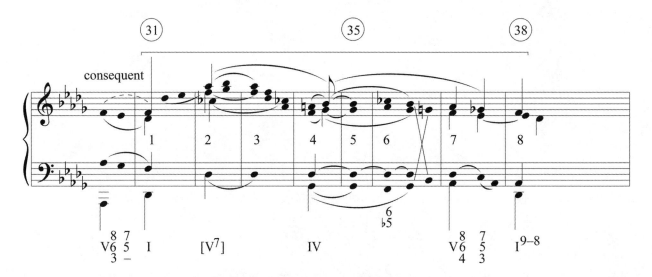

The initial melodic gesture of the first phrase of the B section, the descending third F4–E♭4–D♭4 is answered by the ascending third D♭5–E♭5–F5, the last note covered by A♭5. So the F5–A♭5 of m. 2 is now stated almost simultaneously and then prolonged by its upper neighbors before resolving to G♭4 over E♭4 supported by supertonic harmony in m. 26, displaced momentarily by their upper appoggiaturas. The following three measures, marked *legato espress. e sostenuto*, are, at first glance, a bit difficult to sort out due to the notes of melodic embellishment, but once we sort this all out, the harmony of m. 27 is ii⁵⁻⁶ initially decorated by its secondary dominant, which passes through a tonic chord in first inversion to ii⁶₅ in m. 29. The relationship across mm. 27–29 is a voice exchange between the outer parts prolonging ii and G♭4. The chromatic inflection of this supertonic harmony deflects away from the expected dominant at the end of the phrase to III♮. The result of this surprise is twofold. It not only creates a harmonic reference to B♭ minor, but it also articulates F4 as the melodic goal of the phrase, the completion of the motive F–A♭–G♭–F, while preparing the repetition of the phrase's opening gesture at the outset of the consequent.

Once again the answering third D♭5–E♭5–F5 is immediately covered by A♭5 in the following measure (m. 32). And once again the third F5–A♭5 is decorated by its upper neighbors, first in this octave, then an octave lower in m. 34, where it is supported by IV. The following three measures, which prolong IV, are analogous to mm. 27–29. They are marked *espress. e sostenuto*, but here Brahms allows the dynamic level to rise to *forte*. As before the underlying harmony is temporarily obscured by the numerous notes of melodic embellishment, but once this is sorted out we see (and hear!) the subdominant harmony prolonged by its neighboring V_5^6 followed by the chromatic voice exchange between the outer parts, as shown in Example 8.11. This leads to the $V_{4-3}^{6-7} - I^{9-8}$, the first authentic cadence of the piece. The top voice leads through A♭4 to G♭4 (8–7 of the dominant) to F4/I, completing another clear statement of our identified motive.

In some sources the form of this intermezzo has been incorrectly identified as sonata form. The idea that this intermezzo is written in sonata form may derive in part from the fact that the music to this point consists of two ideas that are linked to form a larger unit that comes to a cadence, a temporary resting point, only in m. 38. Furthermore the following retransition has the character of a development. It opens with a repetition of the initial descending third in octaves: D♭–C–B♭. As shown in Example 8.12, a representation of the voice leading of the retransition, this gesture, beginning from the D♭5, generates an ascending line leading to G♮5, supported by the C^7 chord, V^7 of V, in m. 45. Schenkerian analysts refer to the process by which this ascending line is created as "reaching over," a term which here describes the reaching up to a third above each step in the ascending line to approach the next one from above, similar to the way F5 reaches up to A♭5 in m. 2 to lead to G♭5 on the next downbeat. The last step in this process involves just these pitches, except this time the goal is G♮5, not G♭5. Note how the third above F5, that is, the A♭5, is extended for three measures (mm. 42–44), while the supporting harmony is transformed from a $B♭^7$ into an enharmonically spelled augmented sixth chord by means of a chromatic voice exchange. This is the same chord that was given double meaning in the consequent phrase of the A section (highlighted by the asterisks in Example 8.10).

EXAMPLE 8.12 Voice-leading representation of mm. 38–52

Arrival at the C^7 chord in m. 45 is followed immediately by the statement of the two-note figure D♭–C three times in three successively lower octaves, the last harmonized by V^7 in m. 48. These three statements stand out not only because of the change in the mode of presentation (as chords rather than arpeggios) but also because of their duple rhythmic articulation, which creates a hemiola against the triple meter. It is just at this point that the metric organization of this passage becomes less clear. If we look at the score, we see that the changes of surface design suggest a quadruple hypermeter through m. 46, as indicated between the staves. However, the continuation is not clear, which might very well have been Brahms's intention, since he takes great effort to disguise the return of the opening material. We will return to this thought in a moment.

The melodic gesture that generates the retransition is the descending third D♭5–C5–B♭4 in mm. 38–39, and this third then becomes the overall gesture leading from m. 38 to the B♭4 on the downbeat of m. 52, after the beginning of the A′ section. That is, the voice leading in both melody and bass cross the formal boundary between the retransition and the A′ section, which is indicated in Example 8.12 by the dotted vertical line. The long-range third spanning these fifteen measures is shown by the large slur and extended stems in our example. Brahms takes great effort to help us hear this connection. Though the overall melodic gesture from the pick-up to m. 39 through m. 45 is D♭5 to G♮5, the connection of D♭ to C is established by the insistent repetition of that figure, and the following connection of C to B♭ is then filled in by this third at two levels, as shown by the notation in Example 8.12. Most fascinating is the hesitation after the first two notes of this third in mm. 51–52. At this last moment Brahms rejects D♭–C–B♭ for D♭–C♭–B♭ as the bass leads through E♭ to D♮, not D♭. This creates a dominant ninth chord (B♭–D–F–A♭–C♭), which directs the harmony beyond the beginning of the phrase to the subdominant in m. 54, further blurring the formal boundary between retransition and return.

A representation of the voice leading of the consequent phrase of A′ and the coda, which are linked to form a continuous unit, is provided in Example 8.13. Before discussing this final portion of the intermezzo, we should review the structure of the initial phrase (Example 8.10), since this final section can be understood as an enlargement of that structure. After F5 is established in the top part (m. 2), this voice reaches up to A♭5, then descends by step to E♭5, first harmonized by the supertonic, then the dominant. This is followed by an extension of the dominant, above which E♭5 progresses through the passing tone D♭5 to C5. In other words, D♭5 is never given its own harmonic support in the descent to B♭4. The final portion of the intermezzo, beginning in m. 61, is an expanded version of this opening phrase. The initial four measures involve a motion to A♭5 progressing in parallel tenths with the bass, from which point there is a chromatic descent to E♭5, spelled as D♯5, the third of a B major-minor seventh chord, which enharmonically is ♭II^7, the Neapolitan seventh chord. This prepares the reharmonization of scale degree 4, now transferred to E♭6 in m. 69 as seventh of the dominant. This is the climax of the piece from which point E♭ is transferred down two octaves and the dynamic level gradually decreases in preparation for the coda (*Più Adagio*). This final portion of the phrase extends the dominant for another eleven measures (mm. 72–82), above which scale degree 3, first D♮, then D♭ is extended until finally resolving to C4 and then B♭3, supported for the first time by tonic harmony in root position.[7] As in the opening phrase, scale degree 4 (E♭) is emphasized and extended, and then scale

EXAMPLE 8.13 Voice-leading representation of mm. 61–85

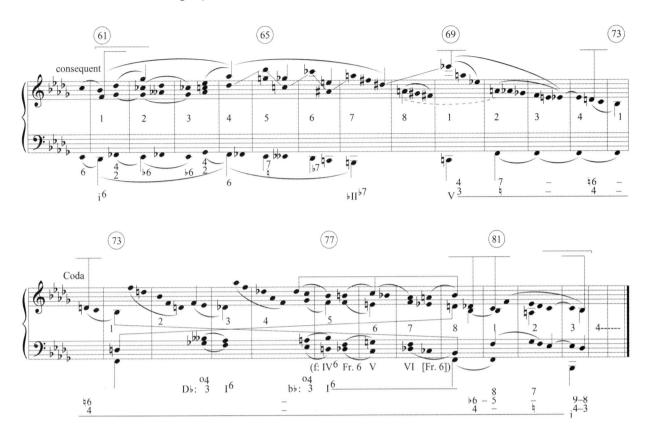

degrees 4–3–2 in the descent to closure all occur over a prolonged dominant. The difference, of course, is one of scale.

The coda is an integral part of the tonal plan, not just a section added at the end. Nevertheless, it does provide in many ways a kind of summary in that it makes clear reference to material from previous sections. As shown in Example 8.13, the $^6_4$ with D♮ is prolonged by a long-range voice exchange between the inner parts from mm. 73 to 80, after which D♭4 is introduced and resolved immediately to C4. The final approach to scale degree 1 involves a diminution of the long-range melodic line, the descending fifth. Internal to the voice exchange, there is first a reference to the key of the B section, D♭ major (III), then within the context of B♭ minor a passing reference to F minor, the key suggested but never confirmed in the parenthetical digression in the second phrase of the piece. This occurs in mm. 77–80 within the context of the descending third D♭5–C5–B♭5 indicated by the beam in Example 8.13.

This intermezzo features many of the most characteristic elements of Brahms's style: elaborate motivic development; complex use of embellishing tones; blurring of boundaries between phrases and larger sections; de-emphasis of root-position tonic harmony and delay of closure; and intricate textures, both contrapuntally and rhythmically. As such, his music presents special challenges to performers, analysts, and listeners.

SUGGESTED ASSIGNMENTS

Beethoven, Piano Sonata in E♭ Major, op. 7, II

Though portions of this movement have been examined earlier in this book, it is worth studying this movement as a whole. The following are some areas to focus on:

1. The form of the A section is a b a′. What are the tonal connections between the a and b sections? How is the a′ section expanded?

2. Analyze the form and harmonic progression of the B section. How is it related to A? How does Beethoven get back to the dominant (m. 37)? You can check your interpretation against the one provided in Example 4.16.

3. What are the motivic and rhythmic bases for the retransition?

4. Analyze carefully the final section (coda) beginning in m. 74.

Schubert, Moment musical, op. 94, no. 2

Portions of this work were discussed in Chapter 4 (see Examples 4.4 and 4.5) in the context of modal mixture. Still there is much to be learned from this relatively short piece. It is written in extended ternary form, by which is meant that it is extended to a five-part form by varied repetition of the A and B sections: A B A′ B′ A″ (coda). Consider the following:

1. Harmony

2. Phrase rhythm, including phrase expansion

3. Schubert's development of the opening neighbor-note motive

Schubert, Piano Sonata in B♭ Major, D. 960, II

1. The A section consists of two phrases, mm. 1–17 and 18–42, where the second is a reharmonization of the melody of the first. Both are expanded. How?

2. The A′ section involves some interesting harmonic digressions. How do you explain the brief passage in C major, mm. 113ff.? The final phrase in C♯ major can be explained as an expansion of eight measures. How so?

3. The B section is more complex. What is its internal form? Can you explain the harmonic progression of the phrases beginning in m. 59 and later in m. 76? These two phrases involve an odd number of measures. Can these be explained as resulting from some kind of phrase expansion? What is the overall harmonic logic of this section? How is it related to the outer sections? (There are probably several correct answers to that question!)

Chopin, Etude in E major, op. 10, no. 3

1. The A section consists of an antecedent phrase and an expanded consequent. How is the antecedent divided? How is the consequent expanded? What is unusual about the resolution of the cadential $^6_4$ at the end of the second phrase?

2. The B section is difficult. First examine the phrases, noting repetitions, and indicate harmonic goals. Do not try to analyze harmonically the extended chromatic passages, mm. 38–41 and 46–53.

3. Examine carefully the retransition. How does Chopin lead back to the beginning?

Brahms, Intermezzo, op. 117, no. 1

1. The A sections of this work are relatively simple and repetitive, appropriate for a setting of a simple Scottish lullaby. What rhythmic effect occurs in mm. 13ff.? How do mm. 17–20 relate to mm. 1–4, and how do they prepare the B section?

2. The B section is contrasting in several respects. How so, and how also is it related to the outer sections? Here you might prepare a simplification of the voice leading and then identify the important harmonies. What is the harmonic progression in mm. 25–26, which is repeated in varied form in mm. 27–28?

9 Rondo Form

In our final chapter, we turn to the **rondo**, which is based on alternations between a recurring theme, known as the **rondo theme** or **refrain**, and contrasting sections referred to as **episodes**. Occasionally, composers wrote rondos as independent pieces, generally for solo piano or for solo instrument with piano or orchestral accompaniment. More commonly, we encounter the rondo as an alternative to sonata form for the last movement of multi-movement instrumental works such as sonatas, string quartets, and symphonies. In concertos, the final movement is much more often a rondo than a sonata form. Rondo forms occasionally occur as slow movements, though less frequently since other formal types, such as sonata form (sometimes without a development section), ternary form, and theme-and-variations form, are found in slow movements in the Classical tradition. After a general discussion of rondo form, this chapter will examine two rondos that serve as finales. The first comes from a piano sonata by Mozart composed in the late 1770s, and the second is from a violin sonata by Brahms written in the mid 1880s. Compared to other rondos by each composer, both movements are expansive and formally complex; in relation to one another, the Brahms movement aptly demonstrates the increasingly elaborate handling of tonal and formal conventions in the late nineteenth century.

Rondo Form

In the previous chapter we studied ternary form, which arises from the restatement of an entire section (A) after a contrasting section (B). Rondo form can be viewed as an extension of ternary form. In a rondo, the initial section (A or refrain) is restated at least *two* additional times. Its first appearance establishes the tonic key and almost always concludes with a perfect authentic cadence in that key. Nearly all refrains have a length between sixteen and thirty-two measures, and they generally feature symmetrical phrases with clear cadences. Sometimes, a rondo refrain contains repeated sections, creating a complete binary or rounded binary form.

The subsequent statements of the refrain can be unaltered, or they can have surface embellishment or be shortened somewhat; the final refrain is often lengthened, especially when not followed by a separate coda. Usually, all statements of the refrain occur in the tonic key, but it is possible for a later refrain to start in the "wrong" key. On *rare* occasions a refrain statement in the middle of the form will occur in a non-tonic key, or it will occur in the tonic key but will proceed into the subsequent section without the expected perfect authentic cadence.

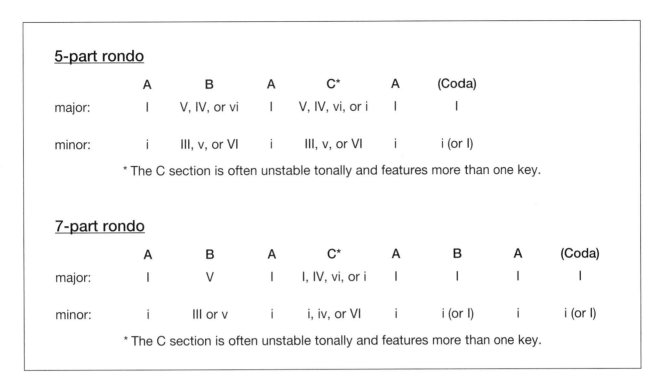

FIGURE 9.1 5-part and 7-part Rondo Forms

In between the statements of the refrain there are contrasting sections which we will refer to as episodes and label with the letters B and C. These sections contrast the refrain both in thematic content but also in key. As with refrains, episodes often have considerable internal repetition.

The most common types of rondo are 5-part and 7-part rondos with the layout of thematic materials shown in Figure 9.1. Except in the case of B episodes in 7-part rondos, there is considerable variety in the key areas found in episodes; Figure 9.1 lists only the most frequent choices. Often the C section will feature more than one key area, although when this occurs it is unlikely that each key would be confirmed with a perfect authentic cadence.

Most rondos have connective material between some of the thematic sections. Nearly all rondos have passages that prepare returns of the refrain. These passages typically sit on the home dominant (usually V^7) and are referred to as **retransitions**. Some rondos also have passages after refrain statements that prepare the key of the following episode; we refer to these as **transitions**. When a rondo contains multiple retransitions, these passages often share similar material; the same is true of the transitions in a rondo with multiple transitions.

Since we have chosen to focus on two complex rondos in this chapter, we offer now brief descriptions of two 5-part rondos by Haydn and Beethoven. The third movement of Haydn's Piano Sonata in D Major, Hob. XVI/37 provides a good illustration of a highly sectionalized rondo form. Its refrain (mm. 1–20) consists of a complete rounded binary form with both halves repeated. The B episode (mm. 21–40), in the parallel minor, is also in rounded binary form with exact repetitions. After an unaltered refrain restatement, the C episode (mm. 61–80) provides yet another rounded binary form, this time in the subdominant

(G major). After the C section, a retransition (mm. 81–93) leads back to the home dominant and playfully sits there for several measures. This is the only connective passage between this rondo's principal sections. The final refrain has its repetitions written out to allow for a livelier sixteenth-note texture in the left hand. The movement ends without a coda; two tonic chords are added at the conclusion of the final refrain.

More elaborate is the 5-part rondo found as the slow movement of Beethoven's Piano Sonata in C Minor, op. 13 ("Pathétique"). The refrain establishes the tonic key of A♭ major through an eight-measure phrase that is immediately repeated an octave higher. The B episode spans a mere seven measures (mm. 17–23) but deceives the listener by tonicizing F minor (vi) before achieving a perfect authentic cadence in E♭ major (V). After a brief retransition (mm. 24–28), the refrain returns (mm. 29–36) but is stated only once. Like the B episode, the C episode (mm. 37–44) touches on two keys; following a tonicization of A♭ minor (i), the episode culminates with a perfect authentic cadence in E major (a convenient spelling of ♭VI). After a short retransition (mm. 45–50), the refrain returns in its original sixteen-measure length (mm. 51–66) but with a faster inner-voice accompaniment (triplet sixteenths rather than sixteenth notes). Unlike the Haydn, this rondo concludes with a coda (mm. 67–73).

Mozart, Piano Sonata in B♭ Major, K. 333, III

Mozart's Piano Sonata in B♭ Major, K. 333, is one of his most popular piano works. In large part, this is due to its masterful coordination of Mozart's characteristically tuneful and charming melodic writing with a number of surprises. In the finale, these surprises include clever manipulations of thematic materials, phrase expansions, and virtuosic passages reminiscent of concerto movements. Our commentary will highlight these important features. Figure 9.2 provides a summary of formal-tonal organization, and Example 9.1 gives an annotated score of the complete movement.

Central to this movement's effectiveness is its innocent beginning. The refrain consists of a single parallel period (mm. 1–8), which is then repeated with louder dynamics and faster rhythms in the left hand (mm. 9–16).[1] As indicated on the score by circles, the melody in mm. 1–8 outlines two descents from F5, the first ending on C5 at the end of the antecedent and the second ending on B♭4 at the close of the consequent. When the antecedent is repeated, its melody remains the same, but when the consequent is repeated its melody is altered and achieves a more emphatic conclusion. This emphasis arises through the higher register and the faster rhythms (compare m. 15 to m. 7). Despite the displacement of embellishing pitches an octave higher in m. 15, the underlying melodic content remains the same. The brief dabbling with this higher register suggests that the music will soon explore it more fully.

The transition is an eight-measure sentence that achieves the most usual tonal goal, V of V (m. 24). Again, structurally important melodic pitches have been circled on the score. The transition's melody comes to a clear termination on G4 on the second quarter note of m. 24, although the left-hand accompaniment already begins the texture that supports the initial measures of the B episode. We will return to the significance of this formal boundary later. A particularly beautiful aspect of the transition is the prominence of the chromatic pitch that signals the modulation, namely E♮ (m. 20). The anacrustic motive *x* (bracketed

REFRAIN (A)				
antecedent	1–4			I – V
consequent	5–8			I
antecedent repeated	9–12			I – V
consequent repeated	13–16			I
Transition	17–24	leads to		V of V
EPISODE 1 (B)	24–36		F(V):	V – I
Retransition	36–40	leads to	B♭(I):	V⁷
REFRAIN (A)	41–56			I
Transition	57–64	leads to	g(vi):	V
EPISODE 2 (C → Development)				
sentence	65–72		g(vi):	i – V
link	73–76	leads to	E♭(IV):	I
development of transition	76–90		E♭(IV):	I – V
development of refrain	91–103	leads to	B♭(I):	V
Retransition	103–111		B♭(I):	V – V⁷
REFRAIN (A)	112–127			I
Transition	128–148			I – V
EPISODE 1 transposed (B′)	148–164			V – I
Transition to cadenza	164–171			I – V
Cadenza	171–199			V
REFRAIN (A′)				
antecedent	200–203			I – V
consequent expanded	204–214			I
CODA	215–225			I

FIGURE 9.2 Outline of Mozart, Piano Sonata, K. 333, III

EXAMPLE 9.1 Mozart, Piano Sonata in B♭ Major, K. 333, III

EXAMPLE **9.1** *continued*

EXAMPLE **9.1** *continued*

EXAMPLE 9.1 *continued*

EXAMPLE 9.1 *continued*

EXAMPLE 9.1 *continued*

EXAMPLE 9.1 *continued*

EXAMPLE 9.1 *continued*

EXAMPLE 9.1 *continued*

on the score) begins both statements of the sentence's basic idea as well as the continuation, but transposed a step higher each time. Due to this process of transposition, we expect E♭ on the last eighth of m. 20 and our attention is grabbed when we hear E♮ instead. Similar prominent handling of a pivotal chromatic pitch will occur in the subsequent transitions.

Like the transition, the B episode begins as an eight-measure sentence, but here the continuation is expanded. Instead of the expected perfect authentic cadence at m. 32, an imperfect authentic cadence occurs, deferring local closure in F major until m. 36. This expanded continuation provides the most exciting music thus far: in addition to its nearly continuous sixteenth-note motion, it touches on a new registral highpoint, D6 (m. 30). Note also that the repeated continuation provides one measure more than necessary. Whereas V^{6-5}_{4-3} span a single measure in that initial statement (m. 31), on the second cadential approach they are stretched across two measures (mm. 34–35). Not only does this extra measure increase the anticipation for cadential closure but it also permits the episode to conclude on a hyperdownbeat rather than a weaker fourth hyperbeat. The end of B elides with a short retransition that transforms the local tonic triad back into V^7 of the home key. Although mm. 36–40 have a connective formal function, they do introduce yet another significant melodic-rhythmic motive, the repeated eighth notes in the right hand.

After an exact restatement of the entire refrain (mm. 41–56), the same transition material returns but leads to a different tonal goal: V of G minor (vi). What pitch most clearly distinguishes B♭ major from G minor? These keys share the same key signature, but in G minor the expression of dominant harmony requires F♯. Notice in m. 62 how prominently the melody moves from F5 to F♯5. This is analogous to the highlighting of E♮ mentioned above in the first transition's modulation to F major. The modulation to G minor is clarified by the augmented sixth chord at the end of m. 63. The choice of vi for the second episode is fairly common in major-mode rondos; almost always, the second episode of a major-mode rondo has a considerable emphasis on the minor mode (if not vi, then usually i). Since major-mode rondo refrains typically have a light-hearted character, the shift to minor during the second episode, or at least a significant portion thereof, brings dramatic contrast.

The second episode starts out as a bold contrast. Besides the shift to a minor key, the large ascending melodic leaps provide a surge in intensity. Despite the rhythmic similarity between the melody in m. 65 and the one in m. 5, the overall effect is contrast, and it seems best to label this new section with the letter C. Mozart, however, gradually returns to thematic materials heard earlier. With the modulation to E♭ major at m. 76, a humorously disguised version of the transition occurs. Although the dotted rhythms are new, the pitch content of the melody in mm. 76–79 is a transposed version of mm. 16–19 (and mm. 56–59). In m. 76, the onset of the harmonic arrival on E♭ major and the long melodic pitch suggest the presence of hypermetric reinterpretation (4 = 1). As the phrase unfolds, it gradually becomes apparent that the anacrustic beginning characteristic of the transition has been preserved. This explains the dual hypermetric reading of mm. 77–81 shown in the score annotations. The music does not attain cadential closure in E♭ major; instead, after a half cadence (m. 88), which is immediately repeated (m. 90), the music passes through C minor and B♭ minor. In these latter key areas, the development of earlier thematic material becomes explicit, as rhythmically unaltered versions of the refrain's beginning occur. The modulation to B♭ minor facilitates the end of this section, since the arrival on its dominant (m. 103) can launch a retransition to prepare the reassertion of B♭ major at the next refrain statement (mm. 112ff.). Due to the extensive manipulation of thematic material from earlier in the movement, this central section of the rondo comes to function more as a development than as a contrasting C section. Since the opening measures of the central section are highly contrasting, the outline in Figure 9.2 suggests a transformation "C→development," but if one were to choose a single label "development" would be more appropriate than "C."

Whether the thematic content of the central section of a 7-part rondo is new or develops earlier thematic material is an important distinction. When this section consists entirely or principally of development, as in this piece, the rondo takes on an attribute of sonata form. For this reason, a 7-part rondo with a development as its central section is often referred to as a **sonata-rondo**. The sonata component is greatly enhanced if there is a transition between the initial refrain and the B episode, as there is in Mozart's rondo. Thus, the initial refrain, transition, and B episode resemble a sonata exposition; the central section provides a development; the return of the refrain after the development, the ensuing transition, and the home-key restatement of the B episode resembles a recapitulation. Of course, compared to sonata form there are two extra refrain statements, one between the "exposition" and "development" and one after the "recapitulation." In addition, the themes themselves usually have somewhat different internal construction than one encounters in a sonata form. As noted above, rondo refrains and B episodes generally have more symmetrical phrase structures and a greater amount of exact repetition than in the first and second themes of a sonata form. Nonetheless, the substitution of a development for a contrasting C episode increases the "weight" or "depth" of a rondo. A sonata-rondo typically provides a more substantial conclusion to a multi-movement work than does a 7-part rondo with a C section.

Returning to Mozart's rondo, we note that after the development section the refrain returns in its entirety and without variation (mm. 112–127). Since the upcoming B episode will occur in the home key, the transition that begins at m. 127 must be modified, as its two previous statements modulated to the dominant and the submediant respectively. Like the earlier transitions, the change is signaled prominently by the introduction of a chromatic pitch, here A♭ (m. 132). Initially, this A♭ is harmonized by V^6_5 of IV, but through a chromatic voice exchange this chord evolves into V^6_5 of ii and sets up a brief descending fifth sequence that leads back to the tonic harmony (m. 137). Compared to the previous transitions, this one is longer and has a thicker, quasi-orchestral texture; as we will see, Mozart revisits these qualities later. The transition attains its expected goal, the dominant harmony, at m. 144 and expands it until m. 148.[2] Where exactly does the transition end? If one compares m. 148 with the corresponding m. 24, it is clear that the melody of B begins in the middle of m. 148 with the C5. But if one listens to several recordings of this rondo, one will discover that many performers connect the preceding F4 quarter note with that C5. This feels quite natural since the F4 is registrally close to C5 and its single-note texture might seem more similar to the lyrical B theme than to the thick F major chord on the measure's downbeat. However natural this feels under the hands, analytically it makes little sense. In the Classical style, when a B episode (or sonata second theme) returns it does so beginning on the same beat. Furthermore, transitions often end with two or three triads or open octaves (less often a single note, as occurs here); these are punctuating articulations that define a formal ending, not a beginning. This is a good example of how thinking precisely about formal boundaries can shape a performance interpretation.

In our earlier discussion of B, we noted that it provides intensification through phrase expansion and registral expansion. Its transposed restatement does so to an even greater extent. Like the initial B episode, the continuation is expanded due to the imperfect authentic cadence at m. 156 (analogous to m. 32). Now, however, the perfect authentic cadence is achieved only after an additional eight measures (at m. 164) rather than four measures (at m. 36). This further expansion arises through an impressive drawing out of the cadential $^6_4$ across mm. 158–162, that is, across five measures rather than the single measure (m. 34) encountered earlier. Since these eight measures are clearly based on a four-measure model, we have shown two levels of hypermeter. There is a periodic surface hypermeter, but one can easily infer an underlying hypermeter wherein a third hyperbeat is powerfully stretched by this stasis on the cadential $^6_4$. In addition to delaying the cadence, this passage includes the highest pitch and introduces the lowest pitch heard thus far—in fact, the highest and lowest pitches available on the five-octave compass of Mozart's instrument. This climactic passage is one of the most virtuosic in all of Mozart's solo piano music.

At this point, we expect a final statement of the refrain, possibly followed by a coda. Mozart does something unexpected: he inserts a quasi-improvisatory section, which he labels as a cadenza, to be played in tempo except for its concluding runs (marked *ad libitum*). In Mozart's numerous concertos with rondo-form finales, a cadenza does precede the final refrain statement. Thus, he is mixing genres by incorporating a feature from the concerto into the piano sonata. In his concertos, cadenzas are heralded by a loud orchestral passage that stops on a cadential $^6_4$. This type of preparation occurs in this piano sonata; the cadential $^6_4$ arrives at m. 171 and is preceded by several *forte* measures with a relatively unusual texture for Mozart's piano music. The left-hand melody in octaves and the violinistic figuration in the right hand conjure up, as best one can on a keyboard instrument, the impression of an orchestra surging towards the cadential $^6_4$ that is the sign for the concerto soloist to improvise a cadenza.

In a concerto, the cadential $^6_4$ preceding the cadenza resolves only at the V^7 near the cadenza's conclusion. Melodically, there is usually a corresponding connection between $\hat{3}$ above the cadential $^6_4$ and $\hat{2}$ above the V^7. For many of Mozart's concertos there exist cadenzas by the composer, and from these it is apparent that while the intervening material explores harmonies other than the dominant—sometimes remote ones, often involving mixture with the minor mode—the organization is such that the underlying sense of the unresolved cadential $^6_4$ is not entirely attenuated. (As the nineteenth century progressed, it became standard for composers to provide written-out cadenzas in the score, and these sometimes have a more innovative tonal function.) In order to clarify what is going on in this piano piece, we provide a voice-leading representation of the cadenza along with an inventory of its thematic content at (a) in Example 9.2.

The cadenza begins with the refrain melody, but its tonal function is changed due to its placement above a dominant pedal. The bass moves deceptively in m. 177, but this bass G♭ serves as a temporary upper neighbor to the dominant. The dominant persists throughout mm. 179–185 as material drawn from the earlier retransitions occurs. Starting at m. 186, Mozart develops the eighth-note rhythmic motive characteristic of the retransition, first with a tonic pedal in the bass (mm. 186–188) and then in the right hand during a descending fifth sequence (mm. 189–192). Although mm. 186ff. are based on a rhythmic motive from

EXAMPLE 9.2 Voice-leading representations of cadenza and transition to restatement of B

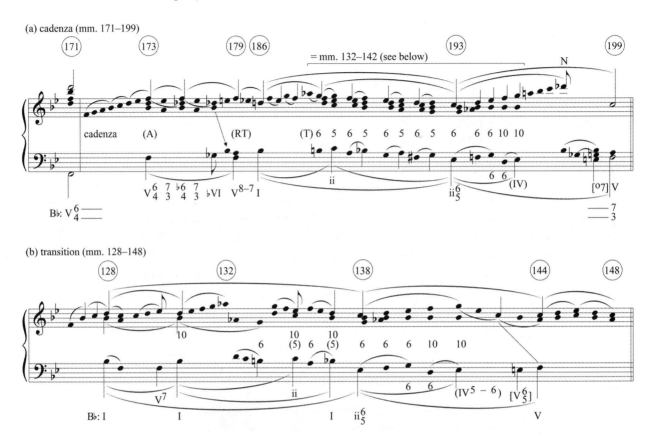

the earlier retransitions, their pitch content is derived from the transition that leads to the restatement of the B episode. Example 9.2 at (b) provides a voice-leading representation of this transition (mm. 128–148) for easy comparison with mm. 186–199 at (a), also in Example 9.2. In both passages, the melody introduces A♭ harmonized with an applied dominant of IV, but this chord resolves deceptively to ii (recall that ii is equivalent to vi in the key of IV). In the earlier sequential passage (mm. 133–137), the harmonic rhythm is slow and the sequence stops at the tonic harmony; in the cadenza's sequential passage (mm. 189–192), the harmonic rhythm is faster, driving the sequence past tonic harmony towards vi which is itself headed to the strong arrival of ii⁶₅ at m. 193. Thus, mm. 191–192 do not actually correspond to anything in the earlier passage, but at m. 193 the correspondence becomes more exact than ever. Except for the doubling of the harmonic rhythm in m. 195, mm. 193–196 (beat 1) recall mm. 138–142 both in harmony and voice leading. After the downbeat of m. 196, the close relationship breaks down; note, however, that the overall harmonic motion remains the same. The bass E♭ prolonged throughout mm. 193–196 passes through E♮ on to F in m. 198, just as happened more directly in mm. 143–144. As shown in Example 9.2, the upper voice extends $\hat{2}$ from the onset of ii⁶₅ until the arrival of the dominant, although in the cadenza its elaboration is considerably more extensive. The cadenza comes to the expected trill on $\hat{2}$, but here again Mozart throws in a little surprise. In a concerto, the trill on $\hat{2}$ generally resolves emphatically to $\hat{1}$, and this perfect authentic cadence coordinates precisely with the triumphant re-entry of the orchestra for its final section. In this sonata, the trill on $\hat{2}$ dissipates into further figuration that decelerates and leads smoothly back to the final refrain statement, still marked *piano*.

Unlike the other refrain restatements, the final one (mm. 200–214) is modified. It consists of only a single period, but one where the consequent phrase is expanded from four measures to eleven. The antecedent remains very close to the refrain's initial antecedent, but the consequent jumps to *forte*, a dynamic previously reserved for the second half of each refrain statement. This dynamic shift signals the elimination of the two-period, soft-loud design in favor of a single period. The consequent is expanded through the use of I^6 (m. 207, m. 210) to delay the cadence. Within the phrase expansion note how the final push to the cadence (mm. 210–213) is itself expanded compared to the preceding unsuccessful attempt (mm. 207–209) through the spreading of the cadential $^6_4$ and its resolution across two measures (mm. 212–213). We observed the same technique in the B section (see mm. 34–35), and as in the B section, this extra measure places the end of the final refrain statement on a hyperdownbeat (m. 214) and thereby gives a bit of extra weight to this moment of structural close.

Since m. 214 corresponds to the end of the refrain material and features a perfect authentic cadence, we have designated the remainder of the movement as a coda (mm. 215–225). The "after-the-end" quality is enhanced through the immediate introduction of $\flat\hat{7}$ as part of V^7 of IV. Unlike the iterations of this harmony in the cadenza and in the transition leading to the restatement of B, this one resolves to IV (not deceptively to ii). The persistence of the tonic pedal in the bass and the shorter lengths of melodic units contribute to a contented conclusion for this bold and expansive movement.

Brahms, Violin Sonata in D Minor, op. 108, IV

Our second rondo form poses numerous analytic challenges, many of which relate to defining aspects of Brahms's language. Foremost among these is the lack of strong arrivals on tonic harmony throughout most of the movement. The deferral of tonal closure occurs on several levels of structure. Also of great importance is Brahms's elaborate development of thematic materials, both within individual sections and between them. These features make the identification and labeling of sections more difficult than in Mozart's rondo. Expressively, these elements contribute to the movement's dramatic sweep towards its tragic conclusion. As we undertake a detailed discussion of Brahms's movement, bear in mind that reinterpreting Classical forms and rendering formal boundaries less clear are typical of much of Brahms's music. Figure 9.3 provides a formal-tonal outline of the movement, and Example 9.3 offers an annotated score.

The movement's first formal quirk occurs at the end of m. 4. After four measures the music suddenly stops and then begins again in m. 5 with the violin spinning a true melody from A5–E5–F5, the pitches in the top voice of the piano chords in mm. 1–2 (labeled *x* in Example 9.3).[3] The first four measures seem like an anticipation of the movement's true beginning—a "false start"; however, this introductory function is not clear because mm. 1–4 are in the movement's main tempo, not in a slower one. This ambiguity about the formal function of mm. 1–4 is why we have placed their introductory label in quotation marks in Figure 9.3. Since rondo forms involve multiple returns of their opening materials,

"Intro"	1–4		V – iv
REFRAIN (A)	5–16		V
Transition (Tx)	17–38		i – V/v
EPISODE 1 (1B)			
antecedent	39–54	C (VII):	I – V^7[iii]
consequent expanded	55–72		I – a (v): VI
Transition (Ty)	73–76	a (v):	V
EPISODE 1 (2B)			
antecedent	77–84		V
consequent expanded	85–107		V – i
Transition (Ty)	108–113		V
"Intro"	114–117		V – d (i): iv
REFRAIN (A)	118–129	d (i):	V
EPISODE 2 (Development)			
part I	130–176	g (iv):	i – f (iii): i
part II	176–194	f (iii):	i – d (i): V
Transition (Tx)	194–217	d (i):	V
EPISODE 1 transposed (1B)			
antecedent	218–233	F (III):	I – V^7[iii]
consequent expanded	234–251		I – d (i): VI
Transition (Ty)	252–255	d (i):	V
EPISODE 1 transposed (2B)			
antecedent	256–263		V
consequent expanded	264–286		V – i
Transition (Ty)	287–292		V
"Intro"	293–296		V – iv
REFRAIN (A)	297–311		V – i
Coda	311–337		i

FIGURE 9.3 Outline of Brahms, Violin Sonata, op. 108, IV

EXAMPLE 9.3 Brahms, Violin Sonata in D Minor, op. 108, IV

EXAMPLE 9.3 *continued*

EXAMPLE 9.3 *continued*

EXAMPLE 9.3 *continued*

EXAMPLE 9.3 *continued*

EXAMPLE 9.3 *continued*

EXAMPLE 9.3 *continued*

EXAMPLE 9.3 *continued*

EXAMPLE 9.3 *continued*

EXAMPLE 9.3 *continued*

(phrase expanded by 2 measures)

continues to tonic resolution

EXAMPLE 9.3 *continued*

the ambiguity about whether mm. 1–4 constitute an introduction to the refrain or the first segment within the refrain is a rich compositional seed for Brahms to sow.

Starting in m. 5, the music proceeds with superficial regularity as the *x* motive launches not only m. 5 but also m. 9 and m. 13. Closer inspection reveals that this strongly projected hypermeter does not correlate with solid tonal pillars. In the initial statement of the *x* motive (mm. 1–2), the terminal F5 was harmonized by root-position tonic harmony, but it occurred in the midst of an ongoing melodic sequence. The larger harmonic connection is between the dominant of m. 1 and that of m. 5, with the subdominant harmony of m. 4 providing neighboring bass motion in between. When the violin takes up the *x* motive in mm. 5–6, the F is a dissonance against dominant harmony and ultimately resolves with a 7–6 motion against the bass of ii$_5^6$ (m. 7). In the next statement, the F is replaced by F♯, which is harmonized with an applied dominant to iv. At m. 13, the *x* motive is transposed to begin from $\hat{1}$ instead of from $\hat{5}$. Here again tonal stability is somewhat undermined by the inclusion of F♯ in the harmonic support of $\hat{1}$, allowing mm. 13–16 to begin with an exact transposition of mm. 1–3 into G minor (iv). Thus, the ambiguity about the formal function of mm. 1–4 is reengaged as its transposed version now serves as the culmination of the rondo refrain. This culmination seems headed for a powerful perfect authentic cadence, but at m. 17 the violin drops out, the dynamics suddenly are soft, and the chordal texture vanishes. These changes affect the degree of tonal resolution between m. 16 and m. 17. Certainly, there is no melodic resolution, but the harmonic resolution is also reduced. While we would not rule out the possibility of hearing an elided imperfect authentic cadence at m. 17, the passage is closer to a half cadence in m. 16 with the root-position tonic harmony in m. 17 serving as a launch to the transition but not also as a conclusion to the refrain. Either way, the degree of tonal closure is significantly less than typically found in this formal location in rondos by Haydn, Mozart, Beethoven, or Schubert.

As expected, the transition (mm. 17–38) modulates and ends on the dominant of a new key, here V of A minor (v).[4] A modulation to the relative major most frequently prepares for the B episode in a 7-part minor-mode rondo, but the minor dominant is the next most common choice. Based on a sixteen-measure sentence (with the goal V harmony expanded), the transition is quite unremarkable except for its deft handling of motivic materials. The transition opens with a new melodic idea moving in eighth notes, which we will refer to as motive *y*, and it is shown by dotted brackets on Example 9.3.[5] In the initial two statements of motive *y*, one is drawn to the interplay between the descending third F4–E4–D4 (m. 17) and the ascending third C♯4–D4–E4 (m. 18), circled in Example 9.3. In mm. 17–20 and mm. 21–24, *piano* iterations of motive *y* are contrasted by *forte* intrusions of motive *x*. In the sentence's continuation, the statements of motive *y* in the violin preserve their ascending thirds (though beginning not with a consonant pitch but with a dissonant D♯4); those in the piano forgo their descending motion in favor of large ascending leaps that prepare the return of motive *x*. Motive *x*, however, is varied (*x′*) through the addition of an appoggiatura (A5 in m. 30; D5 in m. 31). This appoggiatura allows one to hear stepwise motion within the B5–G♯5 and E5–C5 thirds, thereby incorporating into motive *x* an aspect of motive *y*. When the goal V arrives in m. 33, stepwise motion through a third is all that remains of the thematic material (*y′*); simplification of melodic content often accompanies dominant pedals at the ends of transitions, but Brahms's distillation of an element embedded within *y* and subsequently incorporated within *x* is particularly notable.

The juncture between the end of the transition and the start of B involves both continuity and surprise. Melodically, B grows directly from the transition; as shown in Example 9.3, an augmentation of γ' in the bass connects the end of the transition with the start of B, which has a melody that begins with another statement of γ'. This is a good example of linkage technique, whereby a motive near the end of a formal unit is immediately deployed to initiate the next one. The surprising aspect of B is its tonal design; it touches on several key areas before eventually confirming A minor at m. 104 with a perfect authentic cadence, the strongest cadence in the movement thus far. We will now examine the tonal structure and phrase organization of B in more detail.

The B episode contains two periods with contrasting thematic material and keys. Given these strong contrasts, we have chosen to differentiate these periods as 1B and 2B. As noted above 1B has a smooth thematic evolution from the transition, but the expected key of A minor is displaced by its relative major, C major. This initial C major harmony is elaborated through plagal motions, which raise the spectre of F major. The sixteen-measure antecedent phrase features an ascending fifth sequence (mm. 43–48) that leads to the dominant of E minor (mm. 48–54). Notice the treatment of the melody at the highpoint of the phrase. The pitches B3–E4–G4–F♯4–A4–G4–F♯4 are first given by the piano (mm. 47–50) and are then imitated by the violin. The violin's imitation is partial as the melody reverts to the piano at the end of m. 52; observe here the careful upward stemming of the F♯3 to highlight the piano's completion of the violin's imitation. Due to the modulation within the antecedent phrase, the beginning of the consequent back on C major sounds like a deceptive progression within E minor. In fact, C major is only briefly asserted in the consequent, which quickly shifts into F major and then emerges from its ascending-fifth sequence (mm. 61–65) in A minor. The violin, which assumes a leading role during the consequent, provides the melody at the phrase's highpoint: E5–A5–C6–B5–D6–C6–B5–A5 (mm. 65–68). This is a transposition of the end of the consequent from E minor into A minor, but with a terminal $\hat{1}$ (here A5) included within the four-measure unit. This final note is harmonized by an F major chord, VI of A minor; thus, the deceptive motion heard between the end of the antecedent and the start of the consequent is now heard within the consequent's final measure. And, just as at the very start of 1B, F major—the most usual key for B in a 7-part rondo in D minor—seems to be trying to surface. This impression is enhanced through the phrase's striking penultimate chord. While the upper pitches articulate V^7 of A minor, the pianist's left hand plays $\hat{5}$ of F major, C, rather than the expected E. The result is a hybrid harmony that conflates elements from the dominant sevenths of A minor and F major! From a larger perspective, it is clear that the terminal F major functions as VI in A minor, but the preceding bass motion renders it somewhat more stable, as does its placement as goal of an entire musical period.[6]

Following a repetition of the cadence, a brief transition leads to 2B and back to V of A minor. Unlike 1B, 2B begins in A minor, but it still does not assert root-position tonic harmony. Like 1B, 2B consists of a period with expanded consequent but differs in three important respects. First, the roles of the violin and the piano reverse: in 2B the melody is led by the violin in the antecedent and by the piano in the consequent. This is typical in duo sonatas in the Classical tradition. Second, 2B possesses a feeling of acceleration owing to the faster surface rhythms, the shorter phrase length of the antecedent (eight measures compared to sixteen in 1B), and the obvious sentential design of the phrases with fragmentation at the outset of their continuations. Third, the expansion of the consequent phrase in 2B is longer and more elaborate. In 1B, the expansions arise internally through one-measure elongations of two harmonies (m. 57 and m. 60), but in 2B there are multiple expansions. Initially, the consequent's continuation is expanded through thematic fragments that span not one measure—as one expects at the outset of the continuation of an eight-measure sentence—but 1.5 measures (mm. 89–91). These unusual lengths support reading two hyperbeats across three notated measures, an interpretation that responds to the melodic development and preserves quadruple hypermeter. These sequential measures lead from A minor to D minor, a shift emphasized through the deployment of augmented sixth chords (m. 93 and m. 95). An additional passage (mm. 96–104) reattains A minor through a chromatic octave ascent in the bass that connects the A major chord, functioning as V of D minor, with an A minor sonority. The rising bass line, syncopated rhythms, and *crescendo* imbue this phrase expansion with powerful energy that culminates with the melody found at the highpoint of 1B (cf. mm. 104–107 with mm. 65–68), but this time achieving a perfect authentic cadence in A minor. Thus, the drive to this delayed cadence is capped off with a figure that had been left unresolved during 1B, and this thematic recycling helps draw together 1B and 2B into a span of nearly eighty measures all headed towards this perfect authentic cadence in A minor.

The open-octave transitional material that occurred between 1B and 2B returns after 2B (mm. 108–113), but it now leads to $[^{\circ}7]$ V in A minor—an odd goal given that a refrain statement in the home key of D minor is expected. Instead, the quasi-introductory material from mm. 1–4 comes back in A minor. More precisely, its first three measures occur in A minor (mm. 114–116) and its final measure is in D minor (m. 117). This key change is extremely jarring because it creates the progression (in D minor) of V – iv between m. 117 and m. 118. Given its "wrong-key" beginning, this four-measure unit seems even more introductory than in mm. 1–4. The rondo refrain then occurs in its entirety and without variation (mm. 118–129). Since the refrain is not followed by a section beginning with a D minor chord (or even in the key of D minor!), its ending on V is highlighted. We are reminded of the melody's unresolved C♯ due to the linkage technique wherein the D5–C♯5 from the refrain's terminal measure is taken up in the chordal accompaniment of the following section.

At the center of this rondo lies a development section based almost entirely on the initial measures of the refrain (mm. 5–8). The development proceeds in two parts (mm. 130–176 and 176–194), both driven by sequences. In the first part, the thematic derivation is obscured by the slower rhythms and softer dynamics, but a comparison of the melody in mm. 5–8 with that in mm. 134–137 reveals that the latter is a transposed (and reharmonized) simplification of the former: A–E–F–E–(G–B♭)–D–(C–B♭–A–G)–G♯ becomes G–D–E♭–D–C–F♯. In the second part, the thematic connection is more explicit, as the eighth notes in mm. 176–177 clearly arise from those in mm. 7–8. The sequences in the second part are similarly straightforward, proceeding via ascending fifths from F minor (m. 176) and C minor (m. 181) through the key of G minor (m. 187) to the ultimate arrival on the dominant of D minor (m. 194). In the first part, the sequences are more unusual, and we provide a simplification in Example 9.4. Initially, the sequence outlines eight-measure units in rising minor thirds: G minor (m. 134), B♭ minor (m. 142), and C♯ minor (m. 150). This passage has a strong variation component, as the melody always sounds in a different part of the texture and the rhythmic activity continually increases. Thus, the simplification in Example 9.4 shows the "normative" voice leading for the chords involved in the sequence, but this constitutes the actual voice leading only in the B♭ minor unit. Elsewhere, several of the chords occur in inversions different from those shown in Example 9.4, including the all-important augmented sixth chords. At m. 158, a fourth sequential unit in E minor could have begun, but instead the music continues V of E minor from the preceding measure. The eight-measure sequential unit is fragmented to its second half, where the modulation to the next key actually occurs. Beginning with the bass D♯ in m. 158, this shorter sequential module leads to F♯ minor (m. 161) and A major (m. 163). Notice the acceleration of the harmonic rhythm in m. 163 that contracts the latter sequential unit. After m. 163, the sequence fragments further such that the German augmented sixth follows directly after the A major chord; as a result, this unit moves up by a major, rather than minor, third to C♯ major, which Brahms immediately respells as D♭ major. At this point, the goal of F minor could have been reached through one further sequential unit with bass line D♭–C–F; however, the C that occurs in m. 167 supports a passing $\frac{6}{4}$ chord that leads to a new sequence with an urgently brief two-chord sequential unit. The C that supports the cadential $\frac{6}{4}$ arrives only at the

EXAMPLE 9.4 Simplification of sequences in part I of development (mm. 130–176)

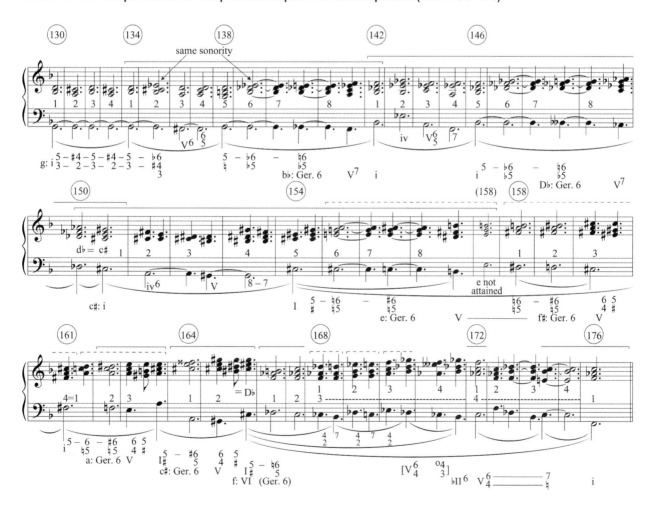

fortissimo in m. 171, which resolves to F minor at m. 176. The progressive reduction in the number of chords in sequential units combines with the acceleration in harmonic rhythm, syncopations, and *crescendo* to produce a powerful—but tonally remote—climax in the middle of this movement.

As noted above, the second part of the development leads to V of D minor (m. 194), and this is the expected tonal goal. Since this movement has been proceeding along the lines of a 7-part rondo, we anticipate a retransition will lead to a restatement of the refrain. However, the material in mm. 194ff. is based on the transition that led from A to 1B, and Brahms does indeed omit the expected return of A. This rondo, then, is a variant of the 7-part rondo that can be summarized as ABACBA, a 6-part rondo not typical of Classical practice but found in a small number of rondos by Mozart. Moreover, Brahms makes a critical change in the transition material: it is entirely set over a dominant pedal (except for the double-neighbor motion in mm. 210–211). Brahms thereby not only avoids thematic return but also tonal return. This is a wonderful illustration of the importance of remaining aware of large-scale tonal structure in addition to chord-to-chord harmonic progression when examining music in the Classical tradition.

The B material returns without alteration, except for transposition down a perfect fifth. Due to its meandering tonal design, this means that a perfect authentic cadence in D minor is not reached until m. 283. Recall that the transition after the initial statement of 2B led to [°7] V in A minor; thus, upon transposition down a fifth, [°7] V in D minor is attained (m. 292), and this leads smoothly into a restatement of mm. 1–4 (in mm. 293–296) to prepare the long-awaited refrain restatement (mm. 297ff.). Except for a coloristic reharmonization of the F♯ in m. 302 and a two-measure phrase expansion (mm. 305–306), the refrain parallels those heard earlier. The enormous change occurs in the measure directly after the refrain where the pianist provides a thunderous D minor chord (m. 311). Unlike the *piano* D minor chord of m. 17 or the abrupt move to G minor after the second refrain statement, this event provides solid tonal closure to the refrain. Experiencing this moment is the payoff of the multiple denials of tonic arrivals earlier in the movement.

The coda returns to materials from the transition that immediately followed the initial refrain. The lilting figure of the transition's opening (mm. 17–19) is transformed from a gesture that leads away from D minor into one that confirms the tonic key (mm. 313–315). The coda then turns to refrain material (mm. 325ff.), specifically its final four measures (mm. 13–16). Neither the violinist nor the pianist can complete the phrase; both get stuck on F with a harmony that includes E♭, a pitch always present in the refrain's penultimate measure (m. 15, m. 128, m. 309) and through which the melody always descended. After the *poco sostenuto*, the players regain their momentum and achieve not only harmonic closure but also melodic closure that involves a descent through diatonic $\hat{2}$ (see circled pitches on the score in mm. 331–335). The coda is still manipulating thematic materials and rendering them more tonally stable. As such, it provides further evidence of Brahms's penchant for large-scale thematic development and for giving all sections of the form dense and piece-specific thematic content.[7] Where composers of the late eighteenth century often allowed closing sections to contain relatively generic melodic materials, Brahms and many other composers of the later nineteenth century maximized the potential of thematic content within the boundaries of the common-practice tonal system, and in this way looked forward to the steps beyond that system in the twentieth century.

SUGGESTED ASSIGNMENTS

Beethoven, Violin Sonata in A Major, op. 12, no. 2, III

1. Consider mm. 53 and 54. Which of these measures should be considered as the first measure of a phrase? Why?

2. There's a very unexpected rest in m. 79, but what does the "breaking down" of the music in these measures also get rid of? (Tonally, what is typically going on at this spot in rondo form?)

3. In m. 120, the piano left-hand note is marked *sf*. What connection is Beethoven highlighting here, and what term describes this type of thematic reworking?

4. What is the form of mm. 120–183? Is this section more like a C section or a development?

5. In mm. 202–205, there are some rather unusual accidentals (for a piece in A major).

    (a) Based on these accidentals, what key is expected in m. 206?

    (b) How does the key identified in (a) relate to the two keys that are tonicized in the two phrases that immediately precede mm. 202–205? (Is there any pattern?)

6. As is often the case, the final statement of the refrain is altered.

    (a) Explain precisely what is altered (measures omitted? added?).

    (b) Explain how Beethoven prepares the final refrain, and explain why this preparation might have suggested one of the alterations identified in (a).

    (c) How do the alterations affect the strength of the refrain's final cadence?

7. Quite near the end a very interesting rhythmic effect occurs. Where is this, and what is it called?

Beethoven, Piano Sonata in D Major, op. 28, IV

1. Compare the initial statement of the rondo refrain with subsequent statements of the refrain.

2. Are there any similarities between the rondo refrain and the thematic materials of the episodes? If yes, describe.

3. Comment on the thematic content of the transitions and/or retransitions (if present). Do any of them re-use the same thematic material? If yes, describe.

4. Some rondo forms are referred to as "sonata-rondos." What feature(s) of this movement would be found in a "sonata-rondo" form, and what feature(s) of this movement are not typical of a "sonata-rondo" form?

Beethoven, Piano Sonata in G Major, op. 31, no. 1, III

1. Compare the initial statement of the rondo refrain with subsequent statements of the refrain. What are the main types of changes introduced in later refrain statements? Which statement of the refrain is most similar to the initial one?

2. Are there any similarities between the rondo refrain and the thematic materials of other sections of the form?

3. Compare mm. 200–205 with the opening refrain. What thematic connection can be observed, and how is the motive transformed from its initial appearance in the refrain?

4. Consider the chord in m. 236. It is marked *rf*.

   (a) What term does *rf* stand for, and what does it mean?

   (b) This is the only time Beethoven uses this marking in the movement. What is so special or unexpected about the chord in m. 236?

Mozart, Piano Sonata in C Major, K. 309, III

1. At what point does phrase expansion occur within the refrain? How is this moment manipulated later in the movement?

2. How does Mozart delay local closure within the B episode? What happens to the moment of closure in the home key restatement of the B episode?

3. What formal similarity exists between this rondo and the one by Brahms studied in this chapter?

4. Comment on the thematic contents of this movement's extensive coda. How does Mozart signify a closing quality in the reminiscence of the refrain in mm. 245ff.?

5. Trace the use of the perfect fifth in the thematic material of each section of this rondo.

Schumann, Piano Trio in F Major, op. 80, II

1. Compared to "Classical" models, what is unusual about the tonal design of the refrain? How is this feature handled (or not handled) in the final statement of the refrain?

2. The chord on the last beat of m. 13 serves as a pivot chord. How would it be analyzed?

3. What is unusual about the key choice for the second refrain statement?

4. Consider the B episode and its transposed restatement.

   (a) By what interval is it transposed when it is restated?

   (b) Other than transposition, in what way is the B material altered during its restatement?

Appendix: Notes On Musical Reductions

In this book we have employed two types of reductions, referred to as simplifications and representations of the voice leading, respectively. The first of these is really a metric simplification of the score, where note values represent relative duration. The purpose of these simplifications is to reveal underlying voice leading and often, as a result, to clarify the harmony. The process of preparing a reduction of this type involves removal of notes of melodic embellishment and normalization or realignment of rhythmic displacements, including suspensions. The process often involves registral normalization as well, particularly in the bass, to show voice-leading connections more clearly. The result should be a recognizable representation of the musical passage, where an assigned note value no longer represents the written value in the score but the total duration of a note and its melodic and/or rhythmic elaborations. Reductions of this sort may vary from person to person depending on how much an individual decides to eliminate or retain in the reduction. In other words, there are different possible "correct" solutions depending on what one seeks to demonstrate through this process.

Consider the opening phrase of the B major Prelude from Book I of the *Well-Tempered Clavier*, which is provided at (a) in Example A1.[1] An important feature of this phrase is the repetition of a melodic-rhythmic figure that occurs in varied form, moving from one voice to another in a three-voice contrapuntal setting. With two exceptions, the pattern elaborates the first note, whether occurring on the beat, either struck or held over from the previous beat, or sounded on the second sixteenth following a sixteenth-note rest. The two exceptions occur in the second measure, where the motion to F♯5 on the second beat (top voice) prolongs E5 and the motion to B4 on the fourth beat (inner voice) temporarily displaces the underlying 7–6 suspension. Removal of these melodic embellishments is the first stage in preparing the reduction at (b). In this instance the 7–6 suspension just noted and its later repetition with the two parts inverted have been retained because of their perceived importance in the construction and flow of the phrase. Note the registral normalization in the bass in the second half of m. 4 and the rhythmic normalization of the inner voice in the second half of the following measure, which helps to clarify the underlying voice leading and harmony. The result of these steps—removal of melodic embellishments, the noted rhythmic and registral normalizations, but the retention of the initial 7–6 suspension and its varied repetition—is the metric simplification at (b).

Our second type of reduction is an interpretation of the voice leading, very much like a Schenkerian graph without invoking all the terminology and notational procedures associated with that approach. Here note values do not represent relative duration, but rather are used to represent hierarchical levels of the voice leading. Such an interpretative representation of the Bach phrase is provided at (c) in Example A1. In this graph the opening melodic gesture is shown to introduce D#5 in the second measure via its upper neighbor note, marked N and given the value of an eighth note to show this neighboring relationship to the note to which it resolves, which has been assigned the value of a quarter note. The diagonal line connecting the D#5 to the bass note B3 indicates their association. Following the establishment of D#5, the top voice is shown to progress by step down to F#4 at the cadence with members of the descent all represented by quarter notes with stems of the same length. This descending sixth is further delineated by a large slur. Extension of G#4 in this encompassing sixth by the descending third G#4–F#4–E#4 is shown to occur at two levels, first in the immediate context, represented by unstemmed note heads grouped by a slur, which is embedded within the harmonized descent represented by quarter notes with short stems and once again grouped by a slur. In this more encompassing version the passing note F#4 is provided temporary harmonic support by vi in the key of the dominant. This deceptive progression is shown to exist within the prolongation of the supertonic harmony leading to the cadence. Slurs in the inner voice and bass indicate extensions of the underlying step progressions, and the Arabic numerals between the staves indicate the intervallic relationship between the outer parts. Though the principles of notation employed here are simple enough,

EXAMPLE A1 Bach, Prelude in B Major (*WTC* I), mm. 1–6

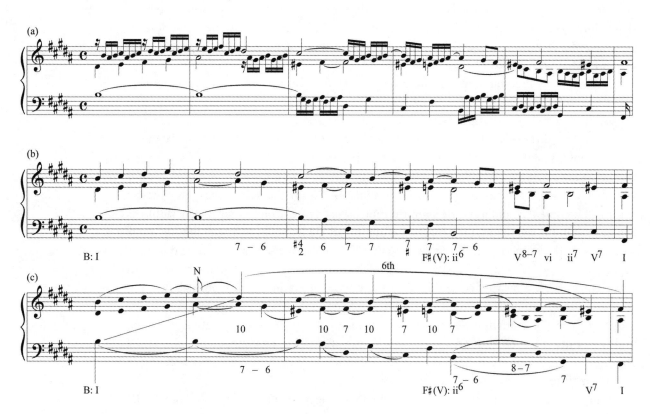

EXAMPLE A2 Mozart, Piano Sonata in F Major, K. 280, I, mm. 17–26

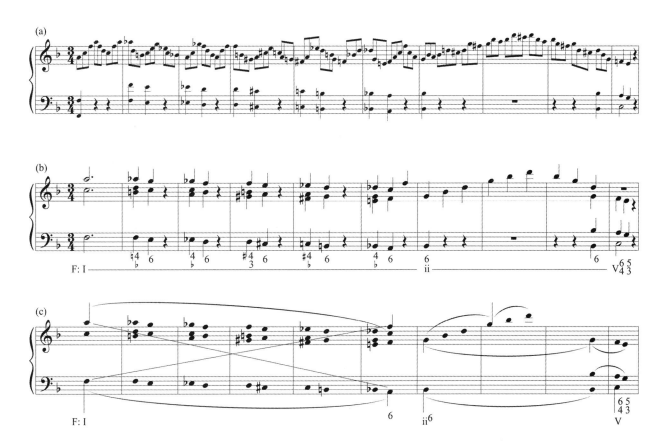

it should be clear from the description above that the decisions involved in this type of interpretative reduction are far more complex than those leading to a metric simplification of the voice leading. This is especially true of the cadential pattern in mm. 4–6.

Two additional examples are provided below. The first of these, the transition passage leading to the second theme in the first movement of Mozart's Piano Sonata in F Major, K. 280, was discussed briefly in Chapter 2 (Example 2.14), where the futility of labeling the chord progression connecting I (m. 17) and I^6 (m. 22) was noted. This passage is reproduced at (a) in Example A2, and a metric simplification of the voice leading is provided at (b). As can be seen in the reduction, the progression of mm. 18–22 is a series of descending $^6_3$ chords, each introduced by an applied $^{o4}_3$, thus preserving the parallel tenths between the outer parts. As shown below the system, the entire passage is controlled by the extended progression I − ii^6 − V$^{6-5}_{4-3}$.[2]

An interpretation of this passage is provided at (c) in Example A2. Here the passing motion connecting I and I^6 is shown to occur within a large-scale voice exchange prolonging the initiating note A5 and the tonic harmony; both the A5 and the supporting bass note have been assigned quarter-note values with long stems. The end points of the voice exchange are also given stems, but short ones to indicate their role in the prolongation of A5/I. The intervening notes are not stemmed. This extension of tonic harmony is followed by the elaboration of both G4 and G5 by arpeggiation of the members of the supporting supertonic harmony. G5 is provided a stem equal to the A5 some seven measures earlier, and, though the cadence follows in the lower octave, this G5 prepares the initial melodic note of the second theme in this upper register (not shown in the example). Here length of stems is used to indicate visually the long-range connections in the outer parts.

Our final example is the opening four measures of the sarabande from Bach's first Cello Suite, which is provided at (a) in Example A3. Though we are focusing primarily on later repertoire in this book, this example was chosen specifically to illustrate how to deal in reductions with music written for non-keyboard solo instruments, where lines often disappear temporarily due to practical limitations of the instrument. A metric reduction of these measures is provided at (b), which retains the second-beat emphasis characteristic of the sarabande rhythm. Though the bass line temporarily drops out, we understand the material up to the second quarter of m. 3, where the subdominant harmony enters, to be controlled by G (I), so that bass note G has been added twice in parentheses. More important to our understanding of this passage is the C4 over subdominant harmony that is implied by the context; it too has been added in parentheses and connected to the C4 that is introduced as a dissonance in the next measure. Finally A3 has been added above the D major chord (V) at the cadence, clearly implied as the local goal of the preceding C4–B3 motion in the top-sounding line.

Our interpretation of the voice leading is provided at level (c). The content of mm. 1–2 is shown to prolong tonic harmony and B3, the latter by its upper neighbor note while the inner voice rises from D3 to G3. The leap in the top voice to D4 while the inner voice

EXAMPLE A3 Bach, Cello Suite in G Major, Sarabande, mm. 1–8

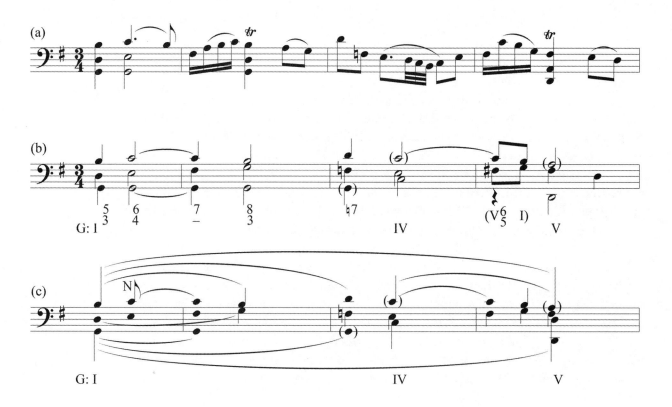

descends to F♮3 predicts the following C4 over subdominant harmony. We might expect this implied C4 to return to B3 as it had before, but this time the motion passes through B3 on its way to the implied A3 at the cadence. The chords during the first beat of m. 4 serve as an elaboration of the underlying harmonic connection between the preceding subdominant and the goal of the phrase, the dominant. As before, our use of note values— quarter, eighth and unstemmed notes—indicates our interpretation of the levels of voice leading, and in this case our understanding of this hierarchy is dependent in part on our awareness of notes missing but clearly implied by the context.

Notes

Preface

1   Taken by itself, Part I is appropriate for a graduate review of tonal theory where the focus is on *understanding* musical structure rather than part writing.
2   For those who want to pursue this topic, we refer you to Chapter 10 ("Text and Music") in David Beach's *Advanced Schenkerian Analysis* (Routledge, 2012), which contains detailed studies of vocal works by Mozart, Schubert, Schumann, and Brahms.

1   A Review of Diatonic Harmony

1   Figured bass is a shorthand system widely used in the seventeenth and eighteenth centuries to indicate to the keyboard (or lute) player the intervals required above the given bass line. The figure 6 for first-inversion triads is actually a short form for $\frac{6}{3}$.
2   Theoretically, all inversions of all triads are possible, but such a listing gives the false impression that all have equal status, which, as we shall see, they do not.
3   Subtonic is sometimes used in the minor mode to designate the triad *below* the tonic, that is, the triad built on the natural seventh degree of the scale.
4   In this opening section we have covered a lot of ground, and in doing so we have assumed a secure knowledge of fundamentals: scales and intervals. If this is not the case, security in these fundamentals, as well as chord construction, must be attained before continuing into the study of harmony.
5   This relationship is sometimes referred to as a question (antecedent) and answer (consequent). We will explore phrase design in more detail in Chapter 3.
6   This type of non-chord tone, which is approached by leap, is sometimes referred to as an appoggiatura.
7   Note that the diminished triad (vii°) is among the first-inversion chords. While diminished triads can occur in root position during sequences, composers tend to avoid them even in these situations.
8   The different types of reductions and their criteria for construction are outlined in the Appendix.
9   The complete descending fifth sequence occurs more frequently in the minor mode because it employs the natural seventh degree of the scale (except with the dominant), thus avoiding the diminished triad vii°.
10 Hemiola involves a conflict between two and three, here created by the repeated duple pattern against the triple meter.
11 Heinrich Schenker, *Harmony*, English translation by Elizabeth Mann Borgese (Chicago, 1954), 133–153.

12 This relationship will be discussed further in Chapter 3, where it is shown to be an important component in the formal design known as a "musical sentence."

13 A voice exchange occurs only between the same two parts/voices.

2 Expanding the Diatonic Palette

1 Secondary chords are often referred to as "applied" chords.

2 One might argue that a reading of ii^6 in m. 43 is equally as logical, but after having heard F so strongly in the previous measure, IV seems the more logical choice. In general, the harmonic interval of a third is interpreted as a root and third of a chord, not the third and fifth, unless there is evidence to suggest the contrary.

3 The effect on the voice leading of substituting a diminished seventh chord for the expected dominant is that the leading tone of the first chord (here A♯) does not lead as expected to B, but instead falls by semitone to A♮.

4 It is significant that the pattern changes as the descending melodic line reaches D♭5 (seventh of the E♭ chord), since an important motivic component of this work is the decoration of C5 by its upper neighbor D♭5.

5 Note values in Example 2.9b do not represent durations.

6 The C5 above the vi chord is implied by the context, but not stated in that octave and is thus placed in parentheses in Example 2.11b.

7 As with Example 2.9b, this graphic representation of the voice leading does not represent relative durations. More will be said about this near the conclusion of this chapter and in the Appendix.

8 The secondary $^{o6}_{\ 5}$ maintains the expected bass pitch A (i.e., as in I^6).

9 Having the pivot occur on a seventh chord is relatively rare, resulting here in the retention of the bass note G♯3 to become the seventh of the following chord.

10 The title *Grande sonate pathétique* was given to this work by Beethoven's publisher, who was impressed by its tragic qualities.

11 The astute reader might have noted that we have not been entirely consistent in how we have notated pivots involving a 5–6 motion. Under normal circumstances we have taken the actual pivot to be the chord represented by the 6 in 5–6. For example, I$^{5-6}$/ii^6 in Examples 2.16 and 2.18, or i$^{5-6}$/iv^6 in Example 2.26. In one instance we have shown the pivot differently, because of the way the harmony is introduced (by its secondary dominant) and its continuation. See Example 2.22. A certain amount of flexibility is needed to adjust to different circumstances. That is, we must be sensitive to the context in which a musical event occurs.

12 This terminology follows that used by William Rothstein in *Phrase Rhythm in Tonal Music* (Schirmer, 1989). Though employed rarely in our text, this terminology is useful in circumstances like this to describe two phrases based on contrasting, as opposed to similar, melodic material that forms a musical period. Phrase design will be discussed further in Chapter 3.

3 Phrase Design

1 We acknowledge the particular influence of two books on our presentation of phrase design and expansion: William Rothstein, *Phrase Rhythm in Tonal Music* (Schirmer, 1989) and William E. Caplin, *Classical Form: A Theory of Formal Functions for the Instrumental Music of Haydn, Mozart, and Beethoven* (Oxford, 1998).

2 When followed by a rest (or extended by a fermata), a V^7 chord—or in very rare instances V^6 or an inversion of V^7—can conclude a phrase. Such instances are best viewed as exceptional cases where a phrase concludes without a normative cadence.

3   A caret placed above an Arabic numeral is a shorthand notation for "scale degree."

4   Our discussion of sentence design follows closely the terminology of William Caplin, as presented in his book cited at the outset of this chapter. Since Caplin's definition of "phrase" differs considerably from ours, however, he describes the sentence as a two-phrase construction. It might be of interest to know that Caplin's theory in turn amplifies observations made by one of the leading composers of the twentieth century, Arnold Schoenberg.

5   Since this is our first orchestral score, we will comment briefly on reading orchestral scores. First, note the larger brackets at the left edge of the score to designate the instrumental families: winds, brass, percussion, and strings. Within the winds—flutes, oboes, clarinets, and bassoons—the clarinets are special. The notated pitch in a clarinet part is not the same as its sounding pitch. Here, the clarinets are "in A," which means that they sound A when C is notated; thus, the sounding pitch is a minor third *lower* than the notated pitch. This is why the clarinet lines use the key signature of F major—the key of F major is a minor third higher than the key of D major. (The other type of clarinet in widespread use is "in B♭," which sounds a major second *lower* than the notated pitch. We will encounter this clarinet transposition in the next chapter, Example 4.14.) The designation "a2" in flutes and bassoons indicates that both players are active, playing in unison. In the brass, Haydn only deploys horns and trumpets in this symphony. In this work, both are "in D," which means that the notated C sounds as D (the horns sound a minor seventh lower, the trumpets a major second higher). As is usual in the Classical repertoire, the only percussion instruments are the two timpani tuned to tonic and dominant pitches; in this excerpt only the timpani tuned to D is used. Finally, the strings—first violins, second violins, violas, cellos, double basses—occupy the lowest four staves. The cellos and double basses are notated together, but the double basses sound an octave lower than notated.

6   Some authors refer to hypermetric reinterpretation as metric reinterpretation. Since it is a hyperbeat that is reinterpreted (not a beat), we prefer the more explicit term hypermetric reinterpretation.

7   As in the Haydn symphony, the clarinet is in A, which means that it sounds a minor third lower than notated. In the text, we always refer to the sounding pitch of the clarinet.

8   Incidentally, at the end of the trio, this period is further expanded. The consequent is expanded by eight, rather than four, measures; the first three measures of the eight-measure expansion are basically the same as in the earlier expansion.

4   Further Expansion of the Harmonic Palette

1   The brackets in Example 4.2 indicate two levels of motivic activity, the shorter idea beginning with the dotted quarter and the larger gesture initiated on the downbeats of mm. 3 and 5.

2   Though the scale is much larger here, note that the excursion to ♭III is brought about by a 5–♭6 linear motion, similar to the approach to ♭VI in Schubert's "Du bist die Ruh."

3   A common pattern involving a voice exchange is IV^6_6 – passing $^6_4$ – $\text{ii}^{:6}_5$, with or without chromatic alteration. Here this common pattern appears as $\text{II}^{\natural 4}_3$ [ ] IV.

4   Note also that the space between E♭2 (V) in m. 41 and G2 (V^6_5) in m. 44 is filled in by the passing tones F♭ – G♭ (supporting IV – V in C♭), though an octave higher.

5   In Chapter 2, we did not explore the use of *half*-diminished seventh chords as secondary chords, since they are used in this way much less frequently than are diminished seventh chords. Half-diminished sevenths can only serve as secondary chords to *major* triads. For another example, see Example 4.10b.

6   The substitution of E♮ for F♭ would normally occur if the line were leading up to F, so this is particularly unusual here, since the line is descending to E♭.

7 The *Lebewohl* motive is the well-known horn call with open fifth. The harmonization of the third interval, the sixth, first by vi and later by ♭VI distorts the pastoral expression normally associated with this idea.

8 The clarinet parts sound a major second lower than written.

9 Another example of modulation to the major mediant is found in the first movement of Beethoven's "Waldstein" Sonata, op. 53, which is in C major. The second theme is in E major, but in this instance the pivot is diatonic as the modulation proceeds first from C major to E minor with pivot vi^6/iv^6 (m. 21).

10 This is the quickest way to return from ♭VI to I, namely, by changing the chord above ♭$\hat{6}$ into an augmented sixth chord leading back to V in the original key.

5 Binary and Rounded Binary Forms

1 When simple binary occurs in the late eighteenth century, it does so most often in themes for sets of variations.

2 For this reason, some authors refer to binary form as "two-reprise form." We prefer the terminology "part" rather than "reprise" since many writers employ the term "reprise" to mean "return" or "recapitulation."

3 Note that sectional binary is almost never found in a minor-mode piece.

4 To conserve space, Example 5.4 employs repeat signs and indicates the changes in mm. 102–103 with annotations above the violin and viola lines.

5 Another defensible interpretation of the first ten measures of B would be 12 1234 1234, where the hypermeter is reoriented around the entry of the flute melody in the third measure of B. (This type of reading will occur at the start of A′.)

6 The motion to the ninth (D♭) does not particularly disrupt the B♭ to A♭ connection. The ninth resolves back to C within the span of the C harmony, and this C becomes the focal tone for the left-hand melody at the thematic return. Although the eighth notes in the first measure of the thematic return touch on C6, the principal pitch for the upper voice in m. 45 is A♭5.

7 We can understand the necessity of this alteration. In mm. 5–6, the right-hand motion from F to G♭ is delayed, creating a subdominant chord before the Neapolitan. When this melody is placed into the bass, extending the F would result in a second-inversion subdominant. A beautiful way of extending the F without generating this $^6_4$ chord is the [V$^6_5$] ♭II.

8 Observe that after the *sostenuto* indication Brahms writes *a tempo* at m. 33. For many composers, *sostenuto* indicates only a shading of dynamics and articulation, but for Brahms *sostenuto* also includes a slowing of tempo.

9 If one wanted to give harmonic labels to these intervening chords, they are best related to the immediately preceding chord. For example, in m. 43 the A♭ major chord is V of the preceding I chord and does not progress to the ii in m. 44. Similarly, in m. 45 the A♭ minor chord is iv of the preceding ii chord (rather than a modally altered dominant chord).

10 The key of D♭ major has a special role throughout the entire sonata. In the first movement, it is the exposition's tonal goal (rather than the normative A♭ major). The second movement (*Andante*) begins in A♭ major but ends in D♭ major—a rare instance of directional tonality in Brahms's oeuvre. As in the first movement, D♭ major is the primary tonal contrast in the finale.

6 Classical Sonata Form

1 Although we do not adopt their terminology, our presentation of the norms of sonata form is informed by the comprehensive discussion in James Hepokoski and Warren Darcy, *Elements of Sonata Theory: Norms, Types, and Deformations in the Late-Eighteenth-Century Sonata* (Oxford, 2006).

2   A second, but less common, possibility for major-mode expositions is for the transition to end on V of the tonic key. Unlike most of the features of Classical sonata form, the non-modulating transition is not generally found in sonata forms composed after 1800.

3   In a significant number of minor-mode expositions, the secondary key is the minor dominant. This tonal alternative is especially suited to movements with a persistently tragic or foreboding nature.

4   Hearing the F4 at m. 7 as subsidiary to A4 is facilitated by the literal presence of F4 as an inner voice beneath the A4 of m. 9. The inner voice in mm. 8–9 emerges directly from the F4 of m. 7.

5   This underlying pattern is discussed by Maury Yeston in *The Stratification of Musical Rhythm* (Yale, 1976), 103–108.

6   In this broader tonal context, the prominent D minor at the outset of the transition can be viewed as a subsidiary 5–6 motion arising within F major harmony.

7   This linkage was pointed out by Oswald Jonas in *Introduction to the Theory of Heinrich Schenker*, trans. and ed. John Rothgeb (Longman, 1982), Example 199.

8   The hypermetric organization of mm. 113–132 is more complex than the duple grouping indicated between the staves in Example 6.1. At the macro level these twenty measures are divided into two groups of 10, which may explain why Mozart instinctively added the two measures of V^7 at the end, namely, to create balance in addition to providing a registral connection to the A major chord of m. 123.

9   We do not refer to these phrases as "part 1" and "part 2" of theme 1, as we did in the Mozart sonata just studied, because they are not separated by a perfect authentic cadence.

10   It is worth noting a long-range pitch connection that goes along with this tonal motion. At the onset of III, the start of theme 2, the *dolce* melody sits on B♭5 (m. 59), and it is from this same pitch that the descent to closure occurs later in the exposition. In the development, the upper line regains B♭5 at the V^7 of iv (m. 152) and then presents A♭5 at the arrival of iv (m. 176) and G5 at the retransition (m. 198). Thus, a stepwise descent through a third associates these key moments melodically.

7   Sonata Form in the Nineteenth Century

1   See, for example, the first movements of Schumann's Symphony No. 2 in C major, op. 61 (1846) and Brahms's Symphony No. 2 in D major, op. 73 (1877).

2   Our observations about this movement have been informed by Heinrich Schenker's discussion and analytic graphs in *Tonwille* 7 (1924) and *Der freie Satz* (1935), Figures 54/8, 114/8, and 154/4.

3   A similar situation occurs in the opening movement of Beethoven's "Waldstein" Sonata, op. 53, where the second half of the exposition features a modal shift (theme 2 in E major, closing section in E minor). Keep in mind that an exposition with a modal shift in the secondary key is not a three-key exposition (where there are three distinct local tonics). Although the exposition with modal shift might be viewed as a precursor of the three-key exposition, it does not undermine the polarity between *two* keys that defines the eighteenth-century sonata exposition. In fact, there are numerous eighteenth-century expositions with a modal shift (e.g., the first movement of Beethoven's Piano Sonata in C Major, op. 2, no. 3).

4   A similar anticipation of the minor mode in the dominant extension before the second theme occurs in the "Waldstein" Sonata (mm. 23–30). It should be noted, however, that even in expositions without a modal shift minor-mode inflections of the dominant extension at the end of the transition are not infrequent; this feature also occurred in the Mozart sonata and Beethoven trio studied in the previous chapter.

5 One comment on our hypermetric analysis of theme 2 is necessary. In Example 7.2, we show successive hypermetric downbeats at the start of theme 2. With the arrival of A♭ harmony, m. 35 provides a hypermetric downbeat, but it ultimately functions as an accompanimental pattern preparing the melody's hypermetric downbeat in m. 36. (Successive hypermetric downbeats occurred for the same reason at the analogous location, mm. 59–60, in the Beethoven trio studied in the previous chapter.)

6 There is an interesting difference between the beginnings of the parenthetical passages in the exposition (mm. 24–34) and development (mm. 94–108). In the exposition, the tonal goal (V^7 of III) coincides with the beginning of the melodic material of the parenthesis; there is thus an elision, and it results in a hypermetric reinterpretation. In the development, the tonal goal (V^7 of VI) is articulated already at m. 93, one measure before the melodic material of the parenthesis begins, meaning there is no elision this time. (Perhaps the very loud dynamics in the development section motivated the extra measure before the *piano* parenthesis begins.)

7 In Example 7.6, we show an implied C4 in m. 231 to complete this pitch motion in a single register, but the actual pitch at the downbeat of m. 231 is C2. C2 has a stepwise connection to the low bass note supporting the ♭II^6 harmony at m. 218 and thereby further clarifies the overall harmonic connection between ♭II^6 and the cadential dominant of mm. 231–238.

8 As shown in Example 7.6, the arrival at m. 239 falls on a hypermetric downbeat, but a statement of theme 2 begins in the next measure. Thus, as with previous theme 2 statements, this one is launched with successive hypermetric downbeats.

9 The close connection between 5–6 motions and modulations by descending third will emerge again in the following Brahms analysis.

10 Beginning a movement with a few quasi-introductory measures that turn out to be thematically integral occurs quite often in Brahms's music. We will encounter this again in the finale of his Violin Sonata in D Minor, op. 108, addressed in our study of rondo form in Chapter 9.

11 Note that in Example 7.8 we have removed rhythmic displacements in order to show the voice leading more clearly. In the bass line in mm. 21–24, for instance, Brahms actually delays the first pitch in each measure by a beat through the use of suspensions. We will continue to remove such displacements in subsequent reductions.

12 The augmentation is not exact. To be exact, the fourth chord would be an eighth note, not a sixteenth. This modification preserves an essential characteristic of the original pattern.

13 Reading of the clarinet line for the remainder of the development section is made more difficult by its notation a diminished third rather than a major second higher than it sounds.

8 Ternary Form

1 There are numerous examples of alternating movement pairs in Bach's suites and partitas.

2 Here, in both mm. 21 and 22, the augmented sixth chord is introduced by a strongly articulated F major chord (VI), anticipating the key of the B section.

3 It might be tempting, though incorrect, to interpret the A♮ in m. 8 as B♭♭, that is, as a G♭ minor chord (vi). The continuation makes it clear that Brahms means what he writes, which indicates an extension of dominant function.

4 It is interesting that scale degree 3 is never supported by tonic harmony in this piece. Even in the coda it is a passing tone—indeed, an extended one—over dominant harmony.

5 We will encounter this chord later in the retransition (m. 44), where it is spelled as a D♭ seventh chord but functions as an augmented sixth chord leading to V^7 of V.

6 See Allen Cadwallader, "Schenker's Unpublished Graphic Analysis of Brahms's Intermezzo Op. 117, No. 2: Tonal Structure and Concealed Motivic Repetition," *Music Theory Spectrum* 6 (1984): 1–13.

7   The employment of both forms of scale degree 3 here reflects their use earlier in the bass at the beginning of the antecedent and consequent phrases, D♮ in m. 52 and D♭ in m. 61.

9   Rondo Form

1   For detailed discussion of mm. 1–8 refer back to Examples 1.9, 1.18, and 3.1.

2   In Example 9.1, the hypermetric reading of this expansion is one of a few possible interpretations of this passage.

3   The emphasis on F, A, and E in this sonata is thought to have programmatic significance, a reference to Brahms's lifelong friend, violinist Joseph Joachim, with whom Brahms had a temporary falling out in the mid 1880s. (Brahms had supported Joachim's wife's position during the couple's divorce negotiations.) Joachim's personal motto from his bachelor years was "Frei aber Einsam" ("Free but lonely"), or F–A–E, and Brahms had encoded this musical cell in a few of his early pieces. Encoding names or words in musical pitches was a favored device in the works of Robert Schumann, a composer who influenced the young Brahms and the young Joachim.

4   Since this movement contains transitions with two types of thematic content, we show this distinction by labeling each transition as either Tx or Ty in Figure 9.3.

5   Motive *y* begins with A–F–E, a permutation of the three pitches in the initial statement of motive *x*. We do not emphasize this connection since the lower register of the A places more attention on the F and E and their continuation rather than on the initial three-note cell.

6   Given the parallelism of antecedent and consequent phrases and the following change in thematic material, this arrival on VI is one of the rare instances where a deceptive progression truly has a cadential function.

7   For a treatment of Brahms's large-scale thematic development see Ryan McClelland, "Brahms and the Principle of Destabilised Beginnings," *Music Analysis* 28, no. 1 (2009): 3–61. This article also discusses the distinction between rondo form and sonata form in relation to the finale of the Violin Sonata, op. 108.

Appendix: Notes on Musical Reductions

1   An analysis by David Beach of the entire prelude is contained in "The Submediant as Third Divider: Its Representation at Different Structural Levels," *Music Theory in Concept and Practice*, ed. Baker, Beach, and Bernard (Rochester, 1997).

2   In this instance Mozart has progressed to the dominant in the original key rather than the dominant in the new key, leaving the process of modulation to occur at the start of the second theme.

Index of Musical Works

Page numbers that appear in **bold** indicate the presence of an annotated score and/or reduction

Index of Names and Terms